The Playing Lesson

A DUFFER'S YEAR AMONG THE PROS

Michael Bamberger

AVID READER PRESS

New York   Amsterdam/Antwerp   London
Toronto   Sydney/Melbourne   New Delhi

AVID READER PRESS
An Imprint of Simon & Schuster, LLC
1230 Avenue of the Americas
New York, NY 10020

First Avid Reader Press hardcover edition June 2025

AVID READER PRESS and colophon are trademarks of Simon & Schuster, LLC

Interior design by Joy O'Meara

Manufactured in the United States of America

1 3 5 7 9 10 8 6 4 2

Library of Congress Cataloging-in-Publication Data has been applied for.

ISBN 978-1-6680-6015-5
ISBN 978-1-6680-6017-9 (ebook)

This book is dedicated to
NEIL OXMAN
who had the best tip of all:

"You should take a lot of lessons."

Do it nice and easy now,
Don't lose control.
A little bit of rhythm—
And a lot of soul.
Come on, come on:
Do the Loco-Motion with me.

—Gerry Goffin and Carole King, "The Loco-Motion" (1962)

Contents

The Playing Lesson

1

Hope

IN THE WINTER OF '66, GEORGE HEADED WEST, SEEKING GOLF. LANKY, patrician George Plimpton, Harvard '48, of New York City, schlepping his brand-new golf bag through California airports and motel parking lots. He was looking to embed himself in the secret society of touring pros and teaching pros, among other high priests in well-traveled Foot-Joys. The final stop on his West Coast swing was the Bob Hope Desert Classic, a five-round pro-am in greater Palm Springs, pros playing for prize money, amateurs beside them, paying for the privilege. George was a shaky 95 shooter. That is, as am as am can get. Our hero. He got himself to the Hope—and inside its rope lines.

In the first round, George sliced a drive that nearly hit Hope and his playing partner, the comedian Phyllis Diller, as they sat in a cart on an adjoining hole. George's recovery shot with a 3-wood flew into a grass parking field. As his caddie chased after it, George bellowed, "Lay it leave!" Diller, wearing a plaid hat topped by a red pom-pom, said to Hope, "Lay it leave?" Poor George. He was looking for *Leave it lay.* Not that anybody said those three words in succession while playing golf, then or ever. But golf promotes all manner of oddness, and does so

1

with stunning efficiency. You can imagine George's get-me-out-of-here 3-wood shot, Bob Hope watching with detached amusement. I see a whirring, blurring swing, George's cheeks turning red as the shot ignores his flight plan for it. Maybe I'm projecting here.

Later, in *The Bogey Man*, George Plimpton's largely joyful and sometimes painful account of his three-week immersion in the pro game and psyche, he wrote this see-through sentence: "I spent a lot of time at driving ranges." Of course you did, George! What golfer seeking improvement can resist a driving range? We always think we're one session, or one shot, away from a revelation, right? We're always close. It keeps us at it and young. Or youngish. *The Bogey Man* was in my high school library, when I was falling into the whole thing. That was a lucky break.

On a bleak Saturday afternoon in January, I flew from Philadelphia (where my wife and I live) to Phoenix, rented a car, drove through an eerie nighttime desert fog, and crossed over the Colorado River and into California. I had, in the back of my semi-large Hertz rental vehicle, a little green golf bag filled with old beryllium copper Ping Eye2 irons with new rubber grips. Also a two-way (lefty and righty) yip-proof (a man can dream) putter and a driver I could hit semi-reliably for second shots on long par-4s and most par-5s. The car's navigation system was out for long stretches, but I didn't need it. My route was a straight shot west on I-10. Palm Springs beckoned. The old Bob Hope tournament beckoned. *Golf* beckoned.

George was thirty-eight when he dropped out of his Upper East Side existence and into golf for three weeks. He asked Jack Nicklaus about his superstitions and tried to ask Arnold Palmer about his dreams. He played lighted courses at night. He was on the prowl, looking for the key to the room where golf's secrets are stored. He read Alex Morrison's *Better Golf Without Practice*. Well, why not? Morrison taught Henry Picard, and Picard taught Jack Grout, and Grout taught Jack Nicklaus. Nicklaus told Plimpton how he wore the same good-luck pants for four straight days through the heat of the 1962 U.S. Open, which he won in a playoff over Arnold at Oakmont, near Pittsburgh. But nothing lasts forever. Lucky pants, like swing thoughts, get hot for a while and then they cool off.

When I headed west, I was sixty-three and had been playing golf, and thinking about the golf swing, for fifty years. Christine, my bride of thirty-plus years, has seen me in front of mirrors many times, dangling and swinging my arms, trying to feel the weight of my hands.

I would need more than three weeks.

In the mid-1970s, when I got snared in golf's web—couldn't play enough, read enough, watch enough—there were professional events named for people, for Patty Berg, for Byron Nelson, for Bing Crosby. Golf was dripping with personality. Johnny Miller in flared plaid pants, smirking as his birdie putts rolled, his hair getting blonder and longer by the week. Lee Trevino wobbling down various fairways—in Dallas, in Canada, in Great Britain—often dwarfed by his enormous caddie, Herman Mitchell. *All putts break toward Herman,* Trevino liked to say. Trevino was Buck, in the stories from writers who knew his nickname. There were tournaments named for cities. Phoenix, going back to 1935. Houston, Atlanta, Hartford, Greensboro. Other tournaments combined people and places: the Dean Martin Tucson Open, the Glen Campbell Los Angeles Open. *M*A*S*H* ended in 1983 and a year later the actor who played Klinger, a cross-dressing enlisted man, had an LPGA event named for him, the Jamie Farr Toledo Classic.

By the time I landed in Phoenix—Saturday night, January 13, 2024—you couldn't find any of that in your rearview mirror. The Bob Hope Desert Classic, the annual five-round tournament in and around

Palm Springs, had morphed, unromantically, into the American Express. Bing Crosby, as a name on the circuit's schedule, appeared for the last time in 1985, replaced by a ticker symbol, AT&T. I get it, we all get it—the lure of money. In that light, more recent developments were inevitable: LIV Golf and its guaranteed contracts; the PGA Tour's for-profit division; so-called Signature Events with no possibility of David versus Goliath; tournaments on both circuits with small fields and no cuts. Indoor, nighttime, made-for-TV events. Does any of this seem like golf? You have your answer, and you can guess mine. In the name of programming, in the name of creating "content," now there is actually too much golf. That is, golf on a screen.

Over the years, what made tournament golf so compelling was its difficulty, its playing fields, its stars, its infrequency. Arnold Palmer, Tom Watson, Tiger Woods: You'd turn on your TV (on those certain and special weekends), and there they were, playing their guts out. We cared because they cared, because golf meant so much to them, and so much to us. Maybe someday order will be restored.

In the meantime, I'm on a mission, in my life and in these pages. I'm seeking the wonder of golf, wherever it might be. *The Mystery of Golf.* It's the title of a cult golf book but also a driving force in my life, and it has been since 1974. (I imagine you have your year, too. We are all shaped by our year.) On the Saturday night of the '74 U.S. Open, Tom Watson had the lead, with Hale Irwin and Arnold Palmer on his heels. You couldn't wait for Sunday afternoon. In the backyard, in the reflection of the garage windows, I was Watson. That summer, the summer of '74, I started playing the public course near my house and broke 100 for the first time, 90 on the bus rides home, 80 in my dreams.

Golf comes out of our dreams. In any given year, we might shoot a save-the-card round. We might play—name your course. We might fall in love with a putter. We might watch people so good at playing golf they don't need another job. Can you imagine? In 1974, Johnny

Miller won the first three events of the year: Pebble, Phoenix, Tucson. Michael Murphy—the author of *Golf in the Kingdom* and the creator of Shivas Irons, the golf teacher-mystic at its center—talks about Johnny Miller in the early months of 1974 as a prime example of a golfing "peak experience," the golfer so dialed in he can just do it. Be the ball, for real.

Fifty years later, I was heading out with no particular plan except to continue an ongoing investigation. *Tour '24: Do the Loco-Motion.* I had my first three stops lined up and nothing beyond that. The Palm Springs event, where I had registered to work as a volunteer. Pebble Beach, where I had work lined up as a caddie. And the Phoenix tournament, where I had signed up to play in the Monday pro-am. Golfing safaris through the Sunshine State, across the Garden State, on the east coast of Scotland—those just kind of happened. Late-season golf dates in Michigan and Ohio and Pennsylvania, the same. Along the way I met *loads* of memorable people. That's the nature of travel, most especially golf travel. I am thinking now of the unlicensed teacher I fell in with late in my *Do the Loco-Motion* tour. You could call this playful man a golfing mystic, but not in a way that brings Shivas Irons to mind. (He could find a money game anywhere.) We hit it off from the get-go. What connected us was the weird riddle that makes your best golf largely elusive. Largely, but not completely. What connected us was the search for golf, real golf, *our* golf.

The Amex, for decades, has been a sprawling event with a huge field, played on three courses. But I was relieved to discover, almost upon arrival, that there was something personal and intimate about it, particularly at La Quinta, the low-buff resort that is the tournament's epicenter each year: made-to-order smoothies at breakfast, small groups in bubbling Jacuzzis at dusk, tumbler drinks by fireplaces at night. Scottie Scheffler with his linebacker's round-shouldered stroll, gliding across a velvety practice green, putter in hand. Do you care how much money he makes? I don't.

I couldn't land a place in the tournament's pro-am, as George had done. For one thing, the spots were way too expensive ($40K-ish), and they were all gone anyhow. My volunteer position was in Amateur Player Services. My job was to distribute tournament gifts—*swag*, in the term of the art—to the amateurs in the field.

One of my colleagues in Amateur Player Services was responsible for handing out caddie bibs to the ams, along with a rectangular white cloth name tag that identified the Amex amateurs in blocky letters, modeled on what the pro caddies wear. An am named Lee Wielansky came through our workstation, in La Quinta's Diego Ballroom. He was a big, tall gent with an unhurried manner. He mentioned, with notable grace, that his surname was spelled incorrectly on his caddie name tag. It would get fixed, immediately—we were all certain of that. The ams are royals in these events. Keith Urban performed at a Friday-night tournament concert held on a driving range, its wide lawn dotted with rhinestoned women in white jeans. The ams picked up the tab for everything.

A band of touring pros traveling from one course to another to play tournament golf is an American invention that dates to the 1930s. Civic leaders invited the fellas into town for a tournament. The organizers sold admission tickets, beer in cans, spots in pro-ams. The players got paid before they left town. If the tournament made more than it spent, the leftover money went to good causes. It wasn't complicated.

When the broadcast networks came in, the purses got much bigger, but nothing really changed. Professional golf has been a weekend staple on TV for decades, but it was never a ratings bonanza, despite Arnold Palmer's broad appeal and Tiger Woods's electrifying play. Golf is slow, contemplative, difficult, not for everybody, not even close. It's a niche sport. For years, NBC sold the Hope on Bob Hope. Bob Hope is in the World Golf Hall of Fame. Bing Crosby is, too.

Bob Hope, in cardboard, Diego Ballroom, La Quinta Resort.

Years after Bob Hope's death, and before American Express came in, Bill Clinton briefly became the tournament host. In his first year, *Sports Illustrated* sent me to the tournament to interview Clinton about his new gig. He spilled some Diet Coke on the white puffy jacket he was wearing, an aide rushed over to dab it away, and Clinton just kept on going, not missing a beat. He talked about golf with ease and joy. I'd brought him a tee sheet from a professional event in Hot Springs, Arkansas, that he had attended as a kid. He pored over the list, remembering names like Ernie Vossler and Al Besselink and how one pro "could play in a telephone booth," his swing was so upright. Clinton said one of his mother's suitors, trying to curry favor with young Bill, gave him a golf club, the first one he ever had. It was a driver. Clinton said, "Michael, I brought that driver to the White House. I had them refurbish it and polish it up. I brought it out to Camp David. And Michael, I could not hit that driver *at all*."

I saw Clinton playing once at Farm Neck, a course on Martha's Vineyard. He had his hands high, admirably so, at the top of his swing, a crazy flying right elbow, and a wicked cut move on the downswing. Still, he could make solid contact. Arnold Palmer once told me that Clinton had "good clubhead speed, but with driver he was all over the map." Arnold was a keen observer of presidents and their swings.

Arnold won the Hope five times. He liked Palm Springs in winter. Late in 1999, I visited with him for several days, seeing Arnold in a casita he owned near the La Quinta resort. This was shortly after the death of his first wife, Winnie, the mother of their two daughters, Peg and Amy. "Winnie never liked it here," Arnold said one morning. "It was a little too fast for her."

We were in the living room. On a side table against a wall, with keys and mail, was a fax machine. It started buzzing with a contract for Arnold. There was glee in his voice as he held the warm sheets in his large hands and described this newest adventure in capitalism. He liked business deals that paid him up front.

One of the few requests Winnie made, when their modest winter getaway home was being planned in the mid-1990s, was for a small backyard pool. Arnold's "too fast" reference was from a lost era—the early 1960s, if not earlier. Over the years and decades, Arnold had logged many rounds, tournament and otherwise, at Tamarisk, a club in Rancho Mirage. Frank Sinatra had a home on the course, with a bar in his backyard, near the seventeenth hole. Arnold played with Sinatra, with CEOs, with stars from every field. He played desert golf with Dwight Eisenhower, Richard Nixon, Jerry Ford, George H. W. Bush, Bill Clinton, and George W. Bush. John F. Kennedy liked

Palm Springs, but he and Arnold never played golf there, or anywhere else. They had been planning a game, and they had settled on a week. Christmastime, 1963.

Hotels in January in Palm Springs and the nearby desert burghs are expensive, but the Courtyard Marriott where I stayed was reasonable, its normal rate discounted due to various construction projects inside and out. My tournament shifts started early and the days were long, so I was barely aware of the ongoing work. The hotel parking lot was dull, gray, urban. But to the west, just beyond downtown Palm Springs, you could see magnificent desert mountains covered with rocks that were almost throbbing in the day's first light. My drive to the La Quinta Resort was forty minutes, and there was never any traffic. Under some of the highway overpasses, you'd see small congregations of homeless people with their shopping carts and plastic bags.

One morning I joined a group of tournament volunteers to work at a food bank, a beneficiary of the tournament. We toured the gleaming facility. We heard about the work done there: getting healthy food to the elderly, the working poor, migrant farmers, needy kids. We unloaded produce and bagged food items on a human assembly line, swept floors, that sort of thing. It was moving, getting a tiny taste of a golf tournament's good works.

Next to the food bank was a flat, sprawling, sunbaked field, and we were told about a plan to expand the facility into this dusty tract. We were invited to look out a large second-floor window at the barren lot and consider its potential. At its center was one worker, shovel in hand, doing nothing and surrounded by nothing. A half hour later, he was gone. Soon after, so were we.

I am drawn to driving ranges, back-road golf courses, shops with second-hand clubs. I prefer used clubs, clubs with life experience. If you're traveling and seeking a good range with a grass tee, look for a First Tee facility. I did that late one afternoon when leaving La Quinta and found my way to the First Tee of the Coachella Valley, where I hit my first shots in this new year. The range was crowded, but the grass was good and so were the balls. Carrying my basket of practice balls to the tee, bag on my shoulder, I had the familiar sense of starting over. Another fresh start in a long series of them. All that hope.

I once asked Tiger Woods what happens when a manufacturer sends him clubs on a tryout basis. It's easy to imagine: Tiger is home in the offseason, the UPS truck arrives and the doorbell rings, Tiger retrieves a knife from a kitchen drawer, slices open a cardboard box, and removes a club still wrapped in protective plastic. (Why should Tiger's experience be any different from yours or mine?) I asked him, "Do you ever get so excited to hit a new club, you don't go through your normal warm-up routine before trying it out?" Tiger *maybe* half-smiled and said, "No, never." There are a thousand things I could say about Tiger and one of them would be that he answers left-field questions with appealing directness.

At the driving range of that First Tee near La Quinta, I made my first swings of the new year. They were hurried and terrible. Just doing everything in too much of a rush, as per usual. Rushed warm-up, rushed backswing, rushed downswing. Blech.

You don't usher in a new golf year like you're dropping a ball in Times Square at midnight. Gradual reintroduction is far better. I should know that. Jack Nicklaus used to start each new golf season by having Jack Grout, his lifelong teacher, look at his grip, his stance, his ball position, and his takeaway. You can read all about it in some of the books Nicklaus wrote, including *Playing Lessons*. Nicklaus and Palmer were prolific writers. I read their instruction books, and Ben Hogan's books, in high school. For better or for worse, they were my main instructors, along with the men I caddied for and the buddies I played with, and what I learned in a gym class during the day and an adult-ed evening class a friend and I slipped into without getting kicked out.

My golf is half-decent, and that's all it is. I can break 90 when the moons align; really, most any day when I'm not distracted by the rest of my life and not flailing around, mentally or otherwise. My problem isn't an inability to hit good shots. It's hitting too many poor ones. (Who wouldn't say the same?) As I started this new golfing year, with George Plimpton as my guide and *The Bogey Man* as my guidebook, my goal was to play golf with more focus and more purpose. To be less rushed and less distracted in every aspect of the enterprise. To hit fewer lousy shots along the way.

There was a nice collection of golf books in the pro shop at the First Tee I visited, *The Bogey Man* among them, along with *The Greatest Game of All* (Nicklaus) and *A Golfer's Life* (Palmer). You could borrow the books, and you could buy used clubs, stuffed into two large golf bags donated by the touring pro Maverick McNealy. I saw Maverick the next day when he was coming out of a scorer's trailer at the Amex, and I showed him a photo of his old bags.

Maverick's father was a founder of Sun Microsystems, but you'd never know it, talking to Maverick. We chatted briefly about pro-ams. At the Amex, a pro plays his own competitive golf alongside an amateur for three straight days. For many years at Pebble Beach, pros and ams played together for as many as four rounds. All garden-variety PGA Tour events have at least one pre-tournament pro-am, and often two. Sometimes there's a Saturday pro-am for players who missed the cut. For years, it was almost a comedy bit for the players to dis the pro-ams they played in. "I think guys used to roll their eyes at them, but that's not true anymore," Maverick told me. Between the pandemic and the launching of LIV Golf, the professional game had been in disarray for a half-decade, pretty much McNealy's entire career. Pro golf, in terms of its payouts, had become way top-heavy. At least some pros had become more aware of who makes their lives possible. People who pay to play in pro-ams would be at the top of that list. Also people who shop at airport golf shops, who buy XL buckets at driving ranges, who watch golf on TV on weekday afternoons.

Maverick told me about the fifty-four-hole golf days he and his father played during vacations when he was a teenager, and how your golf

George Plimpton, the original Bogey Man, putting, Pebble Beach, 1966; bookshelf, pro shop, First Tee of the Coachella Valley.

can improve over the course of single marathon golf day. I've had that experience. At some point, you start swinging without thinking. One little tip if you're planning such a day, and I know Maverick will back me on this: Pack extra socks.

Late on Saturday afternoon at La Quinta, I was in the small gallery that followed Nick Dunlap, an amateur golfer playing on the pro side of the tee sheet. Dunlap was a twenty-year-old sophomore at the University of Alabama and the reigning U.S. Amateur champion, a title that gets you (as long as you don't turn pro) an invitation to the Masters and cheap digs in the Crow's Nest, an attic dormitory in the Augusta National clubhouse. Jack Nicklaus, Tom Watson, and Tiger Woods all stayed in the Crow's Nest when they played in the Masters as college golfers.*

Dunlap looked like a lean, fidgety college kid, but he was playing like a man in full. He was in control of the shape of his shots and how far they would fly. That is, distance control. Harvey Penick, the legendary Texas golf teacher, turned the phrase *Take dead aim* into a life motto for golfers. It's hard to say more in three words. But from what I've seen, tour players don't take dead aim. They take general aim. Their first goal, iron in hand, is to hit a shot hole-high. That is, a precise distance. They have different swings for a 147-yard shot and a 152-yard shot. You can take care of aim as you address the ball. The ball is just sitting there, doing nothing. You have time. Aiming is not that hard. Distance control takes practice, experience, forethought, and *then* you start your swing. On any single shot, there's a lot going on.

Nick Dunlap went out in 30 on his front nine in the third round on the La Quinta course, a short, flat, easy layout with no rough and

---

* At the 1970 Masters, Lanny Wadkins stayed in the Crow's Nest, as did Tom Watson. "Watson was screaming bloody murder every night in his sleep," Wadkins says. "I told him, 'I don't know what you all are smoking at Stanford, but we don't do that stuff at Wake Forest.'"

perfect greens. He was flirting with 59. More significantly, he was trying to become the first amateur to win a PGA Tour event since Phil Mickelson, who did it as a psychology major at Arizona State in 1991. Dunlap's last approach shot in that Saturday round was hole-high and on the money. He made a closing birdie for 60.

On Sunday, after the fifty-four-hole cut, sixty-six pros and young Nick Dunlap, amateur golfer, were playing for the Amex title on the Stadium Course at PGA West. Dunlap, as the leader by four, was in the last threesome of the day with Justin Thomas and Sam Burns, teammates on the most recent U.S. Ryder Cup team. Dunlap's Sunday would not be easy. Even with a four-shot lead.

There were TV cameras in his face. His group got a warning for slow play. Various people had flown in for the occasion and were following him around: Dunlap's girlfriend. His parents. His Alabama coach. His swing coach. His agent (permitted by newish NCAA rules). It was all disorienting, right down to the giant, clicking electronic leaderboards with his name at the top of them, with a collection of familiar names below his own. When you're playing golf on TV on Sunday and you make a mistake, a half-dozen other golfers usually are right there, ready to pounce. It's an opportunistic game, one of the reasons corporate America has always been drawn to it. It's a numbers game with strict rules. On the course, no marketing campaign can save you. You can't fake anything.

Dunlap's lead started to evaporate on the back nine. As he walked off the twelfth green, he let out his own one-word review: "Fuck."

He was clinging to a one-shot lead when he pushed his approach shot into the group of fans to the right of the eighteenth green. Left of the green was a pond. He didn't need to take dead aim. He needed to keep his ball dry.

"Was that your first spectator hit right there?" Justin Thomas said to Dunlap as they walked up the fairway.

"Did I smoke somebody?" Dunlap asked.

"Percentages," Thomas said.

The wayward shot had scattered a small group of clustered spectators. Dunlap's ball caromed off a fan's foot and into an ideal lie, coming to rest on soft, watered grass. There was some cushion, some air, underneath his ball. Without that good bounce, the ball would have stopped on grass flattened by spectators, a much more difficult shot with no margin for error. Golf and luck, good and otherwise, have had a long marriage, with lots of downs and as many ups.

Nick Dunlap got up and down on the last hole and won by a shot. He posed for photos with the winner of the pro-am, Lee Wielansky, 13-handicap golfer, the silver-haired gent who had come through the Diego Ballroom and politely asked for a redo on his caddie name tag. Two amateurs, the youngest in the field and, at seventy-two, the oldest, were the two Amex winners.

The Masters tournament, three months away, immediately became even more interesting. Could Dunlap, as an amateur, contend at Augusta? Could he get himself to Butler Cabin for the Sunday-night CBS interview as the low amateur, a sash previously worn by Ken Venturi, Jack Nicklaus, Ben Crenshaw, Phil Mickelson, Tiger Woods, and other gilded golf names? The Masters was the brainchild of Bobby Jones, trained lawyer and amateur prodigy golfer, and he venerated the role that amateurs played in his tournament. A lot of good karma has come out of that clubhouse attic.

A few days after his win at the Amex, in a meeting room on the Alabama campus, Dunlap announced he was turning pro. He didn't cash a check at the Amex, but to view it another way, he made millions there. The gang was all on hand for the announcement—his agent, his coach, his parents, his swing instructor, his girlfriend, his teammates. He was sniffling and wiping away the occasional tear and wearing an Alabama windbreaker, but he had played his last golf for the Crimson Tide. He was turning pro. Really, he already had.

There was no rain through the week of the tournament. Not a drop. On the day after the tournament ended, it poured. A desert storm. The courtyard at the Courtyard Marriott in Palm Springs: drenched. The shipping containers parked on the edge of town: drenched. The cacti dotting desolate highways, the dormant bushes lining suburban streets, the palm fronds draping over Palm Canyon Drive: drenched, drenched, drenched.

The following day, the sun returned. Lee Wielansky, the Amex am winner, had invited me to his club for a late-morning lunch. (More accurately, I got myself invited, as reporters sometimes do.) His club was Tamarisk Country Club, the old Frank Sinatra hangout, located on Frank Sinatra Drive.

The clubhouse, boxy and bright, is a classic example of mid-century modern architecture, with shiny floors and floor-to-ceiling windows. As we made our way through the clubhouse and to our table, members congratulated Lee on his pro-am victory. Everyone knew him. Mr. Wielansky, I quickly learned, was the club president, the thirty-third since the club opened in 1952.

His well-wishers were women. It was Ladies Day at Tamarisk, as every Tuesday is. There was modern art on display throughout the clubhouse, and a member was leading a group of visiting women through the club to look at the collection.

Lee and I were the only men in the crowded dining room. The lunch menu included all-day breakfast options. (Like!) Lee told me how Tamarisk was founded by Jewish businessmen, lawyers, doctors, and entertainers—Groucho Marx among them—who started the club when they could not get into some of the other clubs in Palm Springs. Tamarisk had been part of the course rotation for the Bob Hope Desert Classic for fifty years, beginning in 1960. From its start, the club aspired to be a central part of the Palm Springs good life. There's something poignant about all this effort in the name of respectability. Exclusion is a powerful motivator.

Lee analyzed his win modestly ("I played well at the right times") and described his pro-am credo: pick up the moment your score no longer matters; don't talk too much; don't complain about *anything*; swing within your means; and always, always, *always* be ready to play.

For some, golf is a ride in the country, and for others it's a hike. I'm in the latter group, and I sometimes think of the golf bag on my back, lunch in a pocket along with a sweater, as my father thought of his canvas rucksack, a tangerine, cheese slices, a Thermos, and a small radio tucked in it. Once, on a hiking vacation, my son introduced me to a website called AllTrails, and I clicked on to it in the Tamarisk parking lot. Within an hour, I was on an arid and remote trail and a world away from Palm Springs country-club living. Three miles in, at fourteen hundred feet, I could see the city for what it is, an oasis in the desert wilderness. On the dusty descent, returning to civilization, I saw something unexpected: a compact green triangle of golf, hugging the mountain on one side, and a dense stretch of developed Palm Springs on the other two. When I got down, I poked around the edges of this toy course. It was the O'Donnell Golf Club, a short, flat, private nine-holer once owned by a Jazz Age oil magnate named Tom O'Donnell. He continued to live on Google, a ringer for Joseph P. Kennedy, JFK's father, right down to his oval banker eyeglasses and stylish double-breasted suits.

Through the kindness of the club's general manager, a stylish gent himself named Koll Farman, I played the course the next afternoon, during the golfer's witching hour, in the hours before sunset.

To get to the club's first tee, you enter the Palm Springs Art Museum parking lot, pass through the club's metal entrance gate, park in a tiny members-and-guests lot, walk by a lovely 1920s stucco clubhouse, and march across two narrow fairways to a small, crowded pro shop with the first tee beside it. It's all charming, if this is your kind of thing. It was not Ben Hogan's kind of thing. As Koll told the story, Hogan shot 30 on his first nine and was two holes into his second nine when he walked off, grumbling about trees in the middle of fairways. This was my first half-round of the new year, and so unexpected. Golf delivers the unexpected on a regular basis. I lost a ball on a blind par-3 (you don't see a blind par-3 every day) but otherwise played pretty well. It was past sunset when I finished. The pro shop was closed. Across the course, you could see the warm yellow lights of the clubhouse, and a cold, inhospitable mountain behind it.

2

George-Abe, Fred-Mike

WHEN GEORGE PLIMPTON WENT WEST IN '66, HE FLEW TO LOS ANGE-les, rented a car, and drove north to Pebble Beach to play in his first tournament, the Bing Crosby National Pro-Am, at a time when the amateur field was crowded with entertainers and athletes and politicians. (In 1977, Jerry Ford played in the Crosby the day after he left the White House. That turned out to be Bing Crosby's final Crosby; he died nine months later, after a round of golf in Spain.) In Los Angeles, a porter helped Plimpton with his luggage. The fellow was a 5-handicap public-course golfer and figured Plimpton was a pro because of his destination and the size of his golf bag. "Well, *pop it*," Plimpton told the gent in a feeble attempt to give him a golf tip along with a real one. The first chapter of *The Bogey Man* ends with Plimpton leaving the airport and his golf-playing porter: "I put the car in gear and started off. As I looked in the rear-view mirror I could see him staring after the car."

After the Amex, my next event was Pebble, listed on the PGA Tour schedule (officially and unromantically) as the AT&T Pebble Beach Pro-Am. As the AT&T, the tournament's original casual vibe had been replaced by something far more rigid, cold, and corporate. There was less public drinking. But the event continued to have a prominent place on the tour's West Coast swing, at least for the ams, for two main reasons: the desire for CEOs to mingle with other CEOs and the lure of Pebble.

I had a layover on my way to Pebble, a five-night stop in Santa Barbara, where Christine had a pet-sitting gig staying in a cozy downtown house where she was looking after two pooches, a short-legged gent named Calvin and his partner Yoshi, rescued from a Tijuana street and apparently able to live on no sleep. (Calvin, in this arranged marriage, had to be the brains of the operation.) Christine and I, during our ventures out, kept an eye on the clock in the name of responsible dog-sitting.

One afternoon, Christine persuaded Vern, the counterman at Sandpiper, a beautiful oceanfront public course up the coast from Santa Barbara, to let me slip out for some walking late-day golf. (Yep, that's the girl I married.) I played the front nine in a long dusk, owing to the heaving Pacific and the light bouncing off it. Christine walked with me. We finished and headed back to Calvin and Yoshi. A few days later, I was behind the wheel of my semi-large Hertz rental vehicle again, heading north on the 101, driving past ranches, farm fields, and mountain ranges, bound for Pebble.

George Plimpton, amateur contestant in the Pebble Beach pro-am, had a short, wheezing caddie named Abe. They were an odd couple. Abe, a former sardine fisherman, didn't have a laser rangefinder, as they did not exist then; nor did he have a PGA Tour–sanctioned yardage book, for the same reason. It wouldn't have mattered.

My path to Pebble was by way of Abe. For decades, the AT&T pro-am field had been massive, one of the biggest in professional golf. But in response to the threat of LIV Golf, the tournament was rechristened by the tour's overlords as a Signature Event (more ridiculous branding), and the size of the field was cut to less than half of what it once was, while the purse was doubled and then some.

Trying to get a job as a caddie in the tournament, I wrote to an amateur I knew in the field, Fred Perpall, the CEO of a large architecture-and-construction company in Dallas and the president of the United States Golf Association. I was Fred's Abe.

Fred, I quickly learned, was a golf-by-numbers guy. (It's all the rage.) His stock 6-iron, per the cheat sheet provided to me by Wes Worster, his Dallas teaching pro who was traveling with him, was his 168-yard club. It gave me pause. The golfing legend Payne Stewart sometimes employed a secret-legend caddie named Linn Strickler, a Vietnam vet who went by "Growler." Payne observed that when Growler worked for Curtis Strange and others, he offered precise yardages—222, 168, 92. But Growler's numbers for Payne all ended in 0 or 5, and Payne wanted to know why. "'Cause you're not that good," Growler said. I viewed the proffered cheat sheet as a guideline.

Fred was in his late forties and athletic. He had a tutored swing and an 8-handicap, the same as another pro-am contestant, Tom Brady. As a dresser, Fred was a scratch, maybe lower. Nobody on the range had a bigger presence, physically or otherwise—except Tom Brady.

Fred, understandably, was doing a lot of sightseeing on the range. All around him were established pros, tour caddies with familiar faces, and princes of finance and sport, among other fields. Wyndham Clark was hitting balls to Fred's left. Seven months earlier, during the U.S. Open at the Los Angeles Country Club, Fred had handed Clark the winner's trophy.

Fred is gregarious. He was at Pebble to play, of course, to try to contend over the thirty-six holes of pro-am play, but also to see and be seen.

A tech investor walking down the range stopped at Fred's workstation and said, "I look like the guy selling Peter Millar. You look like the guy modeling it." Fred was wearing Peter Millar golf pants, a Peter Millar shirt, a Peter Millar quarter-zip pullover—and a Seminole Golf Club visor. (He was a new member to the South Florida club where USGA board members have been prominent for generations.) The whole Pebble scene was recess-gone-wild. On the course, Fred saw somebody he knew who looked like he could have stepped off the set of *Succession*, the HBO series about a feuding family with a media empire at stake. The man saw Fred shove a 3-wood shot and half-sang, "'Push it, push it, push it real good.'" There was something hollow about Fred's laugh.

His innate manner is formal and proper. Maybe you have seen those traits in people who, like Fred, were born and raised in the Bahamas. It might be the European influence in Nassau, coupled with Fred's lifelong church-on-Sunday family life. He told me his surname came from the white French family who once owned his enslaved Black forebears. He had grown up in a working-class family, in a house with two bedrooms, one bathroom, and six people. The defining, and enduring, sorrow of the family's life was the shooting death of Fred's older brother, Randy, in Dallas, at age twenty-five. It fell to Fred to identify the body and bring Randy home. Fred's parents lived for Fred's successes, and they were considerable, starting with his dentist wife, their two daughters, his career, his civic-life prominence, his board seats, his rise in the USGA. Ten years after his first round of golf, not even, Fred had become the president of the USGA, a pro bono position once held by George H. W. Bush's maternal grandfather. He was juggling a great deal.

As a golfer on the rise, Fred had one big competitive advantage: good eye-hand coordination. That and strong hands. I once said to Curtis Strange, "You show me somebody who can shoot pool and make free throws, and I'll show you somebody who can get good at golf." Curtis is one of my favorite people in golf. He is not, by nature, an agreeable person.

He said, "I actually agree with that." *Actually*. Fred wasn't a pool player, but in his basketball prime, he was an 80 percent free-throw shooter. A lot of NBA players would like to shoot free throws at that rate.

Fred played basketball and ran track at the University of The Bahamas and later transferred to the University of Texas at Arlington to play basketball and study architecture. In Nassau, Fred's mother ran a small cafeteria where Fred, waiting on diners, got his customer-service training. Fred's father worked in the avionics department at Bahamasair, the national airline. Neither Fred's mother nor his father had the opportunity to go to college.

One day in his junior year, Fred called his father and said, "Coach wants me to change my major so I can focus more on basketball."

The senior Perpall was not an easy man. He said nothing for five seconds and then hung up. Fred didn't change his major. He did quit the basketball team. He got a bachelor's degree and a master's degree in architecture from UT Arlington.

As a kid, the first golfers Fred met were the wealthy members at the Lyford Cay Club, who gave him money to help send him on his academic way, but there was no obvious path to golf in Nassau for a working-class teenager unless you had a job at a club, and even then it wasn't easy. Fred moved from Atlanta to Dallas in his late thirties with his family and all his basketball gear, but no golf clubs. He didn't have golf clubs. He didn't play golf. In Dallas, he quickly realized, the game was a central part of the city's business culture.

The game became an obsession for Fred. Wes, his teacher, was along for the ride and then some. The USGA was desperate to change its public face—it had been top-heavy with old white men forever—and its leaders found their way to Fred. There were golf games, lunches, phone calls, emails, cigars after dinner. It didn't take long: Fred was on his way. His life story, and his skill with people, was like a wide-open door for him. His impeccable tailoring only helped.

As a USGA board member, Fred met Tiger a number of times, usually at a resort in the Bahamas called Albany, where Tiger held a winter tournament. Fred, like most everybody at the USGA, would like to see Tiger, the winner of nine USGA events—three USGA juniors, three U.S. Amateurs, three U.S. Opens—become the organization's ambassador to the world, as Arnold Palmer had been for many years. In 1975, Arnold became the chairman of a new USGA initiative called the Associates Program, by which regular golfers could become "members" of the USGA. Arnold went to the White House and signed up Jerry Ford for the program. I was in high school then and proud to have a plastic red, white, and blue USGA tag on my carry bag.* I knew plenty of other golfers with the same bag tag. USGA officials have had a long-standing fantasy about what Tiger could do in a similar role.

That first morning, as Wes worked with Fred on the Pebble Beach range, there was a lithe man hitting balls one spot over. The two golfers didn't know each other, but one of the things the tournament does is get like-minded people in the same place.

The man was Dermot Desmond, an Irish billionaire with an impish face and a curling mustache known to many equestrians, European financiers, Caribbean hoteliers, all manner of sportsmen, and hundreds of Irish golf people. Standing behind Dermot that morning was his caddie, Bo Martin, who had worked for Shane Lowry for years. The two Irishmen won the British Open together at Royal Portrush, near Belfast. But they had recently parted ways, as players and their caddies almost always eventually do. Dermot was helping a brother out.

For some years, Dermot's caddie in the Pebble pro-am was Dewey Arnette, an inimitable golf teacher, or maybe I should just say teacher. Dewey

---

* "I played in my first USGA junior event in 1982, and that's when I got my first USGA bag tag," says Lee Janzen, winner of two U.S. Opens, in 1993 and '98. "After I won the '93 Open I got a letter from Arnold. Jack, too. Those letters meant as much to me as the trophies."

was an excellent golfer who once made eight straight birdies at a PGA Tour event. As a golf instructor, he taught no two people the same way. He helped two future British Open winners, Darren Clarke of Northern Ireland and Pádraig Harrington of Ireland, with their short games, though there were some serious disagreements on the road to improvement. "Professional golfers do not want to hear hard truths," Dermot told me once.

Teaching elite players of a certain age—those who got good before the rise of Trackman and other number-spitting machines—can be challenging. For one thing, these players often know more about their swings than their teachers. Also, there's an independent streak in many top players, those who knew golf when it was played with the curving, short-flying balata ball that really did require more artistry. Those golfers—Sam Snead all his life, Lee Trevino in his prime, Ernie Els as a young pro—had to figure out more things for themselves. They learned more on the course than on the range. They taught themselves by playing in all kinds of weather and off every kind of turf. That independent DIY spirit is why I am drawn to many of them. But it is also true that almost nobody gets good at golf, or better at golf, alone. Bobby Jones had Stewart Maiden. Jack Nicklaus had Jack Grout. Dermot Desmond had Dewey Arnette.

Dewey gave Dermot a one-sentence insight into how to use Gene Sarazen's gift to golf, the sand wedge, and it's a keeper: "The edge of the sand wedge is hell, and its bounce is heaven."

It means that when using a sand wedge, especially when playing from a greenside bunker or any fluffy lie, the first point of clubhead-ground contact is with the bottom of the flange—the thick, rounded part on the sole of the club. Bounce is a measurement, the angle between the club's leading edge and the bottom of the flange, but as many golfers use the words, *flange* and *bounce* are the same. The leading edge is hell because it digs. It's a knife. The club's bounce lets the clubhead *slide* under the ball. That's how a ball gets up and out of a trap and up and out of the rough. To me, the shot in golf with the most sex appeal is not the nuked drive.

(I'm dismissive of *Chicks dig the long ball*, among other Nike marketing claims.) It's any take-something-off-it wedge shot, with speed through the ball and a light grip. The wedge's bounce provides the up and out—that's why bounce is heaven. You often hear golfers talk about "explosion shots" out of traps, but that phrase really paints the wrong picture. The clubhead just splashes some sand out and onto the green, like a pizza chef throwing a pinch of white flour on a marble counter.

I realize this is getting technical, but we're here to get better, right? Golf requires technique. The short-game guru Stan Utley likes to say that golf is 95 percent technique, 3 percent mental attitude, and 2 percent luck. The best golf instructors, like Dewey, are teaching technique, logic, fundamentals, physics. That's where they start. But when the teacher-student relationship really clicks, there's more going on.

Dewey once noted that I had no headcovers. (He didn't use headcovers, either.) Everything he gave me started with that, my desire for simplicity. Curtis Strange will sometimes say, "When did the golf swing get so complicated?" It doesn't have to be. Anyway, Dewey's ability to teach the golf swing cannot fully explain Dermot's devotion to Dewey. Not by a long shot.

Dermot was once playing in the Pebble Beach pro-am with Pádraig Harrington as his pro partner and Dewey as his caddie. Pádraig was on the back tee, about to play. Dermot and Dewey were standing nearby, one tee up.

"We better get out of the way or we could be killed," Dermot said.

"I'm ready," Dewey said. He was closing in on fifty. He died at sixty-two. Cancer.

On the Pebble range, Fred Perpall watched Dermot hit a beautiful draw shot (swing by Dewey) using a new toy in his bag, a driver with a hot-pink shaft. They had a quick, pleasant exchange. Soon after, Fred left the range, boarded a shuttle van, and went to the course, talking with the driver along the way. Wes and I were one row back. Wes was from Trinity Forest, Fred's home club in Dallas. He was in his late thirties and square-jawed, built like an NFL wide receiver. Wes had a knapsack packed with anything Fred might require. Fred's clubs, custom-fit to accommodate his six-foot-six frame, were behind us in a stylish blue golf bag. I could see why the two men were close. Casual was not their thing. Cigars had their place; tees another; USGA ball markers another. Fred was the sixty-seventh president of the USGA and the headcover on his driver was stenciled with *FP 67*. He had a handsewn alligator-skin headcover on his Scotty Cameron putter. Fred had told me I could lose anything in the bag—as long as it wasn't that headcover. I think the actual list was far longer.

Getting out of the van, Fred greeted the volunteers at the staging area. On the first tee, he introduced himself to the starter and the marshal. He was a missionary with a message: *It's a new day at the USGA.* He was giving out USGA ball markers like a latter-day John D. Rockefeller dispensing dimes.

While we stood on Pebble's first tee, our first hole together, Fred asked me his first player question, and it was totally reasonable: "How far to that bunker?"

The first at Pebble is an uphill, gently curving dogleg right. Not a special hole except for where you are, at the Pebble Beach Golf Links. As you stand on the tee, your eye goes to the lone bunker on the left side of the fairway. The day was cool, windy, gray, and the ground was soft. Still, that fairway bunker was borderline reachable, if Fred clocked one with a driver.

I fished my tournament-sanctioned yardage book out of my back pocket and tried to decipher the sea of dots, lines, and tiny numbers on the map of the first hole. The modern yardage book is far more detailed and complicated than the ones I had used for some years, starting in the 1980s, and I didn't have my reading glasses on. Fred had not hit even a single shot and I was already choking.

Wes, in his capable way, got out a rangefinder from his knapsack. (I didn't have a rangefinder and had never used one.) He zeroed in on the target and announced the yardage in seconds: 230 to the front of the bunker. Could Fred fly it 230 uphill in cool, damp air? Maybe. *Maybe.* Had it been my own practice round, I would have tried to smash a driver at the trap and let it fade, as my good drives tend to do. If driver was too much (not likely), I'd know for next time. But this was Fred's practice round, and Fred's game, shaped by Wes, was all golf-by-numbers. Most modern golf had gone that way, really. I was hopelessly (pretty much by choice) out of it. Still, I had a job to do. I needed to up my game.

When you have these little episodes where things go awry, I think it's important not to lose your way. I was out of practice, but I know how to caddie. I have caddied in the national championships of Belgium, Canada, Ireland, Italy, Portugal, Scotland, and other countries. I have caddied in the Masters, the U.S. Open, the British Open, and the PGA Championship, among other notable events. I knew Pebble. I know how pro-ams work. I could caddie for Fred.

The joy of being there washed over me. I felt like I was in my midtwenties again, caddying for George Archer, Bill Britton, Tony Cerdá, Mike Donald, Steve Elkington, Brad Faxon, Al Geiberger, Jamie Howell—I could go on. I had a job that was getting me deep into Pebble Beach and its celebrated pro-am tournament, one I associated with the U.S. Open, with Bing Crosby and George Plimpton, with Ben Crenshaw and Johnny Miller, among other people I have known and admired. I watched Tiger, at the peak of his powers, win a U.S. Open at Pebble by fifteen shots. I watched Tom Watson, at sixty, play Pebble in his final U.S. Open, making a cut he had no business making after a first-round 78. I saw Bill Murray perspiring through his flannel shirt on a cold winter day in the AT&T, fooling nobody with his whole nonchalant act. I played Pebble Beach with Michael Murphy and followed the touring pro Jeff Julian around Pebble as he played in the AT&T, ignoring, almost gleefully, the disease (ALS) that was ransacking his body. My friend Sam Reeves, after playing golf around the world for eighty years and counting, says there's no course he loves more than Pebble Beach. Jack Nicklaus says the same. Pebble gets her hooks in you, and I had found my way back to her. I've had a lot of good luck in my life. I put stumbling into golf near the top of the list.

One morning, a tournament official asked me to drive an amateur to a distant tee where he was to join two other players for a practice round. The am introduced himself as Josh as he got into the passenger seat. We headed out, arrived at the appointed tee, and saw that it was empty. Now Josh had neither playing partners nor a slot on the course to call his own. I suggested that he join Fred and Fred's practice-round partner, Thomas. Josh said that sounded fine. As it turned out, Josh was a basketball guy (the president of the Denver Nuggets) and a good golfer. The threesome—Fred, Thomas, Josh—got along well. They talked about golf and basketball and other weighty subjects. When it was over, Josh thanked me for getting him into the game. How nice is that?

Earlier that day, I found myself walking up Pebble's eighteenth hole, green to tee, in a spitting rain, my windbreaker rattling, the cries of the gulls muffled by a ski cap tight against my ears. Imagine bottling all that, the sight and sound and smell. The wind off the ocean. Not to sell it. Of course not. Just to use it now and again. Something you could share with your golfy friends.

The AT&T pro-am, in its first year as a branded Signature Event, was a four-round no-cut tournament for the pros, with the amateurs playing in the first two rounds on two courses before clearing the stage for Scottie Scheffler, Justin Thomas, Rory McIlroy, and seventy-seven other PGA Tour members. With rare exceptions, you have to be a tour member to play in these small-field, big-purse Signature Events, the PGA Tour's misguided (my opinion) response to the threat of LIV Golf, the upstart global golf league fronted by Greg Norman and backed by Saudi billionaires with oil money to burn. LIV had already poached various American-born PGA Tour stars—Phil Mickelson, Bryson DeChambeau, Dustin Johnson, Brooks Koepka, and some less-celebrated PGA Tour veterans like Charles Howell III and Kevin Na—through the age-old promise of more money for less work. The PGA Tour was looking more like LIV Golf with almost every change it was making.

I know of only one golf administrator, my man Fred Perpall, who had an original take on how the PGA Tour could have handled the LIV threat from the start. Early on, I asked Fred what advice, if asked, he would give the PGA Tour commissioner when dealing with tour players who wanted to go LIV. "I'd tell him, 'Let them go,'" Fred said. "It's hard to confer the value of what you have to people who don't appreciate that value." By trying to compete with LIV, the PGA Tour was turning into LIV and losing its own identity. *Let them go* might sound naive or idealistic, but it would let the PGA Tour continue to stand for what it has always been: a merit-based system for players competing in community-minded charity tournaments. Golf—professional golf at its highest levels—was getting hurt by all of this. It made me double down on the ball and what the player did with it. Any ball, any player. Because that part was still loaded with mystery.

Fred's pro partner, for his two tournament rounds, was Lucas Glover, winner of the 2009 U.S. Open at Bethpage Black on Long Island. I've known Lucas for a long time. He's smart and direct and does the *New York Times* crossword puzzle every day. Lucas has no interest in LIV Golf and was even dubious about the Signature Events and all the guaranteed money that came with them. "Meritocracy is dead," he told me. He was one of the few players voicing that view. He was one of the few players who would understand the wisdom of *Let them go.*

Lucas doesn't wear a golf glove, and if anybody since Ben Hogan, another no-glove golfer, has a better grip than Lucas Glover's, I have not seen it. His hands on a club look like Mickey Mantle's on a bat. Lucas has the baseball gene on his mother's side and his father's, too. You need the gift of extreme athleticism to make it as a tournament golfer, but a sentence from Hogan is at the core of the golfing dream machine: "The average golfer is entirely capable of building a repeating swing and breaking 80."

A few years after his U.S. Open win, Lucas told me the best moment of the whole thing was not hoisting the trophy or reciting a Top Ten List for David Letterman. (Number 6: "I had Phil Mickelson in the office pool.") The most powerful feeling, he said, was walking onto the range at the next tournament, in Hartford, and realizing the other players were looking at him in a new way.

But that was then. More recently, Lucas had developed a new take on it all. He had won the Open at age twenty-nine. By his mid-forties, he had endured various setbacks. He had struggled with his short putting—an epic and public battle with the yips—and sought help in uncommon places. He had worked with a firefighter and later a Navy SEAL sharpshooter. Both men were experts in how to breathe in stressful situations, how to still the body and mind, how to move on after things go wrong. In their work, they were trying to save lives amid the prospect of death. Lucas didn't dare compare his job with theirs. But he was committed to getting better at short putting.

Somewhere on his way to middle age, Lucas stopped caring about his status among his peers. He was taking control of validation for himself. (He was not the first U.S. Open winner to go down that path. Hogan once said, "I am the sole judge of my own standards.") Lucas and I were eating lunch at a deli in New York City as we had this conversation, a few months before the AT&T. (Neither of us had any reason to think we'd wind up together at Pebble.) Lucas was in New York with his wife, who was making the rounds at Fashion Week. I had brought him the Sunday *New York Times* crossword puzzle—needlessly, as it turned out. He had already done it. That was in early fall on the Upper West Side at Barney Greengrass. Now it was winter on the Monterey Peninsula at Pebble Beach.

Fred was playing well in that first round at Pebble. On the practice green and in his practice round, you could see he had a rhythmic, flowing putting stroke, as good free-throw shooters often do. But that stroke had gone missing early in this first round. He was struggling to get his putts to the hole.

The eighth at Pebble is both gorgeous and hair-raising, a par-4 defined by an oceanfront teeing ground and a mid-hole cliff with fatal implications for both golf ball and golfer. The goal is to hit a tee shot short of the cliff and a second shot over a swirling cove of ocean water en route to a smallish green. Fred hit a superb tee shot and then a solid approach shot. As a wise man once said, good shots must come in groups of two.

Fred now had a slow birdie putt, twenty-five feet or so. The eighth was one of his stroke holes. I was afraid he'd leave yet another putt short, possibly way short, as golfers in stress often do. Since the first fairway, Lucas had been doing his own thing, pretty much, and he and Fred were not really engaging. It's reasonable to ask the pro in a pro-am for help, but you have to choose your spots with care.

"Luke, would you say Fred's putt here is uphill?" I asked in a loud voice. It was definitely uphill, but I was trying to get Fred in the mood to stroke his putt with more oomph than he had been using. A tap-in

4-for-3 would be just lovely. Hearing some putting insights from Lucas could only help.

"For sure," Lucas said. He considered Fred's putt and said to him, "See that mountain back there?" Beyond the course, beyond the houses beside it, there was a modest mountain. At least, it was more than a hill. "You're putting right up that mountain."

What a green-reading insight: Consider the big picture. At Augusta National, the club caddies like to say the putts break toward Rae's Creek. At the Amex, the resort caddies like to say the putts break toward the city of Indio. (Told that, the actor Samuel L. Jackson said, "Yeah, but where the fuck is Indio?") Now Lucas Glover was bringing in a distant mountain in the name of a twenty-five-footer.

Fred took Lucas's advice, gave his putt a solid rap, and got the ball to the hole. He tapped in. Three good shots. A natural par that, for the purposes of the Glover-Perpall pro-am better-ball score, was a birdie. A 4-for-3, in the language of pro-ams.

Lucas had a shorty for birdie himself, and he was careful with it, a thirty-inch down-the-mountain putt. His stroke had not a bit of indecision in it, and in it went. Nothing but net. You don't have a twenty-year career on the PGA Tour without holing thousands of little putts. It's the misses from a foot that make the rounds on social media. Lucas knows how that goes. You can choose to pay attention or not.

As good as Fred's 4-for-3 on eight was, his play on the par-5 eighteenth, the beauty queen that ends the day at Pebble, was better, in that grind-it-out way that is essential to any good round. Lucas hit his second shot in the ocean on his way to a 6. Not good for Lucas or the team. Fred hit five consecutive mediocre shots. Not good for the team. But then he buried a five-footer for bogey. The eighteenth was a stroke hole for Fred, and that meant it went on the card as a 6-for-5 par. He saved the team a shot right there. They signed for a better-ball 68. Lucas had shot 73 on his ball, so Fred's contributions were significant. He had cut his man five shots. They were in the respectable middle of the eighty-team field, a good way to go out for a Thursday-night dinner and start thinking about the second round.

It mattered for one reason above all others: Fred cared. If anything, he cared too much. But if you don't care, why bother playing competitive golf? If you don't care, why bother counting up your shots at all? Now and again, you'll hear somebody say, "I'm just out here for the walk." How do you figure out where your golf game is if you're just out there for a walk? How are you going to get better with that attitude? When you're playing a match or in a tournament, the course comes alive, and your opponents do, too. Your head gets in it, and so does the rest of you. A round of golf as a walk? If I may take a moment to speak for the Fred-and-Mike team: We can't relate.

For a half century or more, Sam Reeves has been a magnet for golfers. Over the course of Pebble week, all manner of golf people dropped by the Reeves home on a dune between the Pacific Ocean and the Cypress Point golf course. Rory McIlroy came by for a meal. So did Jordan Spieth, Justin Thomas, Jim "Bones" Mackay, Brandon Wu, Nick Dunlap, plus other assorted pros, ams, caddies, teachers, and agents. Sam asked Dunlap if he was nervous over his putt to win the Amex. "What was there to be nervous about?" Nick said. "Either way, I wasn't making any money."

Sam had a young friend staying at the house, a putting coach from Ireland named Stephen Sweeney. Sam had been taking lessons from him and was continuing a lifelong quest to hit his putts from the inside and not cut across them. A sliced putt, breaking away from the hole, will never go in, whereas a putt hooking toward the hole does. That's why you hear the phrase *At least I missed on the pro side.* When

Stephen and Sam talked putting, I hung on every word. Putting is my bugaboo.

One night, as a small group ate leftovers at a round table in the warm Reeves kitchen, steam on the windows, Sam talked about Doug Sanders as an unbeatable amateur in their home state of Georgia in the 1950s, Titanic Thompson as a golf hustler in the 1940s, Bobby Jones as a national sporting hero in the 1930s. For Brandon Wu, a Stanford grad in his twenties, it was like being back at school in a history class, but surely more entertaining.

After last call for cookies came and went, Stephen casually mentioned a departure he had to make long before sunrise. Without hesitation, Sam said, "I'll take you wherever you need to go, whenever you need to be there." I aspire to be a person who can say such a selfless thing and mean it. I aspire, period.

Sam and his wife, Betsy, were both in their late eighties. Sam was born the same year (1934) as my late father-in-law, and Betsy was born the same year (1935) as my late mother-in-law. Sam is an independent thinker, as was my own father, and Betsy is warm and welcoming, as was my own mother. I'm a point-collecting hotel person by road habit (everybody: HO-tel, MO-tel, Holiday *Inn*), but I would never turn down a chance to stay with Sam and Betsy.

Going back to the tournament's earliest years, amateurs at the Crosby were guaranteed three rounds and played a fourth—at Pebble Beach on Sunday, with network cameras rolling—if they survived the fifty-four-hole cut. There were 180 teams in those years, twenty-five of which would play on Sunday. Getting to play on Sunday was the holy grail for every am in the field. That goal became a bit for Jack Lemmon, the Oscar-winning actor, who played year after year with Peter Jacobsen. Every year, upon arrival, Jack Lemmon would tell people that he'd trade one of his two Oscars for a chance to play Pebble on Sunday. "And now here's Jack Lemmon, about to hit that all-important eighth shot," the broadcaster Jim McKay once told a Saturday audience. The TV commentators had to get their good Jack Lemmon lines in on Saturday. He never made it to Sunday.

In his half-dozen or more appearances in the tournament, Sam was going down that same road. And then he became the oldest amateur, at eighty-two, to make the cut. It was not a shocker. For one thing, he could break his age regularly, and he had no issue walking a course for four straight tournament rounds. He was always trying to get better.

Sam and Betsy moved from Memphis to Fresno in 1962 and started going to Pebble for the tournament soon after. They would see Bing Crosby often, at Pebble Beach and at Cypress Point. They fell hard for Pebble and the Monterey Peninsula. Sam's success in the cotton trade—when China opened its docks to American cotton, Sam was bobbing in the Port of Shanghai—allowed Betsy and Sam to buy a sprawling one-story house off 17-Mile Drive. Leaving the Reeves house each morning, I'd coast down their short entrance road, heading for pale green Pacific rollers as they heaved and hoed on their way to shore. The guesthouse, where I bunked, had a bathroom with a heated floor. It's unlikely that another caddie had nicer digs that week.

One night, Sam and Betsy and I went to a club dinner at Cypress Point. A hard rain fell all through the evening, and when we returned to the house, Sam led Betsy on a serpentine path from the car to the front door, avoiding the many puddles. They were under an umbrella and arm in arm. More than once, in a tone that was both lovely and moving, I heard Sam say, "This way, Bets; this way, Bets."

In its new format as a small-field Signature Event, there was no cut for the amateurs, who were done after thirty-six holes, and no cut for the pros, on the docket for seventy-two. The eighty amateurs in the field (180 was history) played one round at Pebble and the other at Spyglass Hill. The ams were playing to win, of course, but the main goal was to get invited back—not at all a given, as there are many more candidates for spots than spots. Returning meant the prospect of making new friends, often new friends in useful places, and going deeper with the guys you already knew. The old-boy network is alive and well in upper-crust golf, and a place in the amateur field of the AT&T is one marker that announces your arrival. The amateur field was pretty much a sea of white businessmen, plus Tom Brady and Larry Fitzgerald, the former NFL receiver. There were only a handful of women in the event, Condoleezza Rice and Heidi Ueberroth, the co-chair of the Pebble Beach Company, among them. (Heidi's father was the former baseball commissioner Peter Ueberroth.) There were Black business executives aside from Fred in the field, but very few. You want to say that something has to give here, but that sentiment has been making the rounds for decades.

Golf pros, the most famous among them, enjoy a path to business leaders in ways you seldom see in other sports. Some sports-section legends—a Joe DiMaggio, a Wilt Chamberlain, a Franco Harris—are adopted by the city where they made their name, their status conferred on them by ordinary fans. That's why so many of them open restaurants and car dealerships. They know their people and their people know them. You could certainly say the same for Arnold Palmer, but he was also right at home in the White House and in any corporate boardroom. I can still see the pride on Arnold's face when he told me he had become the first professional golfer asked to join Augusta National, and how happy he was to be a dues-paying member, not an honorary one. We were in his garage, converted into a workroom, at his Bay Hill condo in Florida. Dow Finsterwald, one of his closest friends, was there, too. The top of the hour came, and Arnold opened a dorm-room fridge and retrieved some cold ones. Arnold joined Augusta in 1999, the same year he and Peter Ueberroth and some others bought Pebble Beach from its Japanese owners. No golfer had more business opportunities than Arnold.

For decades, he was shrewdly marketed and advised by Mark McCormack, the founder of the sports agency IMG, and by McCormack's deputy, Alastair Johnston. Arnold and McCormack were pro-am partners at Pebble Beach going back to its Crosby days. McCormack knew how things worked at Pebble. It was McCormack who urged Ted Forstmann, a well-clubbed golfer and the founder of the investment firm Forstmann, Little & Company, to start coming to the AT&T.

Forstmann Little owned Gulfstream Aerospace, and McCormack told Forstmann that the tournament would be a good place to wine and dine potential buyers of Gulfstream jets (though not Arnold, who flew Cessna Citations). Forstmann did as McCormack suggested. He hosted a series of well-soaked dinners for customers and potential customers at a steak house in the Lodge at Pebble called Club XIX. He started playing in the tournament with Vijay Singh when Singh was one of the best golfers in the world. In Forstmann's office in New York City, high above Fifth Avenue and overlooking Central Park, there were photos of Singh and Forstmann playing golf together, with Singh in a shirt bearing the Forstmann Little name. On an office wall was an Augusta National scorecard with their names and scores on it. You can follow the money in thin-air golf as you can in most anything.

Even with Singh as his pro partner, Forstmann was no threat to win the AT&T pro-am. He couldn't sniff his handicap. Forstmann was the opposite of a sandbagger, a golfer with an inflated handicap. He presented himself as an 8, but from what I saw, he was more like a 16. A vanity handicap if ever there was one. You're tempted to say that golfers with vanity handicaps will overpromise and underdeliver in other aspects of their lives, but it's not a hard-and-fast rule. George Plimpton played as an 18 at Pebble, not that he could play to it. In his case, it wasn't a vanity handicap. It was the highest handicap the tournament allowed in those days.

Fred Perpall's 8 handicap, from everything I could tell, was spot-on. Of course, if the USGA president isn't going to have a legit handicap, who is? In a pro-am format, the amateur rarely holes out on every hole, so there's no real individual scorekeeping. But Fred was hitting the shots of a low-80s golfer, at times lower, in that first round. Then came the second.

I met Fred and Wes at Pebble that morning, a little after seven. Wes was staying at the Lodge. Fred was, too, with his wife, Abi. In addition to being Fred's teaching pro, Wes was also Fred's driver for the week at Pebble. As Wes drove Fred's rental, a big, boxy SUV, on the curvy two-mile ride to Spyglass, Fred tried to catch up on his working life.

The company he ran, the Beck Group, had close to a thousand employees, but the number was about to be reduced by one. Fred was on his cell phone, calmly speaking to one of his lieutenants about a termination package for another executive. Fred said, "I want to give him a soft landing here." He later told me, "Construction is a tough business. Different business units succeed or they don't. I think you have to look hard at the numbers, but be gentle with the people."

For a big, expensive resort course, the arrival area at Spyglass is oddly small and cozy. The course is surrounded by dense forest, vast ocean, and expensive homes. Fred was in the front passenger seat. I was in the SUV's second row, and Fred's clubs were in the boot. We had the first tee time of the day, starting on the tenth, and arrived at the player parking lot with plenty of time to spare. We were one of the first cars of the morning.

As Wes entered the lot, a uniformed officer rushed over and started making hysterical *You ain't parking here* gestures. Wes stopped. Fred rolled down the window and asked what the problem was. The problem was that the parking was for professional contestants only, not amateurs. But from where I sat, the officer's body language and tone did not match the offense. In that setting, at that quiet hour? Fred and I got out of the SUV. I pulled the clubs from the trunk and put on the tournament caddie bib with PERPALL on its back.

Fred had a flashback. In Atlanta, Black executives with big profiles were common, but then the Perpall family moved to Highland Park in Dallas, where Fred became, in his late thirties, the new CEO of Beck. Highland Park is staid, affluent, and overwhelmingly white. In their first eighteen months there, Fred or Abi, a Black mom often driving her two Black daughters, were pulled over by police seven times. To Fred, each of these episodes was a clear case of racial profiling. Neither was ever cited for anything. He went to city officials and offered chapter-and-verse details of what he and Abi had endured. Things changed after that—for them.

There was nothing in Fred's background or nature that was going to let that early-morning Spyglass moment just pass. In a civil tone and with direct language, he told the officer and his supervisor that he had parked in that lot in the past and had not known it was only for pros. He also made it clear that the officer's reaction, in his opinion, was way over the top.

When we talked about the matter later, Fred said, "Old Fred would have gone ballistic there, getting names, badge numbers, plate numbers." But through his forties, Fred had been in therapy for what he called "survivor's guilt," a reference to his brother's murder, along with an effort to understand the various struggles of a hardscrabble childhood in a crowded house in a rough neighborhood. Fred had developed a relationship with a prominent Dallas pastor, T. D. Jakes. Once, in a sermon, Jakes quoted Fred: "'When my partners got better, my business got better.'" A preacherly pause, and then he said it again: "'When my *partners* got better, my *business* got better.'" Fred only wished Pastor Jakes had used the word *life* instead of *business*. Fred had spent the past decade trying to improve himself. In that moment, there at the Spyglass parking lot entrance, he tried to imagine what the officer's morning had been like. Fred was pissed. But you never saw the veins in his neck.

Love-love-love has its limits. Fred told me about a new member of Trinity Forest who had told Fred, a founding member of the club a decade earlier, that he could not park in member parking. Old Fred came roaring out.

Fred and I went first to the Spyglass driving range and then to its practice putting green. Between the two spots, Fred good-morninged his way through his whole new crew. Lucas and his caddie, Tommy Lamb. The other pro in our group, Seamus Power, and his caddie, Simon Keelan, both from Ireland, both well known to Dermot Desmond. Power's amateur partner, Herbert Allen III, president of the investment bank Allen & Company, and Herb's local caddie, Chris Musson. Golf bonds people as few things do. Eight people put together under pretty random circumstances. On the first day, there's a lot of look-'em-in-the-eye introductory handshaking, followed by exaggerated repeat-the-name recitations. By the second day, it's like you've known one another forever: *Where'd you get dinner, where you playing next, can you believe what the dude shot, and what's his handicap, anyway?*

In tournament golf, it's always hard to follow a low round with another low round. That's what the TV commentators say about the pros, and it seems to be true. My friend Mike Donald shot a first-round 64 at the 1990 Masters, followed by an 82 in the second. Spyglass was sopping wet all through our round there. On any hole where you played even a single shot out of the rough, you were likely to make a bogey or worse. Fred had a lot of holes like that. Our Friday was nothing like our Thursday.

On one approach shot, Fred asked for a yardage before playing from a downhill lie out of wet rough on the left side of the hole to a back-right hole location.

"Ninety-eight," I said, giving him the to-the-pin number, calculated off a nearby sprinkler head.

Fred flushed his 50-degree wedge, and his ball pitched over the green.

Herb Allen and his caddie, Chris, were about six yards in front of us, but let's use the Growler rule and call it five. After Herb played, Fred said to Chris, "What'd you guys have there?"

"Ninety-two," Chris said.

A case of the red-ass washed over me.

"Have you noticed," I said to Chris but really to Fred, "that when you play out of wet rough with the grass growing with ya, the shot kinda knuckles and just flies?" I should have mentioned the downhill lie. Shots from downhill lies often go farther than you might expect. For one thing, on instinct alone, you're moving your ball back in your stance.

Chris had a lot of experience in golf, as a caddie and as a player. "For sure," he said. Something close to that.

We all have ways of defending ourselves.

Later, on the long, scenic, and narrow par-4 fourth hole, with a long, scenic, and comically narrow green, I suggested to Fred that he hit driver at a distant crane. This was our thirteenth hole in the second round, and it was here that Fred hit, by far, his best drive of the tournament, taking dead aim at the crane. The shot soared, flew the fairway, and landed in shrubbery. The ball was never seen again.

"That's on me," I said, and apologized. Wrong club, wrong line. What else was there to say? I gave Fred space.

These things are bound to happen. There has to be give and take between player and caddie and an understanding that not everything is going to be perfect or close to it.

The next time driver came out, Fred hit a dead pull. His ball sailed into a tall pine tree before parachuting down, coming to rest maybe a hundred yards ahead of the tee box. We arrived at the ball to see it sitting in a puddle surrounded by soggy rough. Ten yards away, in a large backyard, a midday golf-watching party was under way. One of the guys, maybe thinking that Fred was a well-dressed duffer in over his head, golf-splained to the president of the United States Golf Association that he was entitled to take a free drop because of the casual water around his ball. I felt a sudden urge to come to my man's defense. "He's a good golfer," I said, "and good on the rules, too."

Three holes later, we were done. Our eightsome scattered to the wind, with new phone numbers stored in phones. The Glover-Perpall team was headed to the near-bottom of the eighty-team field. I was relieved that there was no motion for a highlight-reel lunch. I couldn't wait to get back to my car and into dry socks and shoes—I was wet to the bone. Back at Pebble Beach, the sun was finally coming out and a drying wind was starting to blow. I was overcome by the urge to play.

Before George went on tour for *The Bogey Man*, and before going to a Detroit Lions preseason training camp as a last-string quarterback for *Paper Lion*, he had already endured two stints as a writer in the arena. He went three rounds with Archie Moore and lived to write it up. And he pitched in a postseason exhibition baseball game, the basis for his book *Out of My League*. *Paper Lion* had just been released in January 1966 when Plimpton played in the Crosby, accompanied by his dogged caddie, Abe, and his pro, Bob Bruno, mournful (Plimpton's fine word) in his struggles. He and Plimpton missed the pro-am cut by 14 shots. Bruno made the cut for pros and finished in a tie for sixty-second place.

At the Yale library where the writer Herbert Warren Wind's papers are housed, there's a July 8, 1963, letter from Plimpton to Wind that offers a dire sporting prediction.

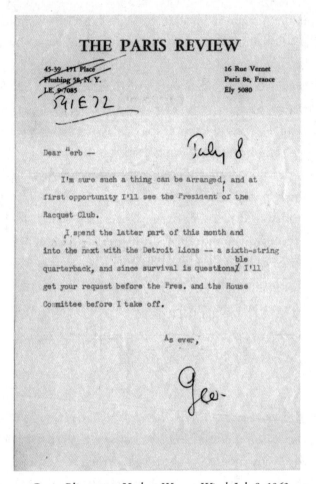

George Plimpton to Herbert Warren Wind, July 8, 1963.

Of course, Plimpton did survive it. We have the book as evidence, and the movie, too (Alan Alda plays Plimpton). George was our vessel: He took a snap, and we took a snap; he played Pebble, and we played Pebble. This is a roundabout way of making a request.

As I write about my own golfing activity here, a request, please: Can you try to view me as a sort of proxy for you? In other words, there *you* are, watching Lucas Glover point to the mountain and realizing that a distant mountain will influence the speed of a putt. My man's birdie putt is *your* birdie putt. ("I'll take you there," etc.) Because if I uncover something on this long green trip that helps you in your golfing quest, well, that would be wonderful. That would be grand.

When Fred and I were done, I gave him a cigar. Knowing nothing about cigars, I did what people do: bought an expensive one. I bro-hugged Fred, shook hands with Wes, ate a free hot lunch in caddie dining, took a cookie to go, got behind the wheel of my own semi-large Hertz rental vehicle, and made the short drive to the Pacific Grove Golf Links, a public course owned and operated by the city of Pacific Grove. As I stood at the pro shop's counter, credit card in hand, I figured I had at least two hours of daylight left, plus dusk, plus the light of the moon, if it came to that.

Is it possible to play the back nine?

The counterman looked at an electronic tee sheet and then out the window. He knew what everybody who has played Pacific Grove knows. Its back nine is duney, old, firm, scruffy—a delight. I'm not saying it's great like Pebble is great, but it is wonderful. The holes are short, and par is a realistic goal on any of them. I have played that back nine, and sometimes just parts of it, many times: by myself, with friends, with strangers. With the late touring pro Jeff Julian, ALS coursing through his body. With Mike Donald after an early-morning game at Cypress Point. With my friend and longtime *Sports Illustrated* colleague Alan Shipnuck, who got his start in golf as a Pebble Beach cart boy. With Casey Boyns, a veteran Pebble Beach caddie and an accomplished amateur golfer. We were joined by a lady who could maybe shoot 120, and Casey could not have been nicer or more helpful to her. Being with Casey makes you want to be a better person.

I paid the eighteen-hole twilight green fee (fifty-two dollars) that Friday afternoon. Happiness washed over me as I made my way to the tenth tee, bag on my back. My bag, my clubs, my golf, my swings, on a course that anybody can play.

Nine holes of golf is sometimes all you need. I have played a lot of golf with Scots in Scotland at courses off the tourist map. They don't view golf as an all-day activity. I feel the same. In the early part of this new year, I had played a quick nine at the O'Donnell course in Palm Springs and a quick nine at Sandpiper, near Santa Barbara. And now I was about to play the back nine at Pacific Grove. One month into it, *Do the Loco-Motion* was off to a good start.

The course nearest to our house in Philadelphia is a pale green nine-holer called St. Martins, in the city limits of Philadelphia, a living antique with spongy zoysia-grass fairways and greens that are almost feminine, they're so beguiling and mysterious. Christine sometimes walks its perimeter with friends, and it's the course I play most often. By myself, I can get in nine holes in an hour on my lunch break and can play them in a twosome in ninety minutes. I am lucky enough to have six annual majors in my life: the four men's majors I cover most years—the Masters, the PGA Championship, the U.S. and British Opens—plus the two St. Martins championships, one in the spring, one in the fall, both handicap events. And maybe I should list one more: the Shivas, named for Shivas Irons. Here's Shivas, from page 67 in my edition of *Golf in the Kingdom*: "My friends, devoted discipline and grace will bring ye knowin's and powers everywhere, in all your life, in all your works if they're good works, in all your loves if they're good loves. Ye'll come away from the links with a new hold on life, that is certain if ye play the game with all your heart." Two sentences that cannot be improved.

Our little gang of Philadelphia golf bums played the first Shivas in 1990, an event put together on short notice, held after the last game of the 1990 World Series and the late-October day Christine and I got married. Had that series gone seven games, Shivas '90 would not have been played. But the Reds beat the A's in four straight, and that made all the difference.

I shot 82 on the Tillinghast course of the Philadelphia Cricket Club, beat the eleven other guys in the field, and have been trying to win it again ever since. I won the *net* side of the event, I should say, where you take handicap strokes off your total score. It did get me the Shivas Trophy. My friend Burt McHugh won the gross event. A few years after our first Shivas, I became a godfather to Burt's namesake son. That's golf for you, one part of life dovetailing into another. After college, Burt played some modest mini-tour golf, didn't make a check, and the USGA still made him wait a year to get his amateur status back. The USGA was a stern father in that era, presiding over all of us. Golfers need supervision.

It was a cool afternoon when we played that first Shivas, and we ate dinner in front of the walk-in fireplace in the Cricket Club club-house, a converted farmhouse. Burt, for his efforts, was given one-year possession of a framed black-and-white photo of the Royal & Ancient clubhouse, the sandstone fortress that looks over the Old Course. The photo is from 1930, but almost nothing since then has changed.

The oceanside nine at Pacific Grove was opened for play in 1932. It was designed by Jack Neville, the co-designer of Pebble Beach. Pretty much nothing has changed there, either.

I played the little par-3 tenth that Friday afternoon and then caught up to a slender college student who was also playing alone. We joined up.

The young man's name was Jason Snow, and he had a wild and energetic swing. His little bag was latched to the back of an electric cart. He played with no glove and a ten-finger baseball grip and wore baggy khaki pants that could not contain his shirttails, not that he cared. He'd grown up in Burbank, near Los Angeles, gone to Burbank High, and started caddying at Hillcrest (long-ago home course of the Marx Brothers) while attending Pasadena City College. When we met, Jason was a student at Chico State, five hours away by car. He had made the drive down to Pebble to watch the tournament, drawn to it as both golf nut and betting man. He was sleeping in his car.

He knew who had shot what and something about every pro in the field at Pebble. He could not believe I had caddied for an amateur in the tournament. He told me his life's dream was to be a full-time Pebble Beach caddie. When I hit a shot into a thick beach shrub, Jason got on his stomach to retrieve the ball. When I asked for a line on a blind shot, he said, "Hit it at the rainbow." He was an interesting kid.

We went around the back once, and then did it again. We played ready golf and were broadly compatible, except I can play happily in silence, and Jason is a compulsive talker. When we came off the seventeenth green the second time, there was almost no daylight left. There was only one group behind us, and they were playing with glow-in-the-dark golf balls. Jason and I made the short walk to the eighteenth tee, a three-hundred-yard par-4. You can see the top of a lighthouse from the tee, beyond the home green. There's a cemetery nearby, which you can't see. Johnny Miller lives down the road. His last win was at Pebble Beach at age forty-six.* He won despite having

---

* "It was a storybook ending to my career," Johnny Miller says. He won the California State Amateur at Pebble Beach in 1968 and the Pebble Beach pro-am in 1974, again in 1987, and finally in 1994, when he was a grandfather and an NBC Sports broadcaster. "Nobody knows and loves Pebble Beach more than me."

the yips. Really, he was pretty much retired from tournament golf by that point, done in by poor short putting. But he played a course he loved as much as any in the world, a course he had played all his life. It was a poetic win.

Jason Snow, sixteenth hole, Pacific Grove Golf Links.

As Jason and I stood on the last tee, something off to the right caught our eye. There, in the fading light, sitting placidly on a bench between a dirt path and a public road with his back to the Pacific, was a powerful-looking man wearing a heavy, colorful woven shirt with the sleeves cut off above the elbow. He had a handful of clubs on his lap and no golf bag. We asked if he wanted to join us for this last hole, and he did. He introduced himself as Chris Wags. His age was hard to guess but I figured he was in his fifties. If you had told me he was a Native American potter, I would have believed it, and if you had told me he was a West Virginia coal miner of German-Irish descent, I would have believed that. His handshake left a lasting impression.

He dropped his clubs to the ground, except for his old driver. He tossed a ball on the back of the tee box and stepped in to hit it without fiddling with the lie. He waggled once or twice but did not take a practice swing. His off-the-deck drive left the tee like a bullet train exiting a tunnel. We could barely see the ball in the gloaming, and I wondered how close to the green it would get. Close, for sure. This single swing was like a roundhouse knockout punch, filled with anger and joy, and there surely had to be ten thousand more in him just like it. It had so much power and rhythm. With one swing, Jason and I both knew: This Chris Wags was the real deal.

While playing a single hole, speaking with little inflection and looking straight ahead, Chris Wags told us that his mother was buried in the cemetery beyond the eighteenth green, that he had played tournament golf as a pro, and that he had caddied all over the Monterey Peninsula, including Pebble Beach. This brief life story actually rendered Jason speechless for a moment. He then told Wags his dream, to become a Pebble Beach caddie.

"I can hook you up," Chris Wags said with no particular emotion.

"Dude! Really? Are you serious?"

"Yeah, man."

Phone numbers were exchanged. Jason and I walked off the course, crossed quiet Asilomar Avenue, and headed to the Pacific Grove parking lot. Chris Wags, clubs in hand, slipped off toward the cemetery to visit his mother, among other departed members of his family. The day's final light came and went. By the time Jason and I started our cars, Friday evening was well under way.

The next day, I asked Sam Reeves about Chris Wags. He knew all about him. It turned out most everybody in greater Pebble Beach, at least those steeped in the local golf scene, did. Chris Wagenseller. Sam knew him as player and caddie. He had sponsored him when Wags tried to play tournament golf as a much younger man.

The bench where Chris Wags sat, Pacific Grove Golf Links.

He could perform astounding athletic feats—he could throw a golf ball more than 170 yards, for instance. He would show off this talent, on a command-performance basis, on the sixteenth hole at Cypress Point, a cliff-to-cliff par-3 over a chasm of ocean. From the tee, he'd throw a ball on the same line that George Plimpton took when he played a 3-wood layup shot there during the second round of the '66 Crosby. It's practically unimaginable, throwing a golf ball that far, especially in heavy ocean air. A golf ball weighs only 1.6 ounces. But Chris Wags could do it without fail.

He was rich in athletic gifts. His best sport was baseball, but he stopped playing after one year at Monterey Peninsula College, where he was a right fielder with a rifle arm and roadrunner legs. There were distractions, family needs among them. But his athletic skills did not suffer from atrophy. Long after his baseball days were over, he continued to have an impressive combination of strength and agility. He could kick his foot from the ground to the top of a six-foot fence and hold it there as long as he wished, standing on one foot. The other caddies couldn't come close.

Late on a misty afternoon in November 1997, using a 90-compression balata ball and a permission driver, Wags made a hole in one on the downhill 290-yard par-4 ninth hole at Cypress Point. This was on a Monday, the traditional day at many private clubs for caddies to play. Wags and a buddy had started on the fourth hole, near a club picnic area where caddies often parked. His ace there got him to five under for the six holes he had played. The walk from the ninth green to the picnic area is a short one. After making that double eagle, Wags and his golf partner called it a day. His friend recorded the shot on a VHS camcorder. Later, Wags distributed some of his mother's ashes on that ninth hole. Nine was her favorite number, and that was the ultimate ace.

It's hard to say why Chris Wagenseller didn't make it in professional golf. Of course, many try and few do. The caddie yards in Northern California and South Florida and the East End of Long Island are filled with guys who can break 70. Golf is hard, and it takes almost unimaginable devotion, in addition to ridiculous amounts of talent, to make a living playing tournament golf, whether it's on the PGA Tour or the Dakotas Tour. I'm not pretending to know the ins and outs of Chris Wagenseller's life. But one hole with him told me that his life had not been an easy one.

Near the driving range at Pebble, and beside a par-3 course designed by Tiger Woods, there's an elevated fifteen-ton bronze sculpture by Richard MacDonald called *Momentum*, three times bigger than life, that depicts the golf swing in all its dynamic roundness. The sculpture brings to mind a drawing by Anthony Ravielli in Ben Hogan's *Five Lessons* that shows Hogan's backswing as a large, swooshing, on-its-side *C*. MacDonald's model was not Hogan. It was Chris Wagenseller.

Wags told me he teaches "this beautiful game to loved ones and close friends who want to get super-good." His teaching, he said, is "unofficial." (Good players are sometimes chased off ranges for teaching.) He means well, you can tell. His obstacles are his obstacles. He opened a door for Jason Snow, aspiring Pebble Beach caddie. His own status in various Monterey Peninsula caddie yards had been made more complicated by various things, including his unwillingness to use a rangefinder.

I asked Wags if he could get the essence of the golf swing down to a single thought, and he offered this: "Timing and tempo." His own timing is off a metronome, and there is a gorgeous sweeping quality to his tempo and to his entire swing, even in its fierceness. At address, his weight is slightly out, toward his toes, like that of an infielder expecting a double-play ball. He looks alive. As Seve Ballesteros took almost no divot, Chris Wagenseller takes almost no divot. My own swing is appallingly steep—I look at myself on video and see a guy chopping wood. Watching Wags makes you want to flatten the path of your clubhead into the ball, so that it comes in like a snowplow clearing fresh powder off a sleeping street.

I mentioned Wags in a story I wrote and sent him the piece. "God bless," Chris Wags wrote back. "Thank you for speaking pleasant about me."

3

By the Time I Got to Phoenix

ON THE SATURDAY OF THE AT&T, I CHECKED OUT OF THE REEVES B&B, had breakfast with a friend who had (by coincidence) clocked many rounds with Wags as his caddie, and started driving south, bound for Phoenix, seven hundred miles away. ("By the Time I Get to Phoenix," etc. You give me a long drive, I'll give you a Jimmy Webb song. "I hear you singing in the wire / I can hear you through the whine," from "Wichita Lineman." Top *that*.) I was driving to Phoenix for the Phoenix Open. Playing the sixteenth hole at TPC Scottsdale was in my near future.

Over the years, the Phoenix Open had morphed (unromantically!) into the WM Phoenix Open, named for the tournament sponsor, Waste Management, the trash collection and recycling company. Before WM, an investment bank was the corporate sponsor. But the real host of the event—and this has been the case going back to the late 1930s—is an all-male civic group called the Thunderbirds, its members easy to spot on the course, then and now, thanks to their roomy blue velvet tunics cinched by heavy leather belts with big silver buckles. Dangling around their stomachs they wear long beaded necklaces with large silver pendants. In terms of dramatic garb, the Thunderbirds put Augusta National members, walking the course during the Masters in their green club coats, to shame.

The Thunderbirds take pride in putting on one of the oldest events on the PGA Tour, the best-attended PGA Tour event, and the most environmentally aware PGA Tour event. They take pride in the millions raised by the tournament each year for local charities. But to a huge number of casual golf fans, the event is known for one thing: the noise that comes from its sixteenth hole, a flat par-3 encircled by grandstands that are so jammed with loud, overserved frat-boy fans that players can barely hear their caddies.

In his first full year on tour, Tiger made a hole in one on sixteen in the tournament's Saturday round. That 170-yard ace with a 9-iron, and his down-the-fairway fist-pumping, was one of his early let-the-legend-grow pro moments. He high-fived Fluff, his caddie, so hard you could practically feel the sting through your TV screen.

Phoenix had two pro-ams. Trying to find a path into either of these one-day pre-tournament events, I consulted with various locals, including Stan Utley, the golf teacher and short-game guru, who lives in Scottsdale, where he oversaw the conversion of Charles Barkley from pitiful hacker to capable golfer. Stan was playing in the Monday pro-am on the pro side of the ledger. I was told there were still a few openings on the am side. When I got in, I let Stan know.

"How'd you get your spot?" he asked.

"I wrote a check."

"That'll do it," Stan said.

I hope Christine skips this part: The entry fee for the Monday pro-am was seven thousand dollars. Yes, one round of golf, although it did come with post-round cocktails and foodstuffs. I imagined that much of the sum would find its way to a worthy charity. Really, I didn't mind paying it. Maybe I'd learn something. Maybe I'd learn something that I could pass on. Anyway, for the first time in my life, I'd be inside the ropes with a club in hand.

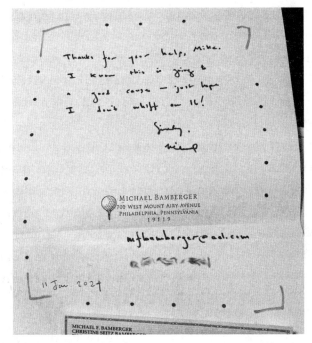

Note and entry fee for Monday pro-am, WM Phoenix Open.

Pro-ams are useful to reporters on the golf beat. Tiger will sometimes do little walk-and-talks with writers, as will other players, if you time it right and don't overstay your welcome. That's how I got John Daly for a profile in 1992, when he wasn't doing any one-on-one sitdown interviews. For a reporter, a pro-am is a gift: There's no place for your subject to run and hide.

I've enjoyed caddying in pro-ams, too. My first exposure to touring pros came in high school and college, when the LPGA had an annual stop on Long Island and I caddied in LPGA pro-ams a couple times. I remember seeing Judy Rankin at close range, wearing sunglasses and a hairband, finishing her swing on her toes. I was starstruck. I caddied in a group whose pro was a young player with wild hair and a casual manner—Lori Garbacz. *Gar-bah-see.* She was only a couple years older than I was. But I was living with my parents on West Lakewood Street in the village of Patchogue, and Lori Garbacz was playing the world. A gulf. Somehow I got up the nerve to say something to her as our group marched down the first fairway: "Lori, there's a beetle on you." There was, on her bottom, seemingly planted there. Lori swiped the bug away and said some amusing thing. I had connected with a touring pro, at least for a few seconds.

Or, viewed another way, much longer. The good vibes that emerge from these pro-ams can have a shelf life of forever. Years after that pro-am on Long Island, Lori found herself enduring an especially slow round at a U.S. Open. On the fourteenth tee at the Colonial Country Club in Fort Worth, Lori instructed her caddie to go to an on-course pay phone and call a nearby Domino's. Their mushroom-and-pepperoni pie was still warm when Lori and a small collection of caddies and players ate it on the seventeenth tee. That funny little episode made the rounds, and if you knew Lori Garbacz for even a day, you enjoyed hearing about it that much more.

Sounds like her!

I followed Lori Garbacz, at least as a name in the Monday agate of various sports sections, for her entire career.

Some pros can see the actual good these pro-ams provide. My star witness on this subject is the veteran golfer and broadcaster Peter Jacobsen, who started to understand the value of the pro-am as a tour rookie playing in his first event, the Crosby pro-am in 1977. Peter was heading out for a practice round by himself, his first start on tour, when Arnold Palmer, playing with Mark McCormack, approached him, stuck out his hand, introduced himself, and said, "Mind if we join you?" From that day on, Peter made a study of everything Arnold did, including how he handled himself in pro-ams. Peter observed that Arnold *never* acted more important than his pro-am partners.

Arnold liked people. They were his fuel. He understood that golf's fans were like company shareholders—they funded the whole enterprise. The ams in pro-ams were your best customers. They were some-times the top executives at companies that sponsored tournaments, or donors to tournament charities. They were often people who knew something about life far beyond the course.

"In these pro-ams, you're meeting people who you'll intersect with in every aspect of your life," Peter told me. I had called him to ask about his long history as a popular pro-am partner and later as a pro-am host. One of his many gigs is to host a pro-am pairings party every March at the Arnold Palmer Invitational at Bay Hill, near Orlando. "They're accountants, they're doctors, they own restaurants," he said. "At some point, you're going to need an accountant, a doctor, a restaurant res-ervation. So I got in the habit of getting business cards at the ends of rounds and writing notes to my pro-am partners." On the final green, when the ams were in their wallets getting out those business cards, they'd also get out something for Fluff (Mike Cowan), who was Peter's caddie for years. Cash money for Fluff, new friends for the pro. What's not to like?[*]

Arnold didn't collect business cards at pro-ams, but he knew the people he met were good for his business. He promoted foot powder, ketchup, motor oil, dry cleaners, cigarettes (until he quit). If there was cash on the barrel, he didn't turn down much. He was a child of the Depression. He despised debt. He was western Pennsylvania through and through.

In fifty years around the game, Peter has realized that professional golf has had few true superstars. Arnold and Tiger in men's American

---

[*] "I never expected it," Fluff says about cash tips at the end of pro-am rounds. "I always appreci-ated it." For Cowan, a native Mainer, taking nothing for granted is a central part of his personality. Cowan is a lifelong baseball fan and a longtime member of Congressional Country Club outside Washington, D.C. When Frank Robinson became the manager of the Washington Nationals, a mutual acquaintance gave Robinson's phone number to Cowan. Cowan said, "I can't fucking be-lieve I got Frank Robinson's phone numbah."

golf. Seve in Europe. Nancy Lopez in the women's game. There have been other notables, of course: Tom Watson and Lee Trevino; Mickey Wright and Kathy Whitworth; Rory McIlroy and Scottie Scheffler. Nicklaus is in a category all his own, and at the height of his fame, he was able to do an American Express spot that began with a question: *Do you know me?* Many did not. As Peter explained it, what has kept professional golf, and the PGA Tour, in business is not the players. It's the marriage of tournament and sponsor. This is not a public service announcement aimed at bratty, clueless players. It's more like a flow chart.

After a few years on tour, Peter made a meaningful realization: For the four or five hours he was with his assigned ams, he was Arnold. He wasn't, of course. But to the amateurs playing with him? Peter was the closest thing they had, so he might as well try to act the part.

Except for bowling, it's hard to think of another sport that has a lower wall between elite pro and ordinary fan. That low wall makes the pro-am possible. Pro-ams in the United States had already been around for almost fifty years before their baseball equivalent, the fantasy camp, started popping up in the mid-1980s. The first widely known pro-am was a one-round event hosted by Bing Crosby in 1937 at Rancho Santa Fe, a course in Southern California, five miles from Del Mar, the racetrack that Crosby owned with others. Sam Snead won the pro division. When Bing went to give Snead his five-hundred-dollar prize in the form of a check, Snead said, "If you don't mind, Mr. Crosby, I'd rather have cash."

For most of its years, the AT&T (née Crosby) gave amateurs the chance to play four rounds with the pros. Many players didn't love it, not if they were playing day after day with guys shooting 100. Still, they got it. Or most did. For decades, there were two PGA Tour events where amateurs and pros played together for up to five straight days, Bob Hope's event and the Las Vegas Invitational. The players *really* didn't like that—five days with ams—but they did like making money.

When Curtis Strange holed a putt to win the 1985 Las Vegas Invitational and $225,000, he did a little jig across the eighteenth green. *So not Curtis.* He got carried away.

I was at the Vegas tournament that year, caddying for an amateur, a Texas oilman named Lee Roy Pearson III, a tall, rangy character, generous in every way. For one of the rounds, Lee Roy drew Nick Price as his partner. (The amateurs got a different pro each day.) Nick read putts, tossed grass, used names. By the end of a single round, Nick had made fans for life. In that same period, I can recall seeing Andy Bean, at the height of his power-fade, country-strong fame, walking up to his pro-am partners, offering his baseball glove of a right hand, and saying, "I'm *AHN-deh-Beeen*," as if the assembled car dealers and insurance agents didn't know. I have seen Tiger, so guarded by nature, chatting with his pro-am partners while walking down a fairway. Talk-talk-talk, sudden stop, burst of laughter. He wasn't worried about where his prize money was coming from, but he could always do some soft selling in the name of his foundation. There's a lot going on in these pro-ams, more than we can readily see.

In *The Bogey Man*, there's a painful moment when George sees his pro, Bob Bruno, emerge from a forest after beating his driver against a tree stump. Capturing the moment and much more, Plimpton wrote, "He was purged and controlled again, but he didn't know how to put it right with us."

If you're in greater Phoenix and have any interest in how golf clubs get made, you might sign up for a tour of Karsten Manufacturing, makers of Ping golf clubs. The company, located on West Desert Cove Avenue in Phoenix, is named for Karsten Solheim, the Norwegian émigré who founded it. Karsten, a trained engineer, was in his mid-eighties and still coming to work every day when I toured the plant. This was in 1996. Ping was launching a new iron called the ISI, but I was face-to-face with Karsten when he said to me, "We never made a better iron than the Eye2." With a few trial separations, I've been playing Eye2s pretty much ever since.

The Eye2 has a wide sole, a high toe, and a heavy head, with a lot of weight distributed around the perimeter of the clubhead. Innumerable golfers were drawn to the engineering of the Eye2, to Karsten's commitment to function over good looks, and to the almost austere way the Solheims ran their family business. For years, Karsten was on the *Forbes* list of the four hundred richest people in America.

Karsten didn't lure top players to Ping with guaranteed contracts, as other manufacturers did. He only wanted players to play his clubs because they liked the performance. He had a formulaic bonus program by which players received a year-end payout based exclusively on how much they made on the course. His company's values matched golf's values. It was all merit-based, all about the numbers. He was an original. Karsten is in the World Golf Hall of Fame, a center of the golf establishment, but there's not another person enshrined there who is anything like him. The Ping ads in the golf magazines made the L.L.Bean catalogs look slick. In the upper left-hand corner, there was usually a small rectangular photo of Karsten in a tie, glasses on his nose, a little white Colonel Sanders goatee at the bottom of his chin. In his right hand was an Eye2 iron, no matter what the company was promoting then.

When other golfers see my old Pings, they sometimes start to talk about Eye2s they have known and loved, sounding like motorists of a certain age remembering the four-speed VW Bugs they drove to school. It was a joy for me to see my Eye2s, among a few other hatless clubs, in a wee bag on the shoulder of my delightful pro-am caddie,

Jessica Marksbury, mother of two, wife of the head pro at the Phoenix Country Club, former Columbia University golfer, and my work colleague. The roles should have been reversed. Jess hits her longest hybrid more reliably than I hit my shortest iron. In her own golf, Jess emphasizes setup. You can't hit a good shot without a sound setup. Now and again, she gets her ball too far back in her stance. Like once every five years.

On the morning of the pro-am, Jess picked me up at my hotel, and we drove out to TPC Scottsdale. The clubhouse parking lot was a zoo, and the valet situation looked complicated. We parked in employee parking. Actually, I'm not sure what it was. Once parked, we slipped out quickly. I was impressed—I didn't know Jess had that move. It was all her idea.

I quickly found out what life was like on the other side of Amateur Player Services. (Jess did, too. Each amateur was permitted to bring along one guest, and Jess was mine.) There were all manner of smiling people serving as hosts and tour guides, more than a few of them Thunderbirds in their blue velvet tunics, pointing you to breakfast, to gift distribution, to the practice green, to the driving range. At the range, one side was reserved for pros and the other for ams. I didn't recognize any of the pros. The pros whose names you know from TV were in the far more expensive Wednesday pro-am, not the Monday one.

The range balls, even on the am side of the range, were shiny and new, without a thick red stripe, and my warm-up went . . . fine. I hit a bunch of irons off tees because the grass was tight and damp, and hitting a series of thin shots or fat ones was not going to be good for anything.

I had been working on something swing-wise, and that morning I continued with it. (My former *SI* colleague Gary Van Sickle, an excellent golfer, likes to say you always have to be working on something. Brad Faxon adds to that: But don't think of it as work.) I had been watching a series of videos featuring a freethinking golf teacher named Jim Venetos, who preaches a *very* closed address position—feet, hips, shoulders pointing to first base if you're right-handed and third if you're a lefty. He wants you coming into the ball on a shallow, descending path from the inside, with most of your weight on your front foot throughout the swing. On his tapes, Venetos hits balls off a driving-range mat in a California desert while wearing Chuck Taylors, Levi's, and a T-shirt. He hits one no-fuss, baby-draw after another. His concept is sound, and I could kind of make the swing work from 7-iron down through the wedges. I struggled with it on longer clubs. So, for this Phoenix pro-am, I figured I'd do Venetos from 7-iron on down. As Nicklaus says, you go to the range before a round to figure out what your swing is doing that day.

Jess and I went to the tenth tee, our first, at the appointed time, and I introduced myself to our pro. I knew Jake Knapp was, at twenty-nine, a PGA Tour rookie—that is, ancient. I knew he had played college golf at UCLA without ever being a star there. And that's about all I knew.

The starter called my name, I put my peg in the ground, and tapped out a rushed, weak, heeled drive. But it was in the air. So not that bad.

Jake had a blond mullet, a matching mustache, and an easy manner. He had a wait-for-it backswing that was out of the Fred Couples–Ernie Els playbook. Jess and I could not believe how far he hit it, given how skinny he was. Then, as the day warmed up, he took off a baggy sweatshirt and we could see he wasn't skinny at all. He had the physique of a middleweight boxer. A lot of young players, raised on Tiger's example, feel like they can't do enough in the gym. Jake was part of that generation. He looked like he could play any sport.

His downswing boggles the mind, there's so much lag in it. When his hands are almost over his ball, his clubhead is still nearly shoulder-high. He combines explosive speed with gorgeous rhythm. A dream. His shots sail, hanging out with other celestial beings before descending back to earth. It's not really a modern swing. Rory McIlroy has a modern swing, with ferocious speed from start to finish. Knapp brings to mind a range of elite rhythm-first golfers. Mickey Wright, for instance. Also Bobby Jones, Sam Snead, Payne Stewart. Fred and Ernie.

Years ago, I saw Ernie Els at the range at Hilton Head on a Saturday night. He had only one club with him, a sand iron. He hit about two dozen shots with it. He was the only player on the range, and he had sent his caddie home for the night, or to wherever he was going on a Saturday night in Hilton Head the week after the Masters. When Ernie was finished, I asked him what he was working on. "Rhythm," he said. That scene shows up in my head on a recurring basis.

Jake had a relaxed, it's-all-good manner, but a distinct earnestness, too. When he talked about the swing, it was in an understandable way. (A tenet of his driving game, he said, was a full, long, don't-rush-it backswing.) But Jake was treating our pro-am round as a practice round, as work, and there were a lot of times when our group just gave him room so he could consult with his caddie, his teacher, his yardage book, his own self. Occasionally, he would stop and look around, taking the course in. TPC Scottsdale, for this Monday pro-am, was an oasis of green, a sparkling temple of mowed grass. By PGA Tour standards, it's an easy course. Still, there are ponds, bunkers, and cacti to consider. A pro playing for keeps always has one eye on opportunities and the other on potential disasters. A golfer plays both offense and defense.

We were a fivesome, and companionable from start to finish. One of the guys in our group was a distiller for Jack Daniel's, and when we were done, he asked each of us for our address. (That portended well.) We were a small army out there: four ams, four caddies; Jake and his caddie, Mike Stephens; Jake's swing coach; Jake's agent for a short while; a tournament scorekeeper; wives and other guests; one or two Thunderbirds; a photographer standing on a tee or a green. There was a lot going on even when play stopped. As we waited on one tee, Jess planted herself on a sunny patch of grass and got in a brief nap.

Despite the pleasures of the day, it never felt like real golf to me. Real golf promotes a tingly anxiety. This was a group activity that centered around golf. We were playing in a scramble format in which all four ams played tee shots, and we anointed one shot as best. From that spot, everybody played a second shot, and the best of those shots was selected again. This pattern continued until the ball was in the bottom of the hole. You're constantly sharing advice on clubs and lines and green speed, and sometimes we had Jake weigh in, too. The hole locations were the easiest that the course setup people could find. Any hole where we didn't make a team birdie using the best of our best, we had done something wrong. It's fantasy golf.

All the while, Jake was playing his own ball. So we had five players on the court. Any hole where Jake's real score was lower than our team scramble score, his score counted. In actual golf, you play all your shots, including your foul balls. In this format, the amateur has either played a shot that counts or done nothing. The whole thing is an exercise in team-building. Jake Knapp led our team for five hours. In return, we will likely be rooting for him forever. For me, he'll be another Lori Garbacz.

From the time Jake left UCLA and turned pro until he became a full-fledged member of the PGA Tour took eight years. (Can you imagine graduating law school and spending eight years trying to pass the bar?) He had endured eight years of on-again, off-again status on various minor-league golf tours. He had eight years of nagging health issues. A long apprenticeship and a lot of years juggling the books of financial insecurity. There was no Plan B. You play where you can. You're looking for status, a term of the profession that means a tour where you can hang your hat. Jake Knapp was "chasing it," to borrow a phrase from my friend Ryan French, owner-operator of a website called Monday Q Info, where he tracks golfers who are chasing it. There's no one way. For eight years, Jake was trying to play his way to status on the PGA Tour. Now he had new things to chase. Keeping his card. Winning. Playing in majors. Getting vested. Making a life of it. Few do.

As a young pro with a Canadian bloodline, Jake wanted to play the summertime Canadian Tour. But you can't just show up in Victoria, British Columbia, at the start of the season with a credit card and two hundred dollars cash and think you're going to play for nine weeks across the Great White North. There are tournament entry fees, caddie fees, airline baggage fees, hotels, food, travel—you pay to play in professional golf. To finance his rookie summer in Canada, Jake took a job as a bouncer at a nightclub called the Country Club. Making it in golf is like making it in any start-up business. You need seed money, and he made some at the Country Club.

Jake ended up playing four summers in Canada and won three times. His first win, in 2019, paid him twenty-five thousand dollars, in Canadian dollars. The Canada Revenue Agency gets a cut, the IRS gets a cut, the caddie gets a cut. Still, money in the bank, and status. The win also earned him Canadian Tour playing privileges for the following summer and a spot in the 2019 Canadian Open, where he made the cut for the first time in a PGA Tour event. Rory McIlroy won that week. Jake finished 29 shots behind him. He knew he needed to get better.

You need a plan to make it in professional golf, a path to improvement. Because wherever your game is, it's not good enough. Everywhere Jake has been in professional golf, he has seen deep fields. At any of the Canadian stops, there could be twenty or thirty guys with his basic skill set. On the Korn Ferry Tour, the number could be sixty.

And then there are players throughout the world whose names you may not know but who are very, *very* good at golf. Sami Välimäki from Finland. Nico Echavarría from Colombia. Takumi Kanaya from Japan. Whoever you are, they can play with you. To make it, you have to play better than hundreds of other golfers who are essentially no better or worse than you are. So who makes it?

I posed this question to Ryan French, the Monday Q guy. He has seen many good players knocking on the door of the PGA Tour door. Some have opened it, many more have not. Ryan, it turned out, had thought a great deal about the question of who makes it, and this is what he said: "The players who make it have a superior ability to identify where they are weak, in body, in mind, in technique. And then they do something about it."

Can you identify where you are weak and actually do something about it? There's a whole world in that, in golf and beyond golf.

By the time we got to the par-3 sixteenth at TPC Scottsdale on that Monday, the sun was high, and there were a few hundred sunbathing fans in grandstands built for ten thousand. From the amateur tees, the hole measured about 120 yards. That's a full pitching wedge for me. When I try to hit a wedge too hard, my head tends to get ahead of the ball, and I hit a dead pull. Certainly didn't want to do that.

Jess angled the bag expertly in my direction. The 9-iron was practically staring at me, and out it came. Excuse the pretention: My hope was to take a little off the shot. I opened the face, assumed a modified Venetos stance, made an unusually rhythmic swing. (Rhythm is contagious—thanks, Jake.) The ball finished about eight feet from the hole. Please don't think this is normal for me.

Jake Knapp celebrating the author's meaningless birdie 2 on the sixteenth hole
at TPC Scottsdale, WM Phoenix Open, Monday pro-am.

Jake read the putt, saw something I didn't, and I stroked it in for birdie. Our little gang bumped and fived.

Stan Utley (you may recall) likes to say that golf is 95 percent technique, 3 percent mental attitude, and 2 percent luck. But you could also say that golf is *all* mental. The basis for everything the golfer does comes out of thought, your brain telling your body what to do. Every sport has a brain-to-body messaging system. But in golf, that role of the messaging system is amplified, because the ball is just sitting there, doing nothing. It's waiting on you. The golfer is over it, deciding what to do and how. Even when the body takes over and muscle memory gets you from the top of the swing to your finish, it's still the mind that starts the engine. Of course, you can't play golf with *only* your mind or *only* your body. You need both. But if you don't have a good plan for what you want to do with your swing before you start it, you have no chance.

My birdie was meaningless. Jake had already made a 2 before I holed my putt. We already had our team birdie. Per the Lee Wielansky pro-am guidelines from the Amex tournament, I really should have just picked up.

But nobody would pick up in that situation. Otherwise, you'd wonder for the rest of your life if you could have made a birdie on sixteen at TPC Scottsdale with a few hundred people in the stands on a lovely Monday in winter. For two shots, I got what I could out of whatever golf skill I have.

I waved my hand to acknowledge the deafening applause and retrieved my ball from the hole.

4

Feherty Does Vegas

HOPE, CROSBY, PHOENIX (AMEX, AT&T, WASTE MANAGEMENT). BEFORE heading home, I had one more stop on this first-leg West Coast swing—this journey into new and improved—and that was in Las Vegas, to see David Feherty.

Feherty was LIV Golf's lead broadcast analyst, and there was a LIV tournament in Las Vegas, a Thursday-Friday-Saturday event making way for the Super Bowl, being held in Las Vegas that Sunday. I was going there to interview Feherty for a Golf.com video experiment called *Golf Originals*. Feherty was our first subject. The drive from the SpringHill Suites (my digs) in Scottsdale to the Paris hotel (David's) in Las Vegas was a little over three hundred miles, a straight shot on U.S. 93. That is, it looked like a straight shot on the tiny map on my tiny phone.

The actual drive was winding and desolate, half-terrifying at times in a steady winter rain. I was not tempted to stop and see Hoover Dam, and it was a relief to get to civilization, to Harry Reid International, where I picked up my colleague Darren Riehl. From the airport we drove to the Paris Las Vegas, and there we collected Feherty. Somewhere in Las Vegas, I celebrated my two thousandth mile in my semi-large Hertz vehicle.

We headed from the hotel to the city's outer limits, to a strip-mall bookshop called the Psychic Eye. I had suggested it, and I believe David's response was something like, "Yeah, sure—whatever." That's how he rolls. A few weeks earlier, I had reached him when he was in (by his reckoning) "Bumfuck, Kansas," because somebody had invited him to hunt quail there. Time on his hands is his enemy. He had dressed with care for our little outing, polished leather shoes, wool vest, crisp checkered shirt. His style is his own—country squire, 1970s, pastoral England—and not anything you'd likely see in the grillroom of a modern American clubhouse. He looked tired.

We drove by Allegiant Stadium. It was empty. In a few days, it would be stuffed with people for the Super Bowl. Feherty likes *football* football, and has no use for American football, with its excessive touchdown celebrations. "Act like you've done it before," he told us.

The conversation was going well; the driving less so. As I missed various turns, Siri blabbered on about corrective U-turns while R.E.M.'s "All the Way to Reno" (my choice) played through the semi-large Hertz vehicle. "Where the fuck are we going?" Feherty asked in his singsong way. "Are we in Reno yet?" I thought I heard Darren laughing in the back. My clubs and lunch leftovers were behind him.

I had first met, or encountered, Feherty thirty-plus years earlier in Europe, while I was caddying for Peter Teravainen. Feherty had jet-black hair and lively blue eyes and, per Christine and others, a most definite presence. Feherty liked Teravainen and would casually use his nickname, Whiplash, for the terrifying force of his second downswing, the one he made after reaching a conventional swing's normal resting place. Feherty and I also shared a fondness for Chuck Will, a legendary and comically profane CBS golf producer from Philadelphia.

Feherty's wit is his stock in trade, but from the moment Feherty got in the car, Darren, operating a handheld camera, and I found ourselves in the presence of a decidedly contemplative man. Within minutes, Feherty told us that his mother, in Northern Ireland—in Bangor, a seaside city in County Down—had been placed that day in palliative care. David, the middle child of three, flanked by sisters, talked about his mother with candor. "She was stoic," he said. "If we fell down and cut ourselves, she'd rub a piece of dirt in it and say, 'Walk it off.'" She had expectations and standards, and she was engaged in the world. She sang and played the piano and passed her love of music on to her son.

Feherty talked about the career choice he had considered as a teenager: music or golf? His musical heroes were Pavarotti and Van Morrison, and he had been studying opera in a serious way. A path in golf seemed more realistic to him. Pavarotti was a voice on the living room record player, while Feherty actually knew club pros. He got a job working for one. He was an apprentice, in the British tradition, and a 75 shooter. He got good by playing as much tournament golf as he could, and by working on his weaknesses. Having the obsessive gene helped. Having the obsessive gene has helped and hurt every aspect of his life.

He liked the Psychic Eye, with its collection of occult curiosities, voodoo charms, healing oils, and the rest. He thumbed through some of the many eclectic books on the racks: *A Brief History of Total Bullsh*t*, for instance. We were with Feherty for about three hours, and there was something magical about the time with him. Feherty is open, funny, aware, vulnerable. He had lost a son to a drug overdose. He had married (second time around) an angel. He had lived through the Northern Ireland Troubles as a younger man and survived accidents and addictions as an older one. He had contended in majors and learned what others have learned, that fourth rounds are played on Mars. He had been told by Keith Richards to fuck off.

The previous week, Feherty had played in a golf event, the Sandy Lane Invitational at the Sandy Lane resort in Barbados, owned by Dermot Desmond and two other Irishmen. (The same Dermot Desmond who was hitting balls next to Fred Perpall on the Pebble driving range.

Dermot gets around.) Feherty said he evades almost every golf invitation he receives by requiring a partner or host he likes and, for proposed road games, transport via private plane. He mentioned three people to whom he could not say no: George W. Bush, Lee Trevino, and Billy Walters, the well-known professional gambler. The invitation to play at Sandy Lane came from Billy Walters, with a ride there on Billy's plane. Feherty described Walters as his "best friend." Such a charming seventh-grade phrase. "If I had to pick someone to hole a three-footer to save my life, it would be Billy," Feherty said.

They got to know each other after Feherty moved from London to Dallas in the mid-1990s, following not so much his first wife—though that's where she was—but their two sons.

"Jesus Christ, did I suck—it was brutal," Feherty said, describing his play at Sandy Lane. "Golf is a perishable skill, like singing. It was probably the fifth or sixth time I had played in seventeen years, since I had been crushed by a truck in a bicycle accident. Billy is the only person who could have gotten me out there to play."

The combination of friendship and golf has been a powerful force in the game for a hundred years. You find yourself playing in a place or on a day you normally wouldn't, were it not for the magnet of friendship.

It was a four-day tournament with eighty players in the field. A lot of horse people were playing, owners and trainers and jockeys. Feherty was the only professional golfer, and that was just a technicality. He was assigned an appropriate handicap for the event, 6. Your foursome was your team, and each day you played with three different players. Every night, a winning team for that day's round was announced at dinner. "I won the third day," Feherty said. That is, his team won, but Feherty was its anchor. I thought I heard an element of chagrin in his voice, but Dermot, in the room that night, detected something else: pride. "People were cheering him on," Dermot told me later. "When was the last time he was in the winner's circle for anything?"

The winner's circle. A horseman's phrase. (Dermot is one.) As a professional golfer, Feherty had represented Europe on a winning Ryder Cup team. He had competed in twelve British Opens. He had won tournaments in Ireland and Italy, in Scotland, in South Africa, in Spain. And most recently, with three others, the third-day competition of the Sandy Lane Invitational in Barbados.

We returned David to his hotel. He told us the walk from the porte cochere to his room was a half-mile. For the week of the LIV event, the Paris Las Vegas, with its thirty-six hundred rooms, was home. His golf skill, and his golf ambitions, had allowed him to see the world. That Tuesday night, he was five thousand miles from his real home, his childhood home, in seaside Bangor. It was Tuesday night in Las Vegas and early Wednesday morning in Northern Ireland. Two days later, David's mother, Violet Feherty, died at home, sharp and alert almost to her end. She was ninety-two. She was proud of her son, of course. Still, she had always wondered where singing could have taken him.

5

Jake Goes Deep

JAKE KNAPP DIDN'T GET INTO TIGER'S EVENT AT RIVIERA, BUT HE played the following week, in late February, when the PGA Tour went to the Pacific Coast resort town of Puerto Vallarta for the Mexico Open. If you want to be a professional golfer, you need an up-to-date passport and a good attitude about getting on planes.

After three rounds, Jake led by four. Not a shocker. He had been playing well, and the course favored long hitters—Tony Finau and Jon Rahm had won there. But final rounds are stressful for any fifty-four-hole leader, and a big lead can actually increase stress, because there's only one outcome everybody expects: The leader closes the deal. Expectation is a killer in golf, as it is in other endeavors.

Jake was playing in the ninth tournament of his PGA Tour career. He was an infant learning to crawl, and here he was with a chance to win. A win would mean a spot in his first Masters, playing status on the PGA Tour for the next two years, and a $1.5 million payday. When Jake Knapp worked nights as a bouncer, he wasn't doing fieldwork for a sociology class. This was what he had in mind—this Sunday afternoon in Mexico, or something like it.

His girlfriend flew in for the occasion. Jake's parents had invited friends and relatives to their house in Southern California to watch the Golf Channel broadcast, screaming because they could while eating supermarket crudités. On the course, a small broadcast team was trailing Jake. He had way more spectators following him than usual. Jake wanted to treat the round like another day at the park, but it wasn't and he couldn't. The guy playing with him, Sami Välimäki, was hanging and then some. When the Finnish golfer made a six-foot putt on the seventh hole for an eagle, he actually had the lead over Jake for a long minute.

Jake's Saturday play was AWOL on Sunday. He was missing fairways and greens left and right. But his little shots were saving him, his greenside pitches, his chip shots, his short, curling putts. He was playing jewel-thief golf. I was texting with some of the people from our Monday golf-with-Jake pro-am group in Phoenix, and we were having a party, even if it was by text. Our rooting and crossed fingers and exclamation marks were not in vain. Jake won, by two. His four rounds were 67, 64, 63, and 71. Three rounds of low. One round of hanging on for dear life. Welcome to the bigs.

About three hours later, Jake, along with his girlfriend—Makena White, a Canadian and (of course) a hockey fan—stepped into a waiting private jet, its engines idling, the other players and their caddies already settled in. Jack Nicklaus has an annual pro-am that raises money for a children's health foundation and honors a family member who died as a toddler. Jake was a late invitation. The event is held each year at Nicklaus's home course in South Florida. The invitation included a lift there. The plane had been waiting on Jake.

By the time the plane reached West Palm Beach, it was two in the morning. Jake went on Travelocity, found a Holiday Inn Express, and got a little sleep. Later that morning, he was in Jupiter with the first couple of golf, Jack and Barbara Nicklaus. Justin Thomas was there, as were Pádraig Harrington, Shane Lowry, and others who had won major golf championships. Jake had never met Nicklaus and was awed by the time "Mr. Nicklaus" took with him. Augusta National had sent an invitation to play in the Masters to Jake's home address in Scottsdale. An Augusta pro had called to tell him the procedure for pre-tournament visits. Pro golf in the fast lane.

The PGA Tour stop that week was down the road from the Bear's Club at PGA National, a course Nicklaus designed. The tournament had a new name, the Cognizant Classic. (After forty-two years as the tournament's sponsor, Honda had been driven off, fed up by the growing financial demands the PGA Tour was making of sponsors in its desperate effort to keep up with LIV Golf.) Because of his win in Mexico, Jake got a marquee pairing at the tournament, playing the first two rounds with the defending champion, Chris Kirk, and Rory McIlroy, who lives at the Bear's Club. One afternoon while Rory was talking to reporters, Jake walked by. Rory said, "I was just talking about you." Doors were opening for Jake. Invitations were pouring in. People were talking.

He was keeping it real. During a practice round at PGA National, Jake turned to another player and said, "What day do we get paid?" The winner's check from the Mexico tournament had not yet landed.

6

Springtime for Duffer

BEFORE I HEADED TO THE SUNSHINE STATE FOR MY OWN HYBRID Florida Swing, I took my car (an Augusta-green Mini Cooper) to the shop for an oil change and tune-up. I figured my clubs were due for a once-over, too.

Except for an old TaylorMade driver, my bag is all Ping, including nine Eye2 irons. I also have three full backup sets, so for good or for ill, I'm set for life.

My putter, a Ping 1A, is the first club Karsten Solheim designed and the product that gave his company its name, for the pinging sound the club makes when your ball meets its sweet spot. I inserted a rubber muffler in a crevice on mine, rendering the club mute, as I am not looking for any extra attention when I putt. I also put in a gooseneck hosel. Normally, a 1A shaft goes straight into the head, like the shaft on a two-way mini-golf putter. The gooseneck gave my putter offset (as most putters have) when putting righty and onset—the bottom of the shaft *behind* the clubhead—when putting lefty.

But I was wondering, in the name of buying improvement, if I was clinging too hard to what Karsten had said—that Ping had never made a club better than the Eye2. "He did say that," Robin McCool, a retired Ping sales rep, told me. For years, Robin was one of the best amateurs in Pennsylvania. "But he also said this: 'We've just started to scratch the surface.'"

It was Robin who pointed me in the direction of a second-generation club fitter and golf teacher in Pennsylvania, Ricky Kline, who learned the craft from his namesake father. Ricky is a fan of Ping clubs and a student of the company's history but is also, as they say these days in the fitting trade, "manufacturer-agnostic." In other words, he'll sell you anything. He works at a golf center his family owns called Sittler Golf in rural Sinking Spring, about sixty miles from our house in Philadelphia. I was lucky to get a short-notice appointment to see him. Everybody, Ricky told me, was doing what I was doing, getting ready for the new season. Punxsutawney Phil had not seen his shadow, which meant spring would be moving in fast. Registration for the St. Martins Spring Championship would be coming soon enough. One of my majors.

I drove out to see Ricky on a weekday in mid-February. The afternoon air was mild for the season, but the Sittler driving range was still half-covered by a thin layer of packed snow. A few people were hitting range balls off plastic mats into the glare of this frozen white sea. Mountains of packed ice marked the corners of the parking lot. On the other side of the lot was a mini-golf course with a tall red pagoda where you might expect to see a windmill. A mother and her kids, released from the tyranny of their winter coats, were playing this little putt-putt course, as if it were late June. People love being outside. It's in our communal DNA.

In between the mini-golf course and the driving range was a no-frills corrugated metal building, seemingly airlifted in from one of the nearby farms. It was inside this building that Ricky and his brother and their colleagues did their winter work, offering consultations in walled-off, high-ceilinged rooms. These chambers were fitting and hitting studios, with machines that could tell you everything your swing was doing, and maybe what you were thinking, too. Ricky was in his mid-thirties and a new first-time father. He was likable, earnest, inquisitive. Even though I was hitting into a padded screen, we could both see, on monitors, the path of my swing and the flight of my ball, its launch angle and spin rate and the rest. Where your clubface is at impact. The path of your swing. The height and distance and shape of your shots. I realize this is familiar territory for many, but it was new to me.

When Ricky was starting in the golf business during his college years and somebody came in with old clubs, his instinct was to explain how modern technology could automatically improve them. Over the years, he developed another approach: What clubs should the person use to get the most enjoyment from the game? Shooting lower scores is not always the main goal, or even a necessary one.

I went to see Ricky to talk about my Eye2s. We ended up talking about swing path more than anything else. My swing path changed radically depending on how I stood to the ball and the swing thought I had in my head.

I had brought two sets of Eye2s with me. I was fully prepared to leave a set with him and get new matching shafts and matching grips installed, along with anything else Ricky thought I needed.

"These clubs are fine for you," he said. "You're going to be playing a lot of golf here. Those Eye2s are some of the best clubs ever made. I wouldn't change a thing."

I headed south.

At the height of his playing fame, Greg Norman liked to begin his golf year—his American golf year, on the PGA Tour—at Doral in Miami in March. He liked the weather and the course, and it was there that his seasons often got off to a good start. He was the tour's leading money winner three times. You used to get a trophy for that, a bronze statue of Arnold Palmer.

The driving range at Sittler Golf, Sinking Spring, Pennsylvania, in February.

The Florida Swing ran four straight weeks back then: Doral, Honda, Players, Bay Hill. A lot of players stayed at Doral, a sprawling resort that once had a "meet George Jetson" shininess about it, but that was a long time ago. Tom Kite made sure to book the same room every year, the one nearest to the driving range. Norman didn't typically stay at Doral. He preferred to commute to and from his oceanfront estate in Hobe Sound, a hundred miles away by helicopter, which he would pilot. Norman, aka Shark, was a big presence at Doral, where he won three times, contended on several other occasions, and designed a course called Great White. You'd see his clothing line, his shark logo embroidered on every shirt and hat, on display in Doral's various shops.

The resort has had a long line of big personalities associated with it, starting with its namesake founders, Doris and Alfred Kaskel. (Doris put the Dor in Doral.) It was a hot spot for Arnold, Nicklaus, Raymond Floyd, Norman, Phil Mickelson, Tiger. You could put Donald Trump on that list. He bought Doral in 2012 and put his name on it, turning the development into Trump Doral. He made some grand entrances at Doral, once in a helicopter on a Sunday, landing on the course during tournament play. The Trump–PGA Tour marriage was bound to be a brief one. The last PGA Tour event at Doral (Trump Doral) was in 2016.

But despite the demise of the tour's Doral stop, the four-tournament Florida Swing continued and, some years more than others, thrived. If you played all four, you could get a taste of professional golf's early days as a true tour, a driving tour, as it was in Hogan's heyday and Palmer's early years. Jake Knapp's plan for his first Florida Swing was to play three of its stops: the Cognizant at PGA National; the Arnold Palmer Invitational at Bay Hill; and the Players Championship at the Stadium Course. Then he'd skip the fourth event, the Valspar Championship, near Tampa, and go to Augusta to see it for the first time. Winning in Mexico gave Jake what every player craves, the ability to make your own schedule, to pick your own spots.

For years, this had been one of the privileges for established players. They picked their spots. They practiced when they wanted to practice. They made their own arrangements with their caddies, teachers, and (eventually) psychologists. They ate where they wanted to eat and stayed where they wanted to stay. The pro on tour was an independent contractor, a cowboy wrapped in tourwear, TaylorMade driver in his hands, unless he preferred Titleist or Callaway or Ping. If you wanted to play the tour successfully, you had to make a long series of good decisions. That was baked into the whole thing. In football, coaches and assistant coaches were always telling you what to do, where to be, and when. Golf was the opposite.

For forty years and counting, March has meant spring-training baseball and the tour's Florida Swing for this reporter. (Gil Hodges, the beloved manager of our beloved New York Mets, had a fatal heart attack after a spring-training golf game. That was a shock for my brother and me.) One year, I stayed for a few days at the Club Med in Port St. Lucie, spring-training home of the Mets. When I checked out, I asked if there was a mistake on my bill. Three fresh buffet meals a day, a good bed, unlimited range balls—the final tab seemed way too low. "No, it's correct," the woman at the front desk told me. "Your roommate was a no-show."

Somewhere along the way, I learned that Mickey Wright lived on the Club Med course. If you got lucky, early some mornings, you could see this legend of legends hitting balls off a plastic mat in her backyard over a metal fence and onto the adjacent fairway. I never did, but a course worker described the scene to me years after Mickey had played her last tournament. Her swing sounded like a mix of textbook perfection and golfing poetry. Mickey believed in a low, long, slow takeaway with the driver. So did Byron Nelson before her and Jack Nicklaus after her. Three great drivers.[*]

I have often returned home from these trips with an important breakthrough, bringing it back to Philadelphia like another visitor might bring back a Margaritaville T-shirt. At tournament ranges, at these Florida events and many others, I can fall into a pleasant golf drift, watching the pros go through their range routines. Almost by osmosis, you absorb what they do. Changes slip in. In the 1970s and '80s and '90s, my left heel (I'm a righty) was well off the ground at the top of my swing; I was taking my cues from Hogan, from Arnold, from Nicklaus, from Tom Watson and everybody else, really. But sometime in this new century—and how and when this happened, I can't say—my left heel remained planted through the backswing. Norman's left heel remained planted at the top. Tiger's left heel is planted. Rory's left foot looks like it's stuck in cement. Maybe it's just a fad, this planted-foot thing. (That's

---

[*] "I know zero-zero-*zero* about the golf swing, but low and long was never a thing for me," says Fred Couples. "I do like slow at the start. But I pick it up. I find it easier to set the club at the top of the swing that way." Couples in his prime drove it as well as anybody.

how I got stuck with an AOL email address, assigned to me when *Sports Illustrated* was jointly owned by AOL and Time Inc. I thought email would be a fad.) Brandel Chamblee, Golf Channel swing guru, doesn't like a planted heel. He wants your front heel lifting to allow more rotation and for the swing to be easier on the body. But can Brandel be right about *everything*?

I made some stops on the drive from Philadelphia to PGA National. In Richmond, I hit balls off the dormant grass at the First Tee's driving range. In North Florida, I spent a night at a Renaissance Hotel off I-95 in a place called World Golf Village, former home of the World Golf Hall of Fame, in a hulking building that had been converted into a megachurch. In a parking lot in North Palm Beach (and with my daughter's help), I turned my phone into a TV and watched the final moments of Jake Knapp's win in Mexico. I had dinner at the Cheesecake Factory (omelets available all day) in West Palm Beach and then checked into the nearby Marriott on Okeechobee Boulevard, crowded, as it always is in March, with young baseball prospects, most of them from Spanish-speaking countries. Scores of kids who, to borrow from Roger Kahn, are good enough to dream.

The next day, I went out the Marriott's back door, heading to a diner I know well. It's an easy walk there, a straight shot east on Okeechobee Boulevard, across a bridge that takes you over the Intracoastal Waterway. That gets you into the town of Palm Beach, and what was a boulevard is now Royal Palm Way. You continue on this palm-lined thoroughfare until you reach South County Road, and there you make a right.

On that corner, where Royal Palm Way meets South County Road, there's an elegant French restaurant, its large casement windows wide open on this warm South Florida afternoon. And sitting right there, at a table for two with their elbows almost over the sidewalk, were Patti Scialfa and Bruce Springsteen.

Bruce is one of my heroes. Imagine stringing together these six

words: *so fast so shiny so sharp*. (From "4th of July, Asbury Park (Sandy),"
if that snippet of poetry is new to you.) Listening to Bruce, I sometimes
feel like I can swim the fifty or sixty nautical miles from the beach in Asbury Park to the dock on the Patchogue River in my hometown, where
the wholesale clam buyers used to pay cash money for littlenecks by the
bushel.

I believe in giving the famous a wide berth, but I also believe what
Christine has often said over the years, that you regret the things in life
you don't do. I took my shot.

"I'm sure this place is great, but you do know there's a diner down
the street, don't ya?"

Diners figure in Bruce's music and life. In Patti's life, too, I would
guess. She's a Jersey girl.

Bruce said, "Yeah? Whadda they got there?"

"You like a tuna melt?"

"Of course."

"They've got a good tuna melt. I put chips in mine."

"I don't do that," Bruce said.

Patti asked for the name of the place, and I told her. The SurfSide
Diner, where the old Hamburger Heaven used to be.

I thanked them for the gift of their music. Bruce put his palms together and made a gentle southbound nod. I made the short walk to the
diner, sat in a swivel seat at the counter, and ordered a tuna melt and an
Arnold Palmer.

A couple days later, I played my first full round of the new year. This
was at one of my favorite golfing spots, the public course in North Palm
Beach on U.S. 1, down the road from Seminole. Jack Nicklaus lives in

North Palm Beach, and as a gift to the village, he took a flat course with sandy soil and turned it into a course with lots of swoops and swales and movement. There's also a lighted driving range, where I often see the same people, and a large public pool. The only thing missing is a soft-serve ice-cream stand. If the place had Carvel—that would almost be too much.

When I told Nicklaus how much I liked the course, he said, "Well, it shows what I can do when you give me a sandy site." Sandy soil is to a course architect what oil paint is to a landscape artist. A sand base gives a course a distinct texture, whether it's on the East Coast of Scotland (the Old Course in St. Andrews), the Sandhills of Nebraska (Sand Hills Golf Club), or in the New Jersey Pine Barrens (Pine Valley). The course architect Tom Doak was building an inland course on a canal about twenty-five miles north of North Palm Beach. His client had one requirement for his dream course, and that was sandy soil. The owner found it in an unlikely area of horse farms and citrus groves. He's calling his new course Sandglass. Donald Ross had the same thing at Seminole, acres and acres of sandy soil, as did Nicklaus in North Palm Beach. Sometimes iron shots at the NPB muni will run like iron shots at North Berwick in Scotland.

My phone rang as I entered the parking lot. It was Jimmy Roberts of NBC Sports, returning my call. He was in town to cover the Cognizant, although everybody was still calling it Honda, no *the* (*See you at Honda*). I told him where I was. He asked who I was playing with.

"Mike Donald and Rees Jones," I said.

"Name-dropper," Jimmy said.

Well, yes, but both are actual friends.

Mike, who is in his late sixties, played in 550 PGA Tour events, starting in 1980. He was the winner of one of them. Rees, in his early eighties, was a busy course architect, though it had been a while since he was the USGA's Open Doctor, a name bestowed upon him when he prepared courses for U.S. Open play. In 1990 at Medinah, Hale Irwin won his third U.S. Open when he beat Mike in a playoff that went nineteen holes. Rees later gave Medinah a makeover. When Mike played in the 1993 U.S. Open at Baltusrol, it was Rees who had doctored it. Yes, Six Degrees of Kevin Bacon, golf-style. A useful activity if you find yourself waiting on a par-3 tee.

Mike, a serious student of the swing (not all tour players are), likes how Rees swings from the inside, promoting a draw. Swinging from the inside is one of Mike's core golf values. (He cannot *stand* it when he sees me swiping at the ball from the outside and across it.) Rees played golf and baseball as a kid in New Jersey and at Montclair High School (Class of '59). If you can pull a baseball—a right-handed batter hitting a line drive over the third baseman, for example—you should be able to draw a golf ball. Rees could do both. The swing paths are similar. The hips clear; the hands, on a circle, follow. I could learn a lot watching Rees. Watching Rees and listening to Mike.

On these annual Florida Swing trips, I often see my former boss Mark Mulvoy, the retired managing editor of *Sports Illustrated*. He caught Time Inc. in its glory years, editorially and financially. The evidence of the latter lingers in Mulvoy's year-round tan, half-dozen club memberships, and multiple residences, including a winter home in Vero Beach. He seems to always be going to Prague for some culture immersion or Ballybunion in Ireland for five rounds in three days. You would never guess the guy is in his early eighties. If he doesn't break his age, he's annoyed.

In 1965, Plimpton and the editors at *Sports Illustrated* cooked up the idea of a series of pieces for the magazine that turned into *The Bogey Man*. Mulvoy was a young *SI* writer, just out of Boston College with an obsessive interest in hockey and golf. The editors gave him an important assignment: Make some calls and help pave the way for George Plimpton, author of *Paper Lion*, to play in three California pro-ams. For Plimpton and Mulvoy, it was the start of a beautiful friendship.

In the years when Mulvoy ran *Sports Illustrated*, Plimpton was one of his go-to writers. It was Mulvoy who published Plimpton's story on a New York Mets prospect and Harvard dropout named Sidd Finch, who had been raised in an orphanage in England and had a 168-mile-an-hour fastball. The piece ran at the start of the baseball season in 1985. The issue date was April 1.

In the next issue, there was a short follow-up: Sidd Finch had retired.

I asked Mulvoy about George's golf game and reminded him that, for the three pro-am events he played, Plimpton was listed as an 18-handicapper. That is, somebody who could shoot in the 90s.

"George couldn't play dead," Mulvoy said. It's a caddie-yard dis (Mulvoy caddied in Boston as a kid) for someone who has no game. The phrase goes back to producers of Westerns who rejected actors so unskilled, they couldn't play a corpse in a saloon shoot-out. "George couldn't box. He certainly couldn't play football, he was so tall and gangly. He could barely dong that triangle or whatever the hell he was doing for the New York Philharmonic. But he could write."

On Monday night of the Cognizant week, some hours after my tuna-melt lunch at the SurfSide Diner, I went to the city-owned course in West Palm Beach for a made-for-TV golf outing called the Match. Match IX, to be more precise. Match I was Tiger versus Phil in Las Vegas, winner takes all for $9 million of somebody else's money. The payday alone was offensive. The golfers were tight, their needling sounded fake, and the event was decided on a 93-yard hole, created on the spot. Mike Mills, the R.E.M. bassist and unlicensed golf commentator, offered this observation: "Where's the windmill? The clown's mouth? A half-wedge to win $9 million?" The naked, ungolfy greed of it all, turning golf into a game show instead of an athletic competition, proved in time to be a precursor to LIV Golf. Match IX had a goofy premise: twelve holes, live in prime time, four players under floodlights and moonlight. But at least it wasn't taking itself too seriously. It was a dressed-up goodwill charity event.

The four players were Max Homa, Rory McIlroy, Lexi Thompson, and Rose Zhang. Each golfer was in a souped-up cart with a cart-cam pointed at the driver-contestant. At times, Rory and Max seemed more interested in their drag racing than in their golf. It's possible that Rose thought it was a team event, girls against boys. (A lot of people did.) When Lexi made a bomb for an eagle and a solo win on the second hole, Rose raised her arms in victory.

It was all good. Rose was a breath of fresh air in the game, a star student at Stanford *and* a rising LPGA star. The LPGA was in a good place.

But more than anything, that Monday-night made-for-TV event was a coming-out party for the host course, formerly the West Palm Beach muni, rebranded as The Park. A group of golf-minded do-gooders had donated millions of dollars to give a course that was dying from neglect a fresh look with old-school touches. The Park has a lighted short course, a lighted putting course, and a lighted driving range, plus a chic pro shop, a lovely restaurant, and teched-out classrooms. The course abuts a neighborhood of modest homes, bordered by I-95 on one side and train tracks on another. Kids who live in West Palm Beach can play The Park for twenty dollars. The whole thing is astounding. You could say the greens and greenside traps are way too difficult for beginning golfers at a busy public course, and maybe they'll soften in the years and decades to come. But that it exists at all is reason enough to throw a party.

The grow-the-game movement, born out of a belief that golf improves lives, became more urgent after the murder of George Floyd and a world slowed by an airborne pandemic. It has been around for a while, but those two tragedies put it on an accelerator. Rich white men have had a stranglehold on the game forever, especially in the United States, and those events sounded a loud and overdue wake-up call. From it came The Park. Other parks are coming. The old West Palm Beach muni was on a death watch. You can hardly get a tee time at the new one.

Brad Faxon, well known for magic-wand putting in his playing days, later a broadcaster and short-game coach, was on the giant practice green at The Park, putter in hand, ready to help those in need. His wife, Dory, was there, too. Dory captured the night's social climate in a single sentence: "Being here is like being under the tree at Augusta." There's an enormous oak at Augusta National between the clubhouse and the first tee, and every April, all through the Masters from morning to night, it's a gathering place for the embroidered-belt crowd, plus a few lucky stragglers.

I first met Brad in 1985, when I caddied for him at Honda in his second year on tour, and we've been comparing notes on our lives in the game ever since. I met Mike Donald at that Honda, too. Mike and Brad played together in the first two rounds. Early that first day, they talked about a Cadillac Mike had won by way of a hole in one. Pros and their cars. Brad once bought a BMW from Payne Stewart after he started cashing some good checks. A lemon, as it turned out. What he earned was directly related to how well he putted. That's true for all touring pros. But it's truer for Brad than most. His four daughters were clothed, fed, and schooled on the miles of putts he holed.

At Honda that week nearly forty years ago, Brad spent hours on the putting green. One of his putting drills was to make fifty straight three-footers. If he missed one on his way to fifty, he started over. He did that at Honda and on hundreds of other occasions over the years. Nobody sprinkled magic putting dust on Brad. He has terrific hand-eye coordination. He can beat almost everybody he plays in Ping-Pong using a cell phone for a paddle. But the real secret to his putting is good technique, good core strength, good thinking—and ten thousand hours of practice. He got to that number years before Malcolm Gladwell did.

My putting struggles developed in an odd way, and Brad knew about them. When I was a teenager and through my twenties and thirties, putting was the, quote, best part of my game and driving the worst. In my forties and since then, that has flipped. My putting woes grow deeper as I get closer to the hole. I'm not a classic yipper. I don't have obvious convulsions and spasms while putting. But hitter always knows. Hitter knows. *My name is Mike, and I am a yipper.*

George Plimpton devoted a chapter in *The Bogey Man* to the yips, a word he first encountered in the second week of his three-week West Coast swing, at Harding Park in San Francisco. He described Byron Nelson stabbing at a four-foot putt and sending it forty feet past the hole. Plimpton's pro partner at Harding Park was Rod Funseth, one of his sources on the malady. Plimpton asked Funseth if there was a cure for the yips. "Golfers who have the yips *try* to cure them, God knows," Funseth said. "There's no sure cure." Why I have read that chapter more than once, I don't know.

For the last ten years—or is it twenty?—I've been carrying two putters or one two-way putter, because I am less apt to yip the short ones as a lefty. With a two-way putter, I can turn any putt into a hook putt, and (as discussed) a hooked putt tumbles end over end, holds its line, and has a chance. Most of us can live with a miss off a good stroke. But a miss by yip sucks the life out of you. Have you ever seen somebody yip a putt and march to the next tee feeling good? No, because that has never happened.

I told Brad I get most nervous, and my putting becomes most erratic, when I'm so close to the hole that there is essentially a 100 percent expectation the putt will be made. And that's when the black clouds come barreling in: *Nothing good can happen here, only something bad.* These situations are hard to practice because you need real-life pressure to get to such a place. Maybe your partner, in the qualifying round for the season-long better ball of partners, is waiting on the side of the green, fingers and legs crossed as you step in. The partner is out of the hole, and everything rests on what you do. The prerequisite to this whole discussion is caring. Caring is great. Caring too much is a killer.

Brad encouraged me to counter such gloomy thoughts (*Nothing good can happen here*) with something productive. Process, for instance: What do you want to do, and how are you going to do it?

"Do you have a routine?" he asked. That is, a method for stepping into the putt, getting over it, making a stroke.

"I really don't," I said. Sometimes my mindset is miss-'em-quick, which lowers expectations and opens the door to a pleasant surprise. Other times I have to go through a long checklist before I take the putter head back.

"Maybe you should," Brad said.

He kindly agreed to give me a putting lesson.

We got together the morning after the Monday-night event at The Park. We went to an out-of-the-way practice green at a course where Brad is a member, Old Palm Golf Club, down the road from PGA National. There's a network of roads in Palm Beach County that lead to all manner of private courses, public courses, municipal courses, development courses, plus driving ranges and gyms and rehab centers with overbooked back specialists.

Brad's teaching method is gentle, positive, and engaged. He asks a lot of questions. The only negative thing he said was about my left-handed putting: "I hate it."

I wasn't expecting a magic solution from one ninety-minute lesson. You cannot turn around years of poor putting with a single putting lesson, even if your teacher is Brad Faxon. Years ago, I got a putting lesson from Dave Stockton, another accomplished player who was a famously great putter. Everything I got from Dave, I gave to my friend David Morse, and he has used it effectively ever since. But I couldn't get comfortable with Stockton's forward-press, short follow-through method. Brad, in our time together, talked some about the path of the putter head but more about what you do before beginning your stroke. Once you take the putter back, he wants instincts and feel to take over. It was terrific, being with him on that practice green.

I'm going to list five of Brad's putting insights, as I processed them. They're being offered in the present tense because this is rest-of-your-life-type stuff.

- *Stand tall to the ball so your arms can swing.*
- *Feel so athletic over the ball that if somebody shoved you, your feet would not move.*
- *Practice holing putts at three speeds to get a feel for how speed dictates line.* *
- *Know where the sweet spot is on your putter, and don't take the manufacturer's word for it. Mark the spot with a Sharpie.*
- *Get a longer putter.*

---

* Mike Donald and Brad Faxon played in the same tour events hundreds of times over their long careers, and Mike was an outstanding putter, too. He was struck by Brad's emphasis on how speed dictates line. "Most golfers underestimate how much a putt is going to break. If you think it breaks three feet, it probably breaks five," Donald says. "You want that ball breaking *toward* the hole as it's dying."

That last one is not universal. Jack Nicklaus, one of the best putters ever, stood with his head four feet over his ball, if that. He didn't need a long shaft on his putter. Brad was saying I needed a longer putter. He wanted me standing taller to it.

Brad recorded me stroking a ten-footer. I have it on my phone. As the ball comes off the face, you can hear him say, "Awesome, Michael."

I'll leave the rest to your imagination.

I know my way around Palm Beach County. It comes with the beat. I've seen Mark Calcavecchia's home bowling alley off U.S. 1, Tiger's restaurant off Indiantown Road, Dustin Johnson's preferred dockside bar off A1A. I know that Donald Ross Road was named not for the architect but for a World War II Army hero, though the broad boulevard offers almost a straight shot off I-95 to Seminole, a Donald Ross masterwork. It was off Donald Ross Road that Jerome Smith, guitarist for KC and the Sunshine Band, was killed while working on a construction site. That was in August 2000, when Tiger's game was on fire. The line from Bobby Jones's waggle to the KC-SB's shake-shake-shake might be circuitous, but it does exist. "One leisurely waggle, and a quick twist of the hips to break up whatever tension may have crept in, and away we go," Jones said. "Shake your booty" arrived forty-five years later, and it came in hot.

After my putting lesson with Brad, I made a beeline down PGA Boulevard to Military Trail and a mom-and-pop golf shop I know there called Rick's, with a locksmith and a liquor store for neighbors. The main man at Rick's is Mr. Jason Page, a warm, tatted man and former college pitcher from New Jersey who has never met a golf club he couldn't improve through ingenuity and craftiness.

Jason's rescue dog, Harper—a tiny pooch named for a large baseball player, Bryce Harper—watched with passing interest as Jason went rooting around for a used shaft in the name of a taller, more free-swinging putting stance for his eager customer.

Jason didn't want to put in a new, longer shaft. His preference was to add length to the existing shaft at its butt end, although that would require removing the putter's black rubber grip. The grip, designed by Karsten Solheim and manufactured by Golf Pride, was sold by Ping as its PP58 model. It's an eight-dollar grip but not much in circulation, as it is a thin grip in an era of fat ones. Tiger has used a PP58 grip throughout his career, yet the grip barely sells. How weird is that? Even as a painfully terrible putter, I much prefer a thin grip. I can't feel the head with a fat one.

Luckily for me, Jason had a PP58 grip in the back room: I wouldn't lose the time it would take to order a new one. On that or any Ping putter grip, you'll see the little white logo, Mr. Ping—a cartoon figure, really, in outline. Mr. Ping looks like a walrus in a bucket hat over a ball. You won't see Mr. Ping on Tiger's putter grip because he blots out the white ink with a black Sharpie. Any new grip feels good, and the fresh-rubber feel of an out-of-the-wrapper PP58 feels especially good. There's a lot of life in it, in its springiness. I don't know how a golfer could not pay close attention to the grip, in both senses of the word. What else connects you to your club?

Jason took a spare shaft and cut off a two-inch piece from its tip end, the narrow end. With the old grip removed, he inserted this invented plug into the top of the existing shaft and glued it in place. He took a wide white roll of tape and, like a nurse tending a wound, carefully wrapped the top end of the shaft, heading south for about a foot. He put on the new PP58 grip.

The putter was now close to two inches longer than it had been. I took some practice strokes on the gray cement floor in Jason's workshop. The new grip, the added length, Jason's enthusiasm, Brad's lesson—I was ready for some better putting. As ready as I'd ever be.

Jason Page, club repairman, with his dog, Harper,
and the author's two-way putter.

The Cognizant Classic had two pro-ams on Wednesday of the tournament week, one big and splashy, the other quiet and tucked away. The big one, held on the tournament course at the PGA National resort, featured Rickie Fowler, Lucas Glover, Rory McIlroy, and other familiar names. The winning team was Nick Dunlap, the Amex winner, and his am Tua Tagovailoa, the Miami Dolphins quarterback. Both went to 'Bama.

Meanwhile, a far more modest pro-am was being held on a nine-hole par-3 course hidden behind the resort's tennis center. I had never heard of such a thing and wandered over to take a look. I bumped into another man and we started chatting. The fella was a lawyer from Philadelphia named Larry Spector. I asked him if he was related to my friend Shanin Specter, also a lawyer in Philadelphia. Turns out, they were second cousins. Their grandfathers were brothers who came through Ellis Island from Ukraine in different decades, were assigned different spellings for their family names by immigration agents, and were reunited on a New York street by bizarre happenstance. Harry Specter had a lawyer son who became a U.S. senator from Pennsylvania and a lawyer grandson who had season tickets to the Phillies behind home plate. Joseph Spector had a lawyer grandson with a winter-break condo at PGA National, right by its par-3 course. Could you have such a what-a-small-world chat at a tennis tournament? Sure. But I think it's more likely in golf.

I saw one familiar name playing in the pro-am on the par-3 course, Robert Garrigus, once a promising country-strong golfer with ridiculous clubhead speed. By his mid-thirties, Garrigus had won one PGA Tour event and lost three times in playoffs. In other words, he was very good. Now he was forty-six, trying to find places to play, trying to get to fifty, and to a second career on the senior tour. There are always several hundred golfers who could say the same thing, hanging around and hanging on, and there might be a dozen new openings on the senior tour in any year. Tough way to make a living.

One of Garrigus's pro-am partners was a woman in her thirties who had never hit a golf ball in her life. She was playing with her husband— they worked together in real estate sales—and they were sharing clubs. After a swing and a miss on one tee shot, Garrigus had a tip for her: Take a practice swing, see where your swing bottoms out, put your ball there, then swing for real. The woman took a practice swing. Garrigus noted where her swing bottomed out and teed up a ball for her there. On her next tee shot, the woman made contact. Her shot was a soft liner that almost reached a greenside trap on a ninety-yard hole. "There you go!" Garrigus said.

Exuberance did not come readily to this young woman, new to golf and the American penchant for public celebration. She picked up her tee like it was a dropped earring. A shy smile crossed her face.

It was impressive, seeing how engaged Robert Garrigus was during that pro-am. "I used to think I was a big deal because I was a good golfer and people knew who I was," he told me. "Now I realize nobody gives a shit." His purpose, he said, was to help who he could, where he could.

Garrigus is a big man with a big personality who turned pro after a brief stint at a community college. He was never the favorite son of the blazer crowd at PGA Tour headquarters, in part because of his history as a drinker and drug user and his candor about it. He has talked publicly about slipping into portable toilets while playing to take quick hits off a joint. Nobody at tour HQ could have been thrilled to see those stories making the rounds. Later, Garrigus was suspended by the PGA Tour after a post-round drug test revealed he had elevated levels of THC, the psychoactive ingredient in marijuana. "If you can buy it in a store, why are we testing for it?" he asked then. He was not trying to make life easier for Jay Monahan, the PGA Tour commissioner.

His buddy Grayson Murray, also a big man with a big personality, had a similar bent. They were both represented by Kevin Canning, the same agent who helped launch Nick Dunlap's pro career. On Tuesday morning of the Cognizant week, Dunlap and Garrigus played nine holes together, the game set up by Canning. You see a lot of that, players hanging with other players who have the same agent. Tiger Woods and Justin Thomas are both managed by Mark Steinberg. Grayson Murray and Robert Garrigus had logged a lot of time together.

Murray found he could talk to Garrigus about the powerful draw of dope and booze, because Garrigus knew all about that kind of lust. They both knew what it was like to swim in the wrong direction in the fishbowl of tour life. Garrigus was born in 1977 and Murray in 1993, but the sixteen-year difference added depth to their bond. Robert Garrigus liked being a go-to person in Grayson Murray's life. He often ended his texts to Murray with *Love you, brother. One day at a time.*

Shortly before the 2023 U.S. Open, there was a players' meeting with Jay Monahan. The meeting was about a possible agreement between the PGA Tour and LIV Golf, one that left rank-and-file players, like Grayson Murray, worried about their future. At the time of the meeting, Murray was the 227th best player in the world, on the Official World Golf Ranking list. He feared he would wind up in a golfing purgatory.

It was a closed-door meeting, but it's hard to keep a secret on the PGA Tour, and Brentley Romine of Golf Channel got wind of who said what.

"We don't trust you, Jay," Murray yelled at the commissioner. "You should resign right now. You lied to our face!"

Rory McIlroy, a PGA Tour board member then and a sort of surrogate for Monahan, was at the meeting. His response to Murray did not come out of a charm-school lesson plan: "Just play better, Grayson." Like, you wouldn't have to worry about playing opportunities if you shot lower scores.

Murray's response was a roundhouse punch from his mouth: "Fuck off."

But Murray *did* start playing better. By the end of the year, he was ranked 133rd in the world. January came, and he won in Hawaii in the first full-field event of the new year. *Just play better, Grayson.* Murray and Garrigus had a field day with McIlroy's phrase, pounding on its every syllable, like third-graders on a pogo stick. *JUST play BET-ter GRAY-son.* "Spite is a powerful motivator," Murray told Garrigus.

When Garrigus finished up his nine-hole practice round at PGA National with Nick Dunlap, he went to the range and saw Murray there. Murray wasn't in the event. He had made the short drive to PGA National from his townhouse in Palm Beach Gardens to get his clubs tweaked.

Garrigus and Murray left the range and got lunch in player dining. Murray was ranked now fifty-fifth in the world. He was thirty and engaged, with his townhouse in Palm Beach Gardens and a membership at the Dye Preserve, a club off Indiantown Road where he could get a game with other good players any day of the week. For the first time in his life, he had a clear path to all four majors, plus the Players. Everything was in front of him. Lunch wrapped up and the two golfers hugged. "One day at a time, brother," Garrigus told him. He thought Murray was in a good place.

It can seem magical. In 2011, Garrigus won on tour and tied for third at the U.S. Open. He was thirty-three and on the rise. Now he was forty-six, with a fiancée, a former wife, an angry ex-girlfriend, three children, and no playing status.

He got his spot in the Cognizant by winning its Monday qualifier, where eighty guys competed for four spots. Garrigus, pushing his bag in a trolley, posted 65 at the qualifier, the low score of the day on a windswept course in Port St. Lucie. Two other players shot 66, so they were in, too.

One spot remained. A half-dozen players shot 67. Two of the six were former PGA Tour winners, D. J. Trahan and Kevin Tway. All six players, in fading afternoon winter light, went into a sudden-death playoff for the one remaining spot. A Canadian golfer named Michael Gligic got the spot with a birdie on the first playoff hole.

There were two tour events the week after the Cognizant. There was the Arnold Palmer Invitational at Bay Hill, with sixty-nine players and a $20 million purse. And there was a so-called opposite-field event, the Puerto Rico Open, with 132 players playing for $4 million. Puerto Rico and events like it exist to appease the tour's underclass.

On Monday Garrigus played in the Cognizant qualifier. On

Tuesday he played a nine-hole practice round with Nick Dunlap. On Wednesday he played in the pro-am on the par-3 course. On Thursday he shot 71 in the first round of the Cognizant. He'd need a good second round to make the cut. He shot 75 on the Friday round. No chance.

The only money Garrigus made for the week was what he earned for playing in the nine-hole pro-am, and the only reason he got invited to that pro-am was because he was close to the man in charge of finding pros for it, a tall, thin, behind-the-curtains tour lifer named Tim West. Garrigus was paid what every other player got paid for the pro-am, fifteen hundred dollars.

There was no Monday qualifier for the Puerto Rico Open, but Garrigus was the tournament's third alternate, so he had a chance to get in. Garrigus and his fiancée, Lauren, were staying at a friend's house in Palm Beach Gardens. They packed up their things and flew to San Juan.

By Wednesday of Puerto Rico week, Garrigus was the first alternate. If anybody scratched, he was in. His plan was to be at the course at sunrise on Thursday, just in case. Early Wednesday night, he and Lauren went for dinner at the players' hotel, a Hyatt Regency. Matti Schmid, a young player from Germany, joined them. Shortly after sitting down, Garrigus received a text message from his buddy Tommy "Two Gloves" Gainey, another tour journeyman: *D. J. Trahan didn't show up for his pro-am tee time. You might want to give somebody a call.*

Gainey knew Trahan was a no-show because he had filled in for Trahan at the pro-am. He also knew what all players know: Missing a pro-am tee time is a cardinal sin. Unless there is a dire extenuating circumstance, when a player misses a pro-am tee time, he is disqualified from that week's tournament. A trip to a hospital emergency room for a heart attack would be an acceptable reason to miss a pro-am, and that's about it. At dinner, Schmid told Garrigus and Lauren in a just-the-facts tone, "I saw him at the golf course. He did not look sick to me." Garrigus figured Trahan had to be out, which meant he'd get his start.

But Trahan did *not* get disqualified from the tournament, and Garrigus was furious. He asked everybody he could why Trahan was permitted to play. So did Kevin Canning, his agent. So did Ryan French, reporting the story for his Monday Q readership. No meaningful answers were forthcoming. Nobody could explain why D. J. Trahan was not disqualified from the Puerto Rico Open for missing a 4:11 Wednesday-afternoon tee time for a nine-hole pro-am appearance.

Garrigus, as the first alternate, was at the course before sunrise Thursday morning. He heard Trahan, huddled with other players in the clubhouse, laughing about something. Trahan approached Garrigus, offering some kind of apology or explanation. Whatever it was, Garrigus didn't want to hear it. "Your job," Garrigus said to him, "is to show up for your tee time." He walked away.

When those places in tournaments are just there for you every week, because that's how good you are, it's easy to convince yourself it will go on forever. Garrigus was once the 35th-ranked player in the world. He was Grayson Murray. He was Jake Knapp. He was any young tour winner with a bright future who could pick his spots. That was then. The final Thursday-morning tee time came and went. Everybody showed. Garrigus returned to the hotel. He and Lauren packed up and flew home.

March in Florida was a four-week golfing bender for your tour guide. I watched, played, played, watched. After Cognizant, I caught some of the Bay Hill tournament, then the Players Championship, and finally the Valspar. I played in three pro-ams on three different tours. At a tournament in Winter Haven, I was paired with a young Chinese woman on the LPGA development circuit, the Epson Tour. I played in the pro-am of the Ocala Open, one of the majors of the Florida mini-tour winter season. I played in the Saturday pro-am at the Valspar. Yes, a Saturday pro-am at a tour event.

One afternoon early in this four-week golfing binge, I met Mike Donald at a Palm Beach County course called Park Ridge, off Military Trail in unincorporated Lake Worth. It's an enjoyable course with modest green fees. I was not surprised to learn that Park Ridge was built on a former landfill because it has elevation and undulation, and Palm Beach County, in its natural state, is as flat as a Publix parking lot. You may know that the early courses in Scotland were established on seaside tracts with sandy soil that could not be farmed and nobody wanted. Talk about repurposing—along the Firth of Forth in Scotland then, off Military Trail in South Florida now.

Mike likes the Park Ridge range. It's wide and deep, with healthy grass and decent balls. A course worker warned Mike that outside teaching was not permitted. Mike, as honest as any person I know, said, "I'm not giving a lesson, I'm just helping a friend with his swing." Mike wasn't there to make money or take teaching business away from anybody.

There are a handful of ranges in Palm Beach County and Broward County where Mike helps his golfing buddies from all walks of life with their swings, always on a pro bono basis. Over the years, simply by calling Mike at random times, I have heard about swing changes being made by his pals Jorge, by Lucky, by Andrew, by others. *Michael, I'm telling you, this Andrew? He just hit three of the most beautiful 6-irons you ever saw in your life.* During the pandemic, Mike stopped going to the barber, and his preferred golf shirt is a loose long-sleeved button-front shirt. Between the hair and the shirt, nobody ever looks at Mike and thinks, *Tour player!* They're more likely to think, *Looks like The Dude from that Jeff Bridges movie.*

But then Mike starts talking with intense enthusiasm about You-

Tube clips showing Hogan or Trevino or a kid in sneakers in Africa hitting iron shots off red dirt with villagers watching and captions in Chinese. Mike sent me that last clip with this note: *I love this video, and the young man has a beautiful swing.*

Mike teaches from his life. He sometimes gives me more credit than I deserve for understanding what he's talking about. But there was one topic from this afternoon session on the Park Ridge range that I definitely got. It related to the start of the swing. He wanted me to kill my pre-swing hovering.

Nicklaus was famous for hovering his clubhead above the ball before starting his takeaway. He did it with every club. One reason Nicklaus never incurred a moving-ball penalty after addressing his ball was because, by the rules, he never addressed his shots at all. The rule book says address begins when you put your club on the ground, but Nicklaus never did, and you can't be penalized for moving a ball if you haven't addressed it. Nicklaus was always careful with his ball. He was careful when marking it on the green, when standing over it in a bunker, when teeing it up behind the tee markers. Golf is not a sport for careless people.

But the main reason Nicklaus hovered was to reduce tension in his grip, through his body, and right up into his head. Hovering prevents you from freezing over the ball. There's a lot to be said for it. Almost everybody who hovers these days got it from Nicklaus. Greg Norman taught himself how to play from Nicklaus's first instruction book, *Golf My Way*, and Norman hovered, too. Nicklaus despises tension in the grip. It prevents proper release of the clubhead, among other issues. It hurts your rhythm. It slows the swing.[*]

---

[*] "Jack Nicklaus and Greg Norman were two of the greatest drivers of the golf ball with a wooden driver ever, and they hovered," Nick Price says. "They were trying to relieve tension with their hovering. But I *wanted* tension. I needed tension in my backswing to give me the compact swing I wanted. Hogan couldn't have hovered. He need that tension in his backswing. That's where his speed came from."

On the eve of the final round of the 1986 British Open, Norman, trying to win his first major, had a chance conversation with Nicklaus about grip pressure. It came at the right time. They were both in the dining room at the Turnberry Hotel. This was on the Saturday night of the British Open. Norman was the fifty-four-hole leader, and Nicklaus had no chance to win. In April, Norman had been the third-round leader at the Masters, but Nicklaus won. In June, Norman had been the Saturday-night leader at the U.S. Open, but Raymond Floyd won. The Open was then the third major of the year. Nicklaus walked over to Norman's table and asked if he could offer a suggestion. Norman said of course, and Nicklaus pulled up a chair. Two golf gods, one looking for his first major, the other with eighteen. Nicklaus, then forty-six, knew that Norman, brash and lively and thirty-one, was good for golf.

Nicklaus's advice for Norman was brief: Be aware of your grip pressure, keep your grip pressure light. A tight grip, Nicklaus said, leads to a tense swing, especially in the thin air of a Sunday afternoon.

Unsaid but baked into the conversation was the hover move. But you have to hover with *intent*. I have watched Nicklaus play hundreds if not thousands of shots. On every single swing, he picked out a spot on the ground a little ahead of his ball and took a concentrated look at it. He had his starting line. He hovered. He moved his chin toward his right shoulder. With that, another swing was under way, not one part of it left to chance. Everything Jack Nicklaus did, he did with purpose. You can't be a rote hoverer. Absolutely not. It requires (to use a word Nicklaus never would) intentionality.

Norman won by five at Turnberry. Whenever he talks about that win, he credits Nicklaus and their Saturday-night dining-room chat.

In an act of imitation—*Be like Jack*—I started hovering as a kid, but only with driver or any shot out of the rough. Over the years, my hovering time got longer and longer. I would hover and start asking myself ridiculous intra-hovering questions, like *When am I going to actually start this backswing?*

And then I played with a good golfer, and his pre-shot thing was hover-drop-go. I adopted it: hover-drop-go. Dropping the club to the ground was my signal to go, to start the takeaway.

But Mike's point, on this afternoon at the range, was that my *go* in hover-drop-go was jerky and fast, like when you pull the starter cord on the lawn mower a *second* time. Too fast in general is a recurring issue in my golf. Mike's suggestion was to scrap the hover and start with the club-head on the ground, as most people do, without getting frozen over the ball. It made sense. I was in favor of anything that would smooth out the takeaway and, ultimately, the backswing, the transition, the downswing, etc., etc. I tried. I'm trying. Change may do you good. But it ain't easy.

On the Wednesday of Bay Hill, aka the Arnold Palmer Invitational, I was invited (got myself invited) to visit the Ping equipment truck. The truck was set up on a vacant lot by the first green, tour trucks from Nike, Titleist, Callaway, and PXG parked alongside it. These air-conditioned, tech-heavy mobile shops for repairs and club-building are equipped with espresso machines, plush seating, flatscreen TVs. They are open for business on Monday, Tuesday, and Wednesday, when you'll see players and caddies popping in without appointments to have lofts and lies adjusted and grips put on, among other tweaks. The techs in these trucks see the most broken shafts on Monday, because players are more likely to snap shafts on Sunday afternoon, when easy money is slipping away with every poor shot. Things can go wrong on Sunday night, too, with clubs in transit, though some players never seem to have any transit issues. Bubba Watson, for instance. When he flies commercial, his clubs are secured with layers and layers of cushiony protection. On private planes, he brings the clubs with him into the luxurious passenger cabin, where his golf bag gets a seat of its own. Bubba is wound tight. Only his nickname is casual.

One of the Ping techs, Jack Ulrich, did a workup on my clubs. Ulrich is a third-generation golf guy. His father worked for Golf Pride, the grip manufacturer, and his father's father played the tour in the 1940s and '50s. Ulrich has seen guys like me all his life, golfers who have no desire to retire their Eye2s. He measured the loft, lie, length, and swing weight of each of my irons and the other clubs, too.

This next little part may be boring for some of you, but understanding these four terms—loft, lie, swing weight, shaft length—can help you improve your golf. You can't wait, right? Okay, here we go.

The loft is the angle of the clubface to a flat surface. The higher the angle, the higher and shorter the flight. Lofts can get altered through play, through travel, through practice, through temper tantrums. It's good to get them checked. A 7-iron with more loft than an 8-iron will result in annoyance, confusion, and bogeys.

The lie is the angle of the shaft to the ground as it comes into the clubhead. The higher the lie angle, also represented in degrees, the higher the golfer's hands are at address. This matters. High hands at address will often promote an upright swing, while low hands a more around-the-body and flatter swing. Karsten Solheim, again ahead of the curve, invented a fitting system called the Ping Dot Color Code that allowed you to find the right lie angle for you depending on your height and the length of your arms.

There are standard norms for the lie angle on every club, and from there, club fitters speak of clubs being 1 or 2 or 3 degrees upright, or 1 or 2 or 3 degrees flat, something in that range. Lie angle matters more than you might realize. A Ping brown-dot iron is 3 degrees flat, for instance, and there are nine other colors and lies as well. As lie defines where your hands are at address, it will influence the shape of your backswing, and therefore your downswing, and ultimately the quality of your round, your day, your golfing life. So know your lie angles. Your partner will thank you.

The swing weight is a measure of the weight of the head versus the rest of the club. The typical range, going from light to heavy, is C6 to D4. The higher the swing weight, the more head-heavy a club is, and feels, but head-heaviness can come at the expense of speed. Longer clubs tend to have a lighter swing weight because you need speed to launch the ball. You used to see, and to some degree still do, players putting lead tape on the backs of their clubs, a legal way to increase the club's swing weight. These are sensitive matters. A single strip of lead tape will increase a D0 club to a D1. One of the reasons I like the Ping Eye2 is because it's a head-heavy club. You can feel where the head is through the swing, especially in the downswing.

Length is length, measured in the United States in inches and in centimeters in many other countries. You want your 5-iron, typically, to be a half-inch longer than your 6, and on it goes from there, up and down the scale. You don't want crazy or inconsistent gaps.

And then there are shafts. Shafts are bizarrely complicated. They vary wildly in terms of flexibility, weight, length, width, tapering, tipping, construction material—and color scheme. A nuanced conversation about shafts is beyond my ken. I once saw the LPGA star Suzann Pettersen on the range at Bay Hill under Arnold's watchful eye, experimenting with different drivers with different shafts and different shaft weights. "What is that one," I asked, "maybe a hundred and twenty grams?" Pettersen, never one to mince words, said, "One-twenty? Are you crazy? It's like ninety!" What was I thinking?

The other basics outlined here are not difficult to grasp. I became interested in them during my high school years on visits to a shop on West Main Street in Patchogue called Scratch Golf, owned by a pilot who was a good amateur golfer. He refurbished clubs and sold second-hand sets. I enjoyed dropping in there and had my eye on a set of sec-ondhand Wilson Staff irons for a year or longer.* They were stamped DYNAPOWER FLUID FEEL, and the typeface alone was part of the ap-peal, but they were sold before I had saved up enough money for them. (Later, I was able to get a set.) It was at Scratch Golf that I was intro-duced to the four main categories of club measurement described here, and despite all the upheavals in club design, nothing has changed since then. Length, loft, lie, and swing weight are the core four. Plus your grips. If your grips are at all slick, you really are hurting yourself. The point of this PSA is that getting your clubs checked out on an annual basis is like seeing your doctor for your yearly physical.

Despite all the jingling and jangling I put my clubs through, I was pleased to learn that the specs for my Pings were spaced out beautifully. For instance, the 5-iron had 27.5 degrees of loft, and the 6-iron had 31.5. Increments of 4 degrees (or close to it) are an established norm, and in my case, that pattern continued in both directions, to the shorter clubs and the longer ones. It's hugely important to feel good about your clubs. Make and model, of course, but loft and lie, too.

Ulrich and his colleagues, when building clubs for the best players in the world, are aware of club issues most of us don't know exist. The Norwegian golfer Viktor Hovland, for instance, likes a loud driver, a driver that makes a distinct sound when you catch it on the sweet spot, and other sounds when you catch it on the toe or the heel, or high or low on the face. The club's acoustics give him feedback with every strike. Louis Oosthuizen, another Ping player, doesn't want any sound, and the Ping techs accomplish that with tiny squirts of hot-melt glue in-

---

* Hale Irwin won three U.S. Opens with three different sets of Wilson Staff irons. "When I went to my first U.S. Open in 1960—I was just a kid, taking it all in—Arnold was playing Wilson Staffs," Irwin says. Palmer won that Open, at Cherry Hills in Denver. "When I turned pro in '68 I hoped I could be a staff golfer for Wilson. Wilson was the superstar of clubs. I wanted to raise my game to the level of those clubs."

serted through a dispenser into the driver's hollow core through a tiny hole normally occupied by a tiny screw. A driver's weight can be fine-tuned in a similar way. Must be nice to be able to feel the difference and tell somebody about it.

The players can develop a strong bond with the techs who work on their clubs. For years, during the week of the Houston Open, Ulrich and other Ping techs would be invited to Ángel Cabrera's house for steaks—deeply salted, beautifully marbled—that the Argentine golfer would grill himself. Cabrera won a U.S. Open and a Masters using Ping clubs.

When Ulrich was done measuring my clubs, he handed me a blue piece of paper with numbers neatly written by hand in little boxes, Wite-Out correction tape applied as needed. I could easily read the loft and lie and swing weight of each club. Also, to the one-eighth inch, each club's length. The top of the page read TOURNAMENT PLAYERS DIVISION SPEC SHEET. Hilarious.

Before leaving, Ulrich alerted me to one problem: "Your driver shaft is a quarter inch over the limit." The USGA limit on shaft length is 46 inches. Mine measured 46.25.

That shaft had been in the driver since the previous summer. All that tainted golf. Kind of makes you ill.

After I left the Ping truck that Wednesday afternoon, Ulrich and his fellow Pingsters packed up the truck and got it on the road to Ponte Vedra Beach for the Players Championship. That drive is only three hours. Ulrich, who has a commercial driver's license, has logged many six-hundred-mile days, as he has driven the Ping truck from one tour stop to another. He and his colleagues from the other companies often wind up in the same places, going out for dinner together. They all know the giant Grand D'Iberville theater in Biloxi, Mississippi, and not because they see movies there. They like the theater's sprawling, safe parking lot and the Courtyard Marriott right beside it. The equipment guys, for all their tech, are about the last vestige of the old tour, when the tour was a tour, and your life was on the road.

The TV compound for the Arnold Palmer Invitational was in the vicinity of the equipment trucks, and when I came out of the Ping truck, the first person I saw, by pure happenstance, was Brad Faxon, who was working the tournament for NBC Sports. I had in tow my Ping putter—my new-and-improved two-way 1A—with the new grip and the extra two inches. When I told Brad about Jason at Rick's Golf Shop on Military Trail, he said, "I bet you Jason's never seen that putter configuration before." Brad gave the putter a few waggles and a pro's nod of approval. Brad Faxon! You can imagine the feeling of confidence that came over me.

I'm not proud of this next part, but it does speak to the compulsive nature of the golfer. I walked over to the large practice putting green at Bay Hill, beside the clubhouse, with Arnold Palmer's office on its second floor, untouched since he had died eight years earlier. (An Arnold Palmer golf bag, stuffed with Callaway clubs, stood on the range in the spot where he hit balls on a daily basis.) The tournament's Wednesday pro-am was in full swing, and the putting green had more than a few golfers on it, pros and ams. Scottie Scheffler was practicing, as were Xander Schauffele, Keegan Bradley, and a bunch of amateurs. I slipped on in.

I wish I could tell you I made everything. But standing taller to the ball did feel like a night-and-day change. I used a departed player's faded chalk line, like the tracer you see in a golf broadcast, and holed one five-footer after another. Why I cannot see a chalk line in my mind's eye when putting for real, I don't know. I wish I could. Maybe everybody feels that way. I made five straight and slipped on out.

From Bay Hill I drove to Winter Haven for the first event of the Epson Tour season: the Florida's Natural Charity Classic, held at the unassuming Country Club of Winter Haven, with special tournament tee markers—weighted containers of various Florida's Natural products, chiefly orange juice in all the popular levels of pulp.

The Epson Tour is the LPGA's development tour, and an LPGA official kindly invited me to play in the pro-am of their start-the-season event. (Yes, got myself invited.) The pro in our group was a former Wake Forest golfer who grew up in Shanghai, Siyun Liu, though she preferred to go by her American nickname, Swing. At Wake, one of the elite American golf programs for women and men, she never tired of hearing her coaches say, "Good swing, Swing." Her father, a Shanghai real estate investor, started his only child in golf at age two. Swing's mother continued to live in Shanghai, where she worked as a financial consultant. Her husband and daughter shared a house in Winston-Salem, near the Wake campus. In China, he was Weiqing, but in the United States and on the Epson Tour, he was William or (more commonly) Swing's dad. Swing's dad was also Swing's caddie, cook, physical therapist, and road manager.

They had made the drive together from Winston-Salem to Winter Haven to start the new season. "It's easy, just ten or eleven hours," Swing told me. One day of driving and done. Nothing for them. They had made several cross-country drives together during the pandemic. She was starting the new season with a new putter. (It's been tried before.) She did not bring a second putter, in an effort to force a commitment to the new one.

The Winter Haven tournament was the first of three consecutive three-round Epson events in Florida. After a first-round 76 in Winter

Haven, Swing was already pining for her old putter, home in Winston-Salem. She missed the thirty-six-hole cut there, and at the other two Florida events as well.

Many of the Epson players stay at private homes during tournaments, happy to have the free digs. Only a handful of players make more than $100,000 in a year. (The top fifteen players on the year-end Epson money list get LPGA playing status for the following year.) In 2023, Swing played in sixteen of the twenty-two Epson tournaments, made eight cuts, won once, finished forty-third on the money list—and made $43,000. The year before that, after getting a master's degree in business analytics from Wake, Swing played in nineteen events and made $10,800. Still, she and her father preferred to stay in inexpensive hotels near the tournament courses. Private homes could come with unreliable plumbing, uncomfortable mattresses, and a lot of forced conversation. "Private homes can be sketchy," Swing told me.

Her English is expressive and fluent. When she works on her game off the course, she told me, she spends a lot of time, too much time, "looking at my numbers," all the pieces of information that a Trackman screen can spit at you after every swing. There was no sign of that in our round together. Swing's swing is free-flowing and loose, and she bombs it. There's no uptight anything in her.

When she did some on-course practicing, hitting short, high greenside pitches over a trap, it was a study in golf by acoustics, ball-turf, ball-turf, like two fast claps. Swing played these shots with the ball back in her stance and with a steep downswing. She was happy to give us some pointers on those shots and others. (It is a truism of pro-am life that female pros are much better than male pros about giving ams the help we need.) After Swing saw me hit a couple of good line-drive, no-tee second shots on par-5s using a driver, she said, "Maybe you should hit driver off the deck from the tee!"

The Epson Tour occupies an unusual place in women's golf. At

Wake Forest, because of Title IX and the school's rich golf tradition, women's golf has the best of everything. A dozen former Wake players have made it to the LPGA tour, where playing and practicing conditions are even better. But the in-between landing place, the Epson Tour, is a world apart from both elite college golf and the LPGA tour. You're in the minors, and that's not meant in a condescending way. It is, by design, a stepping-stone tour.

My one day at the Epson event in Winter Haven was like entering a time machine. A shiny Dodge Charger was on display, part of a sponsorship with a Winter Haven auto dealer. Most of the players didn't have equipment deals or traveling caddies or creased new tour clothes. They're grateful for the starchy all-you-can-eat buffets at breakfast and lunch, where you can load up with needed calories. It's Double-A baseball, a chance to improve and prove how much you want it. In baseball, minor-leaguers have to prove themselves to coaches, managers, general managers, and owners. On the Epson Tour, you're not looking for anyone to approve you. To advance to the next level, all you have to do, and all you can do, is shoot the scores.

The third stop on the tour's four-week Florida Swing, the Players Championship, was at the Stadium Course in Ponte Vedra Beach. I stayed that week down the road at the Courtyard Marriott in St. Augustine Beach, with its wide, flat expanses of packed sand, suitable for SUVs. St. Augustine has been a magnet for spring breakers forever, and up and down the shoreline, people were surfing, fishing, and swimming; walking, jogging, and running; flying kites and throwing footballs. At a small beachside public park, a giant metal mushroom spewed water into a shallow pool crowded with splashing kids. On the edge of the pool was a boy, twelve or older, with no mobility and complex disabilities. His father was nearby, and his eyes never left his son. You try to hold on to that picture. You try.

The early-morning drive from St. Augustine to Ocala is spectacular, all back roads. It's a three-hour drive through the center of the state and a chance to time-travel into old Florida. You can drive for ten minutes without seeing another vehicle, by which I mean a truck. You go through the towns of Hastings and Citra, over rivers and swamps, past orange groves, horse farms, boat ramps, and a slew of dirt driveways. It makes you want to check your phone, not for the date but for the year.

I was heading out to Ocala in the predawn light to play in the pro-am of the Ocala Open, one of the major events on one of golf's most reliable (the checks don't bounce) minor-league tours, the Florida Professional Golf Tour. My friend Ryan French, the Monday Q guy, is an expert on mini tours, and he pointed me to this tour, to the Ocala Open, and to Kevin Aylwin, a 135-pound Florida mini-tour legend with a ten-finger baseball grip. Aylwin aims left and hits fades all day long and into the night. He plays every day. The secret to his golf, he told me, was that he knows how far his shots will go and in what direction. That and outstanding putting. Throughout Florida mini-tour golf, Aylwin is a putting legend, but even for him, putting, the game within the game, comes and goes. "I'll have days when I hit it to thirty feet and walk onto the green and think, *I got this*," he told me. "You're surprised if it doesn't go in. And you have days where you hit it to four feet and it's not close enough, 'cause you know you can't make it."

Aylwin is in his mid-thirties, a lifelong Floridian, born and raised in New Smyrna Beach. He's won almost a hundred mini-tour events, if you count the one-day tournaments, along with two-day and three-day events. When one of the many bad Florida storms turned his front lawn into a lake, Aylwin and his wife, Chelsea, left their house by paddleboard through a first-floor window, stayed with friends for the night, and returned home to find oversize cardboard winner's checks floating in their flooded first floor.

When Aylwin won the Ocala Open in 2018, he made $12,000, the largest check of his career. Now first place paid $16,000. Most of the tournament's prize money comes from the players. There were 144 players in the field for the three-day event, each paying a $750 entry fee. The low forty-eight players, plus ties, make the cut, and those players get paid, though at the bottom the payout is under $1,000. The tournament also had two designated charities, Hospice of Marion County and Interfaith Emergency Services, each of which received $50,000. That money came from the tournament, from the pro-am entry fee (ninety players paying $500 each), and from a dozen or more sponsors: a Marion County engineering firm; an Ocala law firm; a regional bank; a window company, a furniture company. Another time-warp event.

The tournament was played on a public course, Candler Hills Golf Club, part of a massive retirement community called On Top of the World. Business, in the wake of the pandemic, was booming. The two ams I played with in the pro-am were connected to Top of the World housing sales, and they were often on their phones, following mortgage interest rates and addressing other now-or-never matters. The whole tournament was a financial ecosystem unto itself.

The pro in our group, David Erdy, a son of Indiana in his mid-thirties, was a full-time mini-tour player often on the road with his wife, Kristin. It took about three holes to get a sense of his dedication to practice, to diet, to the gym—and to his golfing dreams. By physique and clubhead speed, he looked like a tour player, and he believes if he had a full season of starts on the PGA Tour, he would keep his card. It's impossible to say, of course. But the path is there for him as it is for any golfer.

After the pro-am and a quick lunch, Erdy went to the range, and two hours later he was still there. Hogan Studies 101 ("The secret's in the dirt"). On her Instagram page, Kristin asks, "Where's the dirt they said the secret is in?"

Erdy finished in a tie for eleventh in the pro-am, which paid $5.56. A weird sum to bother with but also, in its precision, a sign of a well-run mini-tour event. The quality of play was high, and everybody at two under or better played the third and final round, which means they were playing for a check. Erdy shot 31 on the back nine in the second round, but with a first-round score of 75, his hole was too deep. He missed the cut by four. In mini-tour golf, there's always a next event, as long as you can cover the entry fee.

In 1953, Ben Hogan won the Masters in April and the U.S. Open in June. Then he faced a dilemma: Commit to the match-play PGA Championship in suburban Detroit, concluding on July 7, or play in the British Open in Scotland, which started with a two-day qualifier that would begin on July 6? He chose Scotland. It was the only Open Championship he ever played. He won it.

As the U.S. Open was the event that meant the most to Hogan, the Ocala Open is the biggest tournament of Kevin Aylwin's annual tour through the dozens of Florida mini-tour events in which he plays. Still, for a decade or more he has harbored a dream, to play in a PGA Tour event. He had entered a bunch of four-spot Monday qualifiers but had never made it through one and into a tour event. The Monday qualifier for the Valspar Championship was on the Monday of the Ocala Open week. If Aylwin somehow got into the Valspar, there was no question what he would do. If you made the cut at the Valspar and finished dead last, you'd make more than sixteen thousand dollars, and that was the least of it. He'd be in the same field as Xander Schauffele, Webb Simpson, Zach Johnson, and all the others. That was the most of it.

He made it through the qualifier for the qualifier, and then he made it through the Monday qualifier itself, shooting 65, the same score Kevin Tway shot. Like that, Aylwin was in his first PGA Tour event. His head was spinning. He needed a caddie, a place to stay, tickets for his wife and parents, a hangtag for player parking, a yardage book. But he was in. He was playing Valspar.

The day after the Monday qualifier, when David Erdy and other golfing road warriors were playing in the Ocala Open pro-am, Kevin Aylwin was playing a practice round on the Copperhead course at the Innisbrook Resort, longtime home of the Valspar Championship. He parked in player parking and said hi to players he knew only from TV. He got a refund on his Ocala Open entry fee, and not because his wife's sister helped run the event.

There were a dozen or more people following Aylwin at the Valspar. Calder Hills to Innisbrook is only a hundred miles, but the trip from the Florida Professional Golf Tour to the PGA Tour is incalculably longer. Aylwin got on the first tee and said to himself, "Holy shit, I am nervous." He shot 75 in the first round and 71 in the second. He missed the cut by four.

I asked Kevin if he found himself thinking about the Ocala Open at all during his time at the Valspar. "Not for a second," he said.

He was driving home to New Smyrna Beach late on Friday when he received a text from Tim West—Robert Garrigus's buddy, the pro-am matchmaker—asking if he wanted to play in the Valspar's Saturday pro-am, at another course at Innisbrook. Kevin made a U-turn.

He hit it off with the guys he played with, and when the round was over, one of the ams got out his billfold and slipped a short, crisp pile of Benjamins to Kevin. One thousand dollars from the gent, on top of fifteen hundred from the Valspar people. Nick Price was there. (He has a

Valspar deal.) Tony Finau was there. (He'd missed the cut.) Some week, and some Saturday. The unexpected payday was great, but that was the least of it. Being in the locker room, eating player food alongside Sam Ryder and Luke Donald, that was the most of it. Sam and Luke talked golf, as golfers do. Kevin was quiet. He was listening. He was hanging on every word.

Tim West got me into the Valspar Saturday pro-am, too, as a last-minute fill-in. The professional in our group was a veteran touring pro from England named Brian Davis. I knew one thing about him: When he could have cheated, he didn't.[*]

In April 2010, Davis was thirty-four and looking to win on the PGA Tour for the first time. At Hilton Head, the week after Phil Mickelson's third win at Augusta, Davis was in a sudden-death playoff with Jim Furyk. While playing his third shot on the first playoff hole, Davis broke a rule while making a swing from the beach beside the eighteenth green. Calibogue Sound and the Hilton Head lighthouse were behind him. Nobody could have seen the infraction, not even his caddie. The rules official for the playoff, Slugger White, was thirty feet away. In golf, the official isn't there to hand out tickets. Golf operates on a different plane, one that is out of step with modern culture. That's what makes it so appealing, at least to some people. Brian Davis, on that Sunday evening at Hilton Head, stood up for the values of the game. Not that he would ever use such an overwrought phrase.

---

[*] Nongolfers often think golf's rule book is fussy. Tom Watson had a long history of demanding that every shot he played, and every shot he saw played, conform to every rule in every way. Without that attitude, tournament golf falls apart. "When playing in formal competitions, playing by the rules is essential in protecting the fairness of the results," Watson says.

By Saturday at the Valspar, Davis was forty-nine and trying to figure out a path to the Champions Tour. He was a past winner of the Spanish Open. He had played in twenty-one majors and contended in events with Phil and Tiger and other golfing legends. He knew Jack Nicklaus and Arnold Palmer. But he had never won on the PGA Tour. When we were deep into our round at Innisbrook, I asked Davis what players had said to him fourteen years earlier, the week after that Hilton Head playoff, with the tour in New Orleans. He summarized what the lodge brothers had told him by way of one communal quote: "You dumbass."

The invention of the Saturday pro-am is credited to Gary Hallberg, who had the idea to find a place for pros who missed the cut to play on Saturday and thereby return home with some kind of check. In the late 1970s, Hallberg had been a star golfer at Wake Forest, thirty years after Arnold, with a putting stroke that made grown men gawk. He went on to have a long PGA Tour career, winning three times, making 288 cuts—and missing 279. He had 279 Saturdays with nothing to do, and 279 weeks when he had spent thousands, and made nothing.

To make the Saturday pro-ams work, you needed four things, three of them relatively easy to find. A course near the tournament course to host the event, amateurs willing to pay to play, and sponsors. Then the fourth piece, the tough one: a supply of pros who didn't really want to be there. Which meant you needed a manager with a unique skill set, somebody who knew how to approach annoyed players on Friday afternoon and cajole them into playing on Saturday morning for a modest payday. Enter Tim West, checkbook in hand.

Ain't much, but what else you got goin' on Saturday morning?

At the Valspar, while Lucas Glover and Justin Thomas and Peter

Malnati (the eventual winner) were playing in a televised event on the Copperhead Course at Innisbrook, a Saturday pro-am was being played a winding mile away, at the resort's Island Course. The PGA Tour's Saturday-morning pro-am, like the Monday qualifier, is a dying tradition, a victim of fewer players playing for more money. But West, looking like he stepped out of the shadows of a Fort Worth rodeo circa 1962, was still at it, wrangling players as needed. Brian Davis wasn't in the Valspar field. Had Tim West not called, Davis would have been teaching that Saturday at his golf academy in Winter Garden, two hours by car from Innisbrook. But West did call, and Davis said yes. He had been saying yes to Tim West for decades. He drove down that morning.

You couldn't have a more entertaining pro-am shepherd. Davis talked about all manner of adventures, with motorcycles, alligators, surgeons, with golfers all over the world, with footballers and snooker players in England, with his wife and their three kids in suburban Orlando.

Not surprisingly, there had been other times he called penalties on himself over a thirty-year pro career, more than he could readily re-member. Not as some sort of ambassador of the USGA and the R&A but because he didn't know any other way to play. He described playing in a tournament (not a PGA Tour event) on a wet course under lift, clean, and place rules. When he lifted, cleaned, and placed, he was care-ful to stay within a club length of his ball's original position, per golf's rules. On the second day, while standing on the first tee, Davis learned that the tournament required, unusually, that the players place the ball within six inches of its original position, the length of their tournament scorecard, not the usual club length.

"Have a good day, fellas," Davis told his playing partners. "I'm off." He DQed himself. He had failed to play by the rules the first day. Nobody would call that cheating. But that first-round scorecard was not close to certified kosher. One of the reasons players turn themselves in is because they're afraid of how they will feel about themselves if they don't.

He has a beautiful swing. Brian Davis making a golf swing brings to mind Gene Sarazen making a swing, or Nick Price, Hal Sutton, Ian Woosnam, Se Ri Pak, and Karrie Webb. It is round, compact, connected. But round, compact, and connected is not what Davis teaches. "Every golfer comes with their own body type, their own athletic ability, their own instincts," he said. "Coming into the ball and leaving the ball, all good golfers look pretty much the same. But there are a lot of ways to get to impact." Davis cited Jim Furyk, whose swing is an odd series of contortions, but at impact, he's the picture of convention.[*]

Davis teaches a lot of talented junior golfers. The parents always want to know the same thing: How talented is my kid? *We talking college level?* And Davis always tells the parents the same thing. It's not just talent. It's talent along with temperament, attitude, and desire. Without the whole package, your kid doesn't have a chance of playing any serious tournament golf, at any level. Davis told our foursome about giving a full refund to a wealthy father who had prepaid for a series of lessons for his son. The son had Division I talent, but he was late for the first lesson and then the second. Davis had seen enough. He couldn't teach the kid to care. The father couldn't make the kid care.

Junior golfers need more tough love, Davis said. He recounted this conversation with one young student: "We were by a green and he had his lob wedge out, and every time he played a shot, he gave himself a perfect lie. I started giving him some nasty lies. He said, 'I've never seen a shot like that.' I said, 'You will.' He said, 'I don't know how to play this shot.' I said, 'Figure it out.'"

---

[*] Jay Haas, the nephew of Bob Goalby, the 1968 Masters winner, has an unconventional backswing. He has also had one of the longest careers in the history of tournament golf. Over the course of half a century as a touring pro, Haas has been the model of convention at impact. "Uncle Bob thought that the address position and the impact position should be fairly similar," Haas says. "For most of the best players, impact looks like address, except at impact the hips have cleared and you're getting your weight to your forward foot. In my opinion, that's the number one key to the golf swing."

Brian Davis turned pro at nineteen. He didn't know what he was doing. He figured it out.

The beach to the left of the eighteenth green at Harbour Town Golf Links in Hilton Head is in play. It's basically a giant sand trap. The rule book changes periodically, and now you can ground your club in the sand. But in 2010, when Davis called that penalty on himself, you could not. You hovered your club above the ball.

And that's what Davis was doing as he prepared to play his third shot in that playoff with Jim Furyk. He was hovering his wedge over his ball. There were marsh grasses and reeds in the vicinity of his ball. As he made his backswing, he could see, out of the corner of his eye, a fluttering reed. He knew he must have made contact with it. He completed his swing, and his ball stopped about thirty feet from the hole.

As soon as his ball came to rest, he waved in Slugger White. If the reed was fixed—growing, alive, attached to something—Davis was fine, per the rule book. But if it was loose, he was not. The logic behind the rule was that golfers should not be able to improve their lie by dislodging loose impediments with an actual swing or with a practice swing. The rule book wants you to play the ball as it lies. Golf preaches, *Own it*. You got yourself there. Now deal with it.

Ticking that reed had no impact on the shot Davis played, but the rule book doesn't allow for such nuance. It seeks to turn every situation into a binary choice: You play by the rules or you don't. The rule book is not a static document, and the rule book is not the enemy. It's the spine of the game, as the Constitution is the central document of American life. The rule book is reviewed constantly and revised occasionally, and players may now move loose impediments in penalty areas. The rule book is becoming kinder and gentler with every new edition. What Davis did then is permitted now. Maybe it's a good change. I could argue either side. Now you can leave the flagstick in while putting—a welcome change, I think. Maybe you don't. Golfers love arguing about the rules. But in 2010 in Hilton Head, Davis did something the rules did not allow. He broke a rule. There were consequences.

He has never pretended to be a rules expert or some kind of golf philosopher. "I played that shot and thought, *What just happened?*" he told me. "I called in Slugger to make sure I did things the right way."

He hadn't. He caught that reed, that loose impediment, on his back-swing. It's not complicated. You can't have one rule for one guy and another for somebody else. The system works when everybody plays by the rules, all the rules, all the time, and not just the ones you think make sense.

Late on Saturday afternoon at the Arnold Palmer Invitational, the week before the Valspar, Wyndham Clark drove his ball into deep rough on the right side of the eighteenth hole. He could see maybe a third of his ball, with the rest of it engulfed by the rough. Clark, then the reigning U.S. Open champion, was in contention. He was playing with Scottie Scheffler.

There was nothing Clark could do from that lie except hack it out and avoid the pond that lines the hole's right side. He took a wedge, with its heavy flange, and shoved it behind the ball four or more times. The rules permit you to place the club "lightly" behind the ball. If this was light, I wouldn't want to see Wyndham Clark coming at me with a dental drill in hand. As he pushed the flange into the grass behind the ball with repeated stabs, the ball sank deeper into the rough. He was making things worse. No wonder he stopped. You could see it on the videotape, which means (I believe) Clark could see it in real time. Professional golfers watch their balls like hawks watching newborns in their nests. But even if he couldn't see it, the jabbing alone was beyond the pale.

When Clark came in from his round, a rules official showed him a video replay. Scheffler was in the room, too. Clark could have said, "Wow, that's *way* too much. Man, I shoved that club in there. For sure, that ball did move. What's the penalty?" But he didn't say anything like that. (In golf, as in life, people see what they want to see.) The rules official could have decided to penalize Clark on his own authority, but didn't. On Golf Channel, Brandel Chamblee said, "You begin to wonder: What does a tour player have to do to get a penalty?"

At a tournament in suburban Chicago eleven years earlier, Tiger Woods was preparing to chip a ball out from under a stand of trees. A stubby and inconvenient twig that looked like a stogie was leaning against his ball. Woods attempted to move the twig, as the rules allow, and his ball moved ever so slightly, movement he had to account for. Woods's eyes were about two feet over his ball, and he was staring right at it. Logic and experience would tell you Woods stopped trying to remove that twig because either the ball moved or he was afraid it might.

After the round, Slugger White, the chief rules official at that Chicago event, showed Woods the video of his attempted twig removal. Woods said the ball didn't move. White, a study in calm during tense moments over a long career, said it had and, by implication, that Woods knew it in real time. When Woods would not assess himself a penalty, White did it for him. A rare circumstance, but no player can be above the rules. Ideally, a golfer of Woods's stature is setting an example for by-the-book play. He didn't that day.

Arnold Palmer took great pride in Bay Hill and its difficulty. He liked lush, nasty rough on his course, the kind of rough that Wyndham Clark found his ball in on eighteen that Saturday afternoon. Brian Davis played often at Bay Hill, and when he refers to Arnold, it's always as *Mr. Palmer*.

Two of his three children were born in the Arnold Palmer Hospital for Children and for years Davis has helped raise money for the hospital at outings. He played often in two tournaments, the Honda and the Memorial, that raise money for causes dear to Nicklaus, including the Nicklaus Children's Hospital, and when Davis refers to Big Jack, it is always as *Mr. Nicklaus*. (Nicklaus and Palmer both found their way to the cause of children's health care through their wives and children.) It's impossible to imagine Nicklaus ever getting himself in a rules situation like the one Wyndham Clark was in at Bay Hill. For one thing, the rule book was sacred to him. Also, the hovering thing.

I asked Davis if Arnold or Jack had ever mentioned anything to him about how he handled that situation at Hilton Head while trying to win on tour for the first time. "No, but they wouldn't," he said. "You're just doing what you're supposed to do."

That round with Brian Davis in the Saturday pro-am at the Valspar was the last moment of my self-made Florida Swing, the Sunshine State portion of *Tour '24: Do the Loco-Motion*.

I realize you're not hearing much about the competitive aspects of these pro-am rounds. There's not much to report. With Davis, we all played off our fivesome's best shot, which, of course, was often his. It's fun. I wouldn't call it competitive golf.

I did have one unlikely moment. On a long par-5, Davis hit a good tee shot. The five of us motored on up to it in our carts. The three other ams played first, and none of their shots was anything to text home about. Davis had his 3-wood in hand. I was the fourth to play and smashed (a smash for me) a driver off the turf. The ball was a hot, sliding line drive that took a big bounce and kept on rolling. It went more than 240 yards and finished a half-wedge from the green. Davis said, "Let's go. No way I can hit three-wood closer than that."

I said, "You can hit driver farther than that."

How often can an am tell a pro something about his own game? Never.

Davis put his 3-wood away, got out his driver, and smashed it. We watched his ball sail past mine and finish within spitting distance of the green.

There were unexpected moments all through the month. One day I played the city-owned course in Largo, near Clearwater, where the Phillies train. It was crowded but pleasant, and I had never seen a course with greens that more resembled perfect flat circles. There were nine of them. I played, by random luck, with a man named Douglas Jacobs, a professor at Southern Adventist University in Chattanooga and an ordained pastor. He had traveled and lived all over the world. Dr. Jacobs and his family owned a vacation home in a mobile home community near the golf course. He told me about a day when he was hitting balls at the Choo Choo Golf Academy in Chattanooga when the serenity of his practice session was shattered by the sickening sound of rapid gunfire. He saw a shooter open fire, twenty-five rounds in all, at a car wash directly across the street from the driving range. People were struck and injured, but nobody was killed.

A day or so after our game, Dr. Jacobs sent me an essay he had written about the incident for *Adventist Review*. For a lede, he borrowed from Psalms: "Even though I walk through the valley of the shadow of death, I will fear no evil, for you are with me." A student who had seen combat duty once told Dr. Jacobs how to respond in an active shooting, and on the Choo Choo range that day, Dr. Jacobs did as his student had instructed him. He laid low on muddy ground in front of a driving-range mat, facing the terror. In the wake of the shooting, a police investigator asked Dr. Jacobs if he had been carrying a gun. No, Dr. Jacobs said. Just a driver.

Earlier in the month, I went to see Tom Doak at Sandglass, the private inland, canal-front golf course he was building on a sandy tract near Hobe Sound. I was with my Golf.com colleague Darren Riehle, just as we'd been together in Las Vegas to see David Feherty. Doak was sitting on a John Deere tractor when we had the following exchange, Darren recording all the while.

"This is really morbid, but do you have any postpartum plans, and do they involve golf courses?"

Doak considered the question, exhaled, chortled, and said, "Technically, it's illegal to just spread your ashes wherever you want to. But I might have a few courses where a superintendent will get a small amount of . . . *that*, 'cause I've left myself in some of these places." Doak's arms were crossed on the tractor's steering wheel. His baseball cap was high on his head. You could see his farmer's tan under the raised sleeves of his golf shirt. You could see how much his career, his life building golf courses, meant to him. "That seems fitting to me." He went quiet and still.

Golf offers so much surprise, and travel does, too. There was Donna, a housekeeper from Jamaica at the Courtyard Marriott in St. Augustine Beach, singing beautiful hymns in a full voice as she worked her way in and out of first-floor rooms in need of fresh towels and vacuumed carpets. Donna liked the blanket I traveled with, pale green and heavy, crocheted by a friend, Stephanie French, wife of Ryan, the Monday Q guy. Christine and I have watched many movies under that blanket, bringing it into the different theaters in our rotation. I like traveling with things from home, starting with my own coffeemaker.

I had already signed up for one of my majors, the spring St. Martins championship, a match-play event. For the first time, there was an entry fee, ten dollars, to cover prizes for the eight players who made it to the quarterfinals. The winner gets something money can't buy: your name in gold paint on dark wood in the locker room.

The clubs went in the boot, and I pointed the Mini north. I stopped for a night at the Fairfield Inn in Roanoke Rapids, North Carolina. You can cover a lot of America in any two-day drive. I don't push myself on these drives, and I often do a little accidental-tourist sightseeing along the way. (Drives down small-town main streets, for instance, on the prowl for ice cream.) When I had left it was winter, and I came home to early spring. Christine's crocuses and forsythia were waving their colors.

Paint, St. Martins men's locker room, Philadelphia Cricket Club.

7

Miami → *Augusta*

"COME ON IN HERE, YOU ASSHOLE," GREG NORMAN SAID. HE BROUGHT me in for a manly hug.

Despite forty-plus years in the United States, Norman remained Aussie to the bone. He was in his late sixties but as trim as a middle-weight boxer ready for fifteen rounds. He was wearing a shirt with ep-aulets, the sleeves rolled up. His eyes were blue, electric, intense, as they have always been. You don't have to look for Norman's charisma—it hits you when you enter his orbit. He was standing at the guarded en-trance to a tent where a pro-am party was under way.

This was at Trump Doral in Miami, where LIV Golf was conduct-ing an event the week before the Masters. Donald Trump and the PGA Tour had parted ways, and now Trump was in deep with LIV Golf, and with Greg Norman, LIV Golf's chief executive officer, a big title but the least of Norman's roles. He was LIV Golf's founder, public face, and ambassador to the world. He helped convince various elite players to leave a freighter for a luxury yacht.

I had been invited (got myself invited) to play in the LIV Miami pro-am. Norman and I, as newsmaker and reporter, had been talking about LIV Golf since before it had a name (and on other subjects long before that). If he cared at all, and I doubt he did, he would have known that I had barely concealed disdain for this new league. Among a dozen other things, the launching of LIV Golf revealed a show-me-the-money greediness. Greediness, grubbiness, guaranteed money. Prior to LIV, the dreamers among us didn't know such greed existed, and I'm counting Scottie Scheffler in the dreamers' club. "They didn't have to say yes," he said. Flawless logic. Phil Mickelson, Dustin Johnson, Brooks Koepka, Bryson DeChambeau, eventually Jon Rahm—they didn't have to say yes. But they did. They left their golfing homes and proved that golfers are *not* our high priests, that they can be bought, that they were happy to populate a league created out of whole cloth. They turned their backs on the institutions that made them, and the people behind those institutions, for paltry sums like $200 million or $400 million or whatever.

That Wednesday night at Doral, the wet-wool game of our shepherd forebears was lost in time and space. Norman was welcoming guests to the party, and the band played on, its brass section practically moaning. Under the tent's roof there were serving tables piled high with colorful fresh food and bars with all manner of wine and drink. The whole space was awash with a distinctive Latin American brio, young people, many of them speaking Spanish, enjoying a warm spring night, their wealth, their jewelry, their immense sense of style. Norman and his Saudi backers weren't just selling golf. They were selling reinvention.

I was sure I'd know nobody there, but I was wrong. About the first person I saw was Slugger White, one of my go-to guys, in fresh Tommy Bahama-wear. If I had a rules question, for years, I went to Slugger. You don't have to be a lawyer to be good on the rules, or a good rules official. You do have to be logical, precise, and willing to speak truth to power, without being obnoxious about it. Enter Slugger.

When Norman first came to the United States in the early 1980s, Slugger was playing the tour. Later, as a rules official, he made a thousand rulings with a walkie-talkie in his left hand and a Panama hat on his head. After forty years, in a period when veteran staffers were leaving the tour, Slugger retired and LIV Golf swooped in, making him an offer he couldn't refuse. In the name of credibility, Slugger was a smart early hire.

He and Norman were buds. They had a history. In 1995, on the seventh hole of the first round of the World Series of Golf, Norman accused a playing partner, Mark McCumber, of cheating, saying that he had removed a tiny tuft of rooted grass on the line of the eight-foot par putt he was about to attempt. McCumber said the object was a bug, a small brown insect with a hard shell. In the absence of proof either way, McCumber's word was accepted. When Norman refused to sign and thereby attest to McCumber's scorecard, a rules official did it for him. When Norman, who had a tendency to run hot, threatened to withdraw from the tournament, Slugger talked him out of it. Three days later, Norman won the tournament and $360,000.

"Slugger!" I said, glad to see his good-ole-boy self among all these shiny young people with their colorful cocktails. Slugger, not for the first time in his life, was nursing a cold one. He had grown up in West Virginia and came of age in New Smyrna Beach, Florida, where he and his gang had daylong triathlons that revolved around bowling, golf, and shooting pool, hydration supplied by Miller Lite. He logged a lot of rounds with Kevin Aylwin's father.

"Michael!" Slugger said. "How's our boy?" That is, Mike Donald. He's known Mike forever.

"Just talked to him," I said. My clubs had not made it to Florida with me, and I had called Mike from the airport, looking to borrow a set for the pro-am.

"Say hey to him for me," Slugger said.

The old tour, the one Slugger came up on, was more Southern than anything else, *say hey* and *our boy* and all the rest. It was Charley Pride in a Dallas pro-am, fans in Lynyrd Skynyrd T-shirts at the Atlanta Golf Classic, guys calling Andy Bean *Mongo*, the cowboy (played by Alex Karras) in *Blazing Saddles* who punches a horse in the neck. Everybody was called something. Mike Donald was Statman, Fuzzy was Fuzzy, the caddie Sam Foy was Killer. Slugger was Slugger. Norman was Shark. Norman would go out in 31, and somebody would say, "Shark on a *heater*." It was primitive and great and not complicated. All that energy and commentary coming out of shots played and numbers on score-cards. Golfers played the shots, and golfers put numbers on cards for all to see.

Greg Norman was everywhere at Doral. At the entrance to the party tent. In the hotel lobby. At a restaurant in the clubhouse, eating dinner with a handful of people half his age. He wasn't glad-handing. He was being Greg Norman, winner of eighty-eight professional events across the world, for people who had never seen him play a single shot in a tournament and never would.

LIV Golf was up and running, with stops in Australia, Saudi Arabia, the United States, and some other places. It was in its third year, and there were growing pains. It was struggling to attract a meaningful broadcasting audience and large crowds of fans or get sustained coverage on the major golf websites. But it did exist. Thirty years after Norman first announced his world golf tour, he finally had one.

Playing in the pro-am qualified me for a couple meals in player-caddie-family dining, in one of the Doral ballrooms. I made a trip to the omelet station and listened as a young man at my table, a LIV caddie, talked about new plantings for his backyard landscaping project. I went to a Saturday-night tournament concert where a rapper named Akon performed. "LIV, how you feelin'?" he asked the crowd, his band's bass so loud it felt like your cell phone was buzzing through your heart. The crowd was young, not golfy. No club belts, no FootJoy socklets.

I sat in on press conferences in another ballroom and interviewed the golfer Anthony Kim, attempting a long-shot comeback, by the scorer's room. The tournament was expertly run. It was never close to crowded, but neither was it a ghost town. For the people there, LIV Miami at Trump Doral was an opportunity to hang, drink, eat, buy, see, be seen, take selfies, get some sun, watch golf on clubhouse screens, and maybe even watch live golf, as long as it was near the clubhouse and you had your sunglasses. People were having a good time. A lot of the fans seemed new to golf—nothing wrong with that. Golf always needs a next generation. The Doral crowd would not know that blaring music on the first tee is not something you would ever hear up the road at the Cognizant Classic at PGA National, to say nothing of the Masters at Augusta National. They wouldn't know, and they wouldn't care.

There were many fans at Doral in their twenties, meaning they were not yet born in late 1994, when Norman announced he was launching something he called the World Golf Tour. Tim Finchem, then the tour's commissioner, used his considerable political skill to squash it. When Arnold Palmer, a god to the players, spoke up against it, the burial was complete. Mark McCumber, a tour loyalist, said then, "Who does Greg think he is, God?" McCumber's rules incident with Norman came nine months later.

But nobody shared the death certificate with Norman. He knew what others did not: His dream had not died.

During the pandemic, I talked regularly with Norman about a new version of his old idea. This was before anybody knew the phrase *LIV Golf* or (in a golf context) the name Yasir. To me, the timing seemed beyond off, as an airborne disease was killing innumerable people. "The backers I have will wait it out," Norman said. It was a striking comment, because patience was never Greg Norman's strong suit. Of course, the best investors see opportunity in inopportune times.

That conversation took place when Norman was in an office in West Palm Beach and I was on a cell phone, standing outside my neighborhood coffee shop. You placed your order online, and your coffee came through a sliding window in a gloved hand. Most people were trying to figure out ways to get through the pandemic. Norman and his people were planning for a world after it.

In another phone interview, I asked Norman which player he would most want to sign. He couldn't say. I suggested a quick game of Twenty Questions, and when I got to Hideki Matsuyama of Japan, we stopped. Norman's unnamed golf tour had no announced timeline. It had no signed players. It had no announced backers or even a name. But it had global ambitions. Hideki, for instance. And this was before he won the 2021 Masters. The final frame of that event was so lovely—his caddie, on eighteen in the Sunday twilight, bowing to the course. The world took notice of the gesture.

A half-year later, a group of reporters was invited for a daylong meeting at a chic hotel in New York City where Norman laid out his plan, except for the names of his players. Norman and others told us about the backers, the league's name, the span-the-universe schedule and global roster, the funny-money (my phrase) payouts, the simultaneous individual and team competitions. That meant a player would be rooting for a player he was also trying to beat. That was new. All of it was, really. Part of Norman's bet was that professional golf needed something different, that moved more quickly. It did not need more seventy-two-hole stroke-play individual events. Slugger was there, silent but very much present. "This can be additive," Norman said. More golf for fans to enjoy. The PGA Tour surely did not share that view. Tour executives and board members had no interest in talking to Norman or his minions. Why would they? The tour was happy with the status quo. Its leaders didn't want Norman as a partner. They wanted him to go away. But they underestimated the irresistible lure of money. Nobody made any sort of declaration, but golf's unseemly turf war had already begun. Everybody was digging in. Damage, collateral and otherwise, would soon be coming.

LIV Golf is pronounced to rhyme with *give*. The name represents, as a Roman numeral, the number of holes in a LIV event (fifty-four) and the score you'd shoot if you made eighteen straight birdies on a par-72 course (54). Its financiers were Yasir Al-Rumayyan and a small group of his Saudi countrymen who controlled the vast sums broadly invested by the Public Investment Fund of Saudi Arabia. To the PIF, $100 million here and $100 million there, in the name of R&D, was like the loose change you leave in the plastic tub at McDonald's for a Ronald McDonald House. Tournament golf didn't even exist as a business, not in a conventional let's-make-money sense, but the Saudis were prepared to spend billions to try to turn it into one. It made your eyes glaze. It made you wonder what they were trying to do.

Fortunately, none of this had any impact on the joy and challenge of playing a pitch shot from a thin lie over a yawning trap to a downhill pin. Real golf, our golf. We own it, and it's not for sale.

Norman was mesmerizing in the hotel meeting room that day, and later that night at an elaborate dinner. (I didn't go but friends did.) Even with all he had accomplished, the league he envisioned seemed to be his life. He described how he and his partners were enthralled by the excitement of Ryder Cup golf, by *team* golf. Of course, what makes the Ryder Cup the Ryder Cup, the U.S. versus Europe, is that the pros are playing for national pride. Professional golf is a niche sport. Arnold and Tiger were outliers. There had been Seve Ballesteros in Europe, Jumbo Ozaki in Japan, and Nancy Lopez in women's golf—and that's about it. People overstate its popularity. About the only way to make big money in golf is to sell golf balls, because golfers lose them frequently and like to start rounds with shiny new ones. Or to be a true innovator, like Karsten Solheim.

But professional golf *is* an efficient way to get near big money and close to the people who control it. The various pro tours are a portal to hundreds of corporate boards in the United States and around the world. You could see why Saudi oligarchs would want that in an on-going effort to diversify their incalculable oil wealth. LIV Golf could help them appear more Western and more modern, alongside Saudi women getting the right to drive. It fit with their investments in professional tennis (for men and women), Formula 1 car racing, Premier League football. But those leagues were looking for new investors with new money. The PGA Tour reveled in its autonomy and its king-of-the-tours status.

I'm speculating here. I wish I could offer you more, but I don't know what the Saudi investors want out of professional golf. Are they making a long-term bet on Donald Trump in the name of selling oil and building golf courses? Seems half-crazy but also possible. I don't know that Greg Norman could ever have known the Saudis' true goal. My efforts to get an interview with Yasir Al-Rumayyan have fallen into a cyber hole. If golf-obsessed Saudi billionaires are trying to get into Augusta National and Seminole, taking on the PGA Tour and the golf establishment is an odd way to go about it. I do think that reinvention is at the core of the whole enterprise. Sell reinvention while reinventing yourself. Ralph Lifshitz of the Bronx becoming Ralph Lauren, Colorado rancher and East Coast man-about-town, billionaire and philanthropist with his name sewn into the blue blazer every American player wore when the Ryder Cup went to Paris. Something like that.

It took me a while to figure out what bothered me most about LIV Golf: The underlying premise for it was subjective. Greg Norman and peeps were swiping left and swiping right. *We want you, we don't want you. We want you but not at your price.* It was leading with commerce, marketing, fan engagement. It had everything backward. As our hunting forebears once lived off their kills, professional golfers lived off their scores. Our interest in them followed from that. The players announced themselves with their scores, their shots, their swings, their interviews in victory and defeat, and then we swiped. Nobody did it for us.

The three-round events with tiny fields and no cut, the shotgun starts and shotgun finishes, didn't help matters, not for those of us who were raised in the orthodox tradition. Neither did the manufactured enthusiasm for the teams, the Crushers, the Iron Heads, the Fireballs, and the others. For this reporter, and surely for other people, official Saudi intolerance for gay unions, along with restrictions to free speech, assembly, and religious choice, is far more troubling. But even if you could somehow leave all that aside, LIV did not have *May the best man win* in its DNA. To get a LIV guaranteed contract, you had to win some kind of beauty contest first.

With rare exception. I played in the Doral pro-am with Andy Ogletree, one of the few golfers who played his way onto the LIV roster by way of scorecard, although even his path has an odd asterisk.

Ogletree won the 2019 U.S. Amateur despite being four down after five holes in the thirty-six-hole match-play final. That victory got him into the 2020 Masters, which was delayed by seven months because of the pandemic. But he waited it out and stayed amateur so he would not have to forfeit his place in the tournament. By Masters custom, the reigning U.S. Amateur is paired with the defending Masters champion, so Ogletree played those first two rounds with Tiger Woods—a big part of his incentive to stay amateur through that Masters.

It all worked out. On Sunday night, when Dustin Johnson went to Butler Cabin to slip on his new winner's green jacket for the CBS audience, Ogletree sat beside him, as the tournament's low amateur. That's a serious way to turn pro, with a win in the Amateur and a low-am finish at Augusta on your agent's pitch deck. Jack Nicklaus, Phil Mickelson, Tiger Woods, and Bryson DeChambeau had those two titles on their CVs, too.

And then Ogletree woke up. He turned pro, didn't play well, had hip surgery, recovered slowly, played indifferently, couldn't find a golfing home on any major or even minor tour. Jake Knapp before he won in Mexico, and a thousand others on the bumpy road to status, could have sung the same song. I heard a lot about Ogletree's travails because his renegade agent, Mac Barnhardt, is a buddy of mine. Then Ogletree played in a LIV event. It didn't go well.

The inaugural LIV Golf event was played in London in June 2022. Norman and Co. struggled to fill the field. Ogletree, desperate to play anywhere and aided and abetted by Mac, got a spot. He finished last, which paid $120,000. The PGA Tour, and by extension the Korn Ferry Tour, suspended him for the rest of the year for conspiring with the enemy, though you won't see that phrase in any tour statement. The LIV folks did not invite him to play in any other tournaments. In London, he finished 31 shots behind the winner. He was in a tough spot.

Mac was, too. He once had a thriving agency based in Sea Island, Georgia. He had a dozen or more players with Southern ties including Davis Love III, Lucas Glover, Brandt Snedeker, Brian Harman, and Hudson Swafford, among others who had won on different tours. He sold his agency and got pushed to the sidelines for a two-year period by a noncompete clause. He was planning to stage a comeback, putting to good use everything he had learned over thirty years in professional golf.

In his second stint as an agent, Mac was determined to be honest with his clients and his prospective clients. That was a problem, because the things he'd say would make young promising pros run for the hills: *No, I can't promise you any starts on any tour. No, I don't think you should change your irons, your swing instructor, your girlfriend. No, you should not buy that house. Have you thought about buying a used truck? Oh, you're going to need to get better at golf, and you're gonna need a plan to do it.*

Mac was trying to stage a second-act comeback as an agent by making a big bet on one player, Andy Ogletree. If you know the movie *Jerry Maguire*, you'll get this: Mac was in the Tom Cruise agent role, and Ogletree was his Cuba Gooding wide receiver.

Mac enjoyed giving me the play-by-play on a regular basis. I knew about Ogletree's boyhood in Union, Mississippi, where his family owned a Piggly Wiggly grocery store. I knew about his transition from golfer with glasses, struggling to play in rain and heat, to (post–Lasik surgery) golfer without glasses. About his fights with his own swing, his efforts to get more golf-fit. Also, his sessions with the trainer Kolby Tullier, who works with Tiger Woods, and the swing coach Tony Ruggiero, who teaches Lucas Glover. Mac believed the modern professional golfer needed to be surrounded by a team. A person to help the player with travel, another to be with the player during practice sessions. Mac had trainers on call for physical fitness, along with therapists for mental fitness and advisers for club fitting. He viewed the modern golfer as the CEO of a small company, surrounded by a support team.

After Ogletree's poor LIV performance at the first LIV event, and largely as a thank-you, the LIV folks gave him a spot on the Asian Tour for the rest of the year. (LIV Golf had made a major investment in the Asian Tour.) Unrelated to that, and in a nod toward golf's meritocratic tradition, LIV was giving the leading money-winner on the Asian Tour's International Series a one-year deal to play LIV Golf, longer if the player could make a deal with one of the LIV teams.

Ogletree played well enough over the rest of 2022 to qualify for the Asian Tour in 2023. That year he won the tour's "order of merit" (a quaint and telling phrase for money list), which earned him a one-year invitation to play LIV in 2024. Mac shopped him around to different teams and signed Ogletree to a three-year deal with Phil Mickelson's four-player LIV team, the HyFlyers. That deal was worth millions, guaranteed. None of this would have happened had Ogletree not played in the first LIV event. Yes, this is all strange and new and convoluted. No, it was never like this before.

Still, Andy Ogletree was chasing it. No doubt about that. In a professional career that was just getting started, he had won events in

Egypt, Qatar, and England. He had cashed checks playing in China, Oman, Scotland, and Singapore.

I once asked Mac what he saw in Ogletree that convinced him to make such a big bet on him. "When he was four down after five in that that U.S. Am, if you looked at him, you would have thought he was leading," Mac said. "You could see how much he believed in himself. A lot of guys have the talent to make it. There are literally thousands of 'em. But to actually make it, you need two things: heart and balls."

Mac had enough sway with the LIV people that he could get me into the pro-am at the LIV Miami event. He caddied for me there. Mac is a good golfer and if he could reinvent himself, he'd want to be a teacher. He had one telling observation about my golf: "You got a draw stance and a fade swing." Yikes.

Andy Ogletree was with our group for nine holes, per LIV Golf pro-am custom. At the turn, we were supposed to pick up the Australian golfer Cameron Smith, winner of the 2022 Open at St. Andrews, but he called in sick. Before disappointment set in, Smith's replacement showed up on the tenth tee, a LIV Golf reserve player named Ben Campbell, from New Zealand. Campbell had one of the oddest jobs in professional golf, understudy touring pro, showing up at LIV events with the promise of a chance to play only if a roster player pulled out on short notice. His status made me think about the first Walker Cup, played at the National Golf Links on Long Island in 1922, when the British golf writer Bernard Darwin was a twelfth-hour fill-in for an ill British team member. I didn't mention that to Campbell, the winner of the 2023 Hong Kong Open, but I'm sure he would have found it interesting. He was a delightful playing partner, interested in golf history, course architecture, the Blue Monster course, our play, wondering all the while if he'd get a Friday tee time, when the tournament began for real, with a guaranteed payday for everybody in its field.

My most painful experience at the LIV Miami event was interviewing Anthony Kim, pushing forty and playing in his first professional golf event in the United States in almost twelve years. When he was in his twenties, he was a radical talent who choked up close to an inch on the club. Distance came naturally to him. He choked up for control. Tiger Woods was probably more interested in Kim's mechanics than Kim was. Anthony Kim was the opposite of a golf nerd, carrying himself with so much *whatup* nonchalance that he didn't seem like a PGA Tour player at all. In his play, you could see shades of Tiger. In his casual, brash manner, there was some John Daly. In body type—small, slight, strong in a sinewy way—he brought to mind Rickie Fowler. People were drawn to him. One night years ago, at a cavernous indoor beer garden in greater Palm Springs, Kim deposited two young women at my table and kept on going, chasing something and likely burying something, too.

The ensuing years brought injury, addiction, marriage, fatherhood, mystery. He had been missing in action for a long time—that twelve-year span could have been the prime of his career. At Doral, I interviewed him early on a Friday night, after he had signed for a first-round 76. That's about where his golf was. Whether he could become a 67 shooter again was unlikely, but the chance was there. That's golf, at every level: there's a chance.

The shape of his swing had not changed, but his speed was slower and his contact less precise. Playing tournament golf is not like riding a bike. As I talked to him, Kim was holding his daughter, a toddler, and not saying much. All his brashness was gone. You could see his hard living, and hard life, in his body and on his face.

The most delightful experience I had at the LIV Miami event was meeting a young married couple, Carla and Rafa Flores. Rafa, who worked in a family construction business, was one of my playing partners in the pro-am, along with Josh Moser, a young sports anchor for a Miami TV station. Jane MacNeille, a LIV Golf communications executive, had met Carla and Rafa years earlier on a college graduation trip to Honduras, where Rafa grew up. Carla and Rafa lived in Miami, where they were raising their three children—"Four is showing off," Carla said casually—and the parents went from English to Spanish and back to English effortlessly. Rafa's golf was my golf, some duffs, enough good shots. He did *not* take himself or his golf too seriously. We talked about baseball, golf, family, Miami, Honduras, and the nonstop flights there and back from Miami. What other sport can give two strangers an opportunity to cover all that ground in such an intimate way?

I saw Carla with Jane on Friday night at Doral, shortly after I interviewed Anthony Kim. When his name came up in our conversation, Carla said, "*Arropado. Arropado!*" A Spanish word to describe what she felt Anthony needed: to be wrapped in blankets, in warmth.

I don't know how they got it, and I don't know how to define it, but we all know it when we feel it—Rafa and Carla had the warm gene themselves. This happens a lot in golf: You're with people for a day, you may never see them again, but you feel better just for having met them.

Cameron Smith played the Friday round at Doral. Ben Campbell did not. Smith shot 75 and withdrew from the event, and Campbell took his place, which meant for two rounds he was a Ripper, the name of the team Smith captained. The Rippers finished tenth out of the thirteen teams in the field. The HyFlyers—Phil Mickelson, Brendan Steele,

Cameron Tringale, Andy Ogletree—finished last in the team competition. Ogletree had a rough three rounds, shooting 79, 73, and 74. He finished in fiftieth place and made $60,000. Anthony Kim finished last, shooting 76, 81, and 80. It hurts to type those numbers. He made $50,000, but his LIV deal dwarfed that. For a while there, negotiating the terms of his attempted comeback, Kim had leverage. He was a complete unknown: Could he become a world-class golfer again? Greg Norman and his people were betting that an Anthony Kim comeback story as a LIV player, twelve years after walking away from the PGA Tour, would be good for Anthony Kim and good for LIV Golf.

Ben Campbell, in his two weekend rounds, shot 71 and 73. He got last-place money, too—$50,000. More like an appearance fee. Dean Burmester of South Africa won the event and $4 million. Legion XIII, captained by Jon Rahm, won the team competition, worth $3 million to the team. If you know a term more appropriate than *funny money*, please let me know.

Over nearly thirty years, I can recall Mark Steinberg, Tiger's agent, asking me one question: "Have you ever been to a LIV event?" I hadn't. (None of Steinberg's players, tellingly, were LIV golfers.) The LIV Miami event was the first I had ever attended. In ways, it felt like an ordinary tour event. On Sunday, for the third and final day, I followed Sergio Garcia. If you focused solely on Garcia making swings, it seemed like another golf tournament featuring mega-talents. I knew he was in contention for the title. And yet I found myself not caring, and I *never* don't care. In the end, Garcia and Burmester were in a playoff. A playoff for what? A payday. The runner-up would get $2.25 million. It gets boring. Boring and numbing.

When Tiger or Phil or Ernie won at Doral, it made you think about Greg Norman or Raymond Floyd winning there. I can remember unlikely wins at Doral by Craig Parry and Rocco Mediate—all part of the fun. The fields had 144 players, the tournaments were four rounds, and there was a thirty-six-hole cut. You could play your way into the Masters, with a win at Doral. More significantly, victory got you a two-year tour exemption. You were doing whatever you could to avoid getting a real job.

And there was Greg Norman, on Sunday night of the LIV Miami event at Trump Doral, at the awards ceremony, held on the Blue Monster's eighteenth green. He had been on that green many times as a player. Now, in his role as the public face of an upstart golf league, he was congratulating Burmester on his win. It was a beautiful April night. Burmester was not in the Masters, in part became his LIV play did not earn him Official World Golf Ranking points. Norman would be going to Augusta as a paying spectator and not as an official guest of the club. That told you something about the state of the game, at least at its elite professional level. By custom, past winners of golf's major championships, professional and amateur, had always been welcome to come to the Masters and, for many years, to play in the Wednesday par-3 tournament. Norman won the British Open twice. On eight occasions, he had finished fifth or better at Augusta. For years afterward, he was on the invitation list. I don't recall ever seeing Greg Norman at Augusta after he stopped playing in the tournament, but I've seen Al Geiberger, winner of the 1966 PGA Championship, and Lou Graham, winner of the 1975 U.S. Open, and Nathaniel Crosby, Bing's son, winner of the 1981 U.S. Amateur. The Masters did a lot to hand down the game from one generation to the next. Everything was broadly off now in the pro game. All this new money floating around golf was good for a few players and their agents and caddies, and that was about it.

There were thirteen LIV golfers going from Miami to Augusta for the Masters—and nearly as many private jets.

One afternoon during the Doral event, I went to the grass range at a public course called Miami Springs. There was a guy hitting balls near me with an exaggerated late-career Trevino move. This player took the club way outside going back, dropped his hands at least six inches at the top, lowered the clubhead below his right shoulder, then made a powerful pass at the ball from the inside. He hit one draw shot after another.

One of the regulars walked by him and said, "How you hittin' it, Noonan?"

"Better every day," he said.

Right next to me a man named Luis was hitting balls. We started talking about the swing, and the conversation quickly became technical. Luis had taken several lessons from Jimmy Ballard, a golf instructor who played an instrumental role in the professional careers of Curtis Strange, Hal Sutton, and Rocco Mediate. Ballard had made an intensive study of Ben Hogan and his "half a left arm." It was a phrase Hogan used, as a right-handed golfer, to keep the left arm, from the top of the shoulder to the elbow, connected to the body throughout the swing. Ballard devoted his teaching life to this principle. All Ballard players—Curtis, Rocco, Sutton, Luis—make that move. They're zealots about it.

I asked Luis if I could videotape his swing. Of course, he said. He was looking to spread the gospel of half a left arm. The line here is so clear: from Sam Byrd (Babe Ruth Yankee teammate turned professional golfer) to Hogan, Hogan to Ballard, Ballard to Luis, Luis to me, and now me to you. Sam Byrd, a right-handed hitter, used to take batting practice with a towel between his left arm and rib cage. Hogan ran with that.[*]

I have never been able to make that connection thing work for me,

---

[*] "Through college and into my first win on tour, I had a long upright swing—I could have never kept that towel there," Curtis Strange says. "Then I wanted to start hitting it shorter and straighter and play out of the fairway. I began focusing on pushing my left armpit into my rib cage." Strange won two U.S. Opens with that swing.

not before I met Luis, not with Luis, not after I left Luis that day. I've tried. I'll try anything. Maybe you're the same. Maybe that half a left arm will be a breakthrough for you.

On Saturday night at Doral, after sunset, two players, and only two, were on the putting green. Brooks Koepka and Bryson DeChambeau. You could hear the Akon concert in the distance. Before they went to the putting green, they were on the range, the only golfers on it. They weren't talking to each other or ignoring each other. Each was doing his thing.

When he was done, and before he slipped back into the Doral hotel, I asked DeChambeau if he found himself thinking about Augusta and the Masters during that Saturday-night practice session.

"The whole time," he said.

Don't get the wrong idea here, because I do love going to the Masters each April, but there is something weird about both the club and its rite-of-spring tournament. Augusta National has an almost comical level of reverence for its own history, its own nomenclature, its own authoritarian rule. Bobby Jones, the cofounder of the club with Clifford Roberts, was named "president in perpetuity" in 1966, a half-decade before he died.* Fans are *patrons*, tickets are *badges*, and prize money is

---

* "Privately, Bub was *not* happy about it," says Jones's namesake grandson, Dr. Bobby Jones IV, a psychologist in Atlanta. "My grandfather wanted my father to succeed him as president. Bub and my father believed that Cliff came up with that 'president in perpetuity' title to keep my father out as president. Bub would never use *perpetuity* like that. He wanted the golf course to be his monument."

not discussed. Only the club chairman speaks for the club, and he gives one press conference per year, on the eve of the tournament. The State of the Masters.

But when you consider the entire week in toto, it's astounding how well everything comes together, and when you consider the years and decades as a collected work, it's more amazing yet. There are Sunday afternoons at Augusta, when the shadows are long and the leaderboard is tight, when your skin will tingle for hours. Now and again, there's a dull finish—or Patrick Reed wins—but over the sweep of time, the Masters packs some wallop. When I was a kid and Dave Anderson had a Masters write-up with an Augusta dateline in *The New York Times* I could smell spring in the newsprint. Nothing has changed for me, and for a long while now, I have typed the dateline myself. Luck. Luck, luck, luck, luck, luck.

Some years my Sunday-night assignment has been to write (in our crude deadline shorthand) "the loser." Losing anywhere, in any endeavor, is poignant, but especially at Augusta because winning is *so* celebrated. Winning gets you in the club forever. The sting of second can also last forever. Ken Venturi, Roberto De Vincenzo, Tom Weiskopf, Johnny Miller, Greg Norman, Curtis Strange, Ernie Els, and Davis Love III are all Hall of Famers who know the sour taste of *almost* at Augusta does not go away.

It's stunning how much it all means, the winning and the losing, not just to the few dozen men who know what it's like in the mix and inside the ropes, but to the millions of us watching. Bob Jones and Cliff Roberts and the stewards after them, take a bow. None of this happens by accident.

Tom Weiskopf finished second four times, and you could hear his unrequited love for the course in his CBS commentary and see it in at least some of his design work. Johnny Miller had three second-place finishes and has joked for years that the club could at least give him a green vest. Greg Norman's three seconds at Augusta defined his playing career and dented his heart. In 1986, he finished a shot behind Nicklaus with a closing bogey off a shoved iron when a par would have meant a playoff. (It was later that year that Nicklaus advised Norman to be careful with his grip pressure.) Norman had his second second the next year, when Larry Mize, an Augusta native, chipped in from 140 feet on the second hole of a sudden-death playoff. Then a third and final second in 1996, when Norman had a six-shot lead over Nick Faldo through three rounds, and Faldo won the tournament by five. Norman's grace through that remains a model of sporting decorum, and the Norman-Faldo embrace on eighteen, a bear hug between two men who did not like each other, is one of the game's most powerful and lasting images.*

If Norman had won at Augusta even once, maybe his compulsion to create a world golf tour would have fizzled out. It's easy to imagine: Norman in his sixties, mellow and content, enjoying his place in the Augusta lineage, the one that goes from Bob Jones to Hogan-Nelson-Snead to Arnold to Nicklaus to Watson, and on from there, with Greg Norman in the lineup. Here's Greg Norman, in the second-floor locker room for players with green coats. He'd be different.

The week after the LIV event in Miami, Norman was all over Augusta National, wearing his trademark straw hat with the colorful shark emblem on it, a golf shirt embroidered with a LIV logo, and his purchased grounds-only spectator's badge hanging on a lanyard around his neck. He said hello to players, LIV and otherwise, and to fans young and old. He talked to reporters and ate his first Masters sandwich from a concession stand. He was having a good time.

Bryson DeChambeau, one of his LIV golfers, was the leader after a first-round 65 and the coleader after a 73 in the second round's windstorm. But Scottie Scheffler was the leader after the third round, and by Sunday, with no other LIV player in contention, Norman was gone.

---

* "Faldo was an aloof, self-centered enigma, which made him the player he was," Greg Norman says. "So I cannot explain the hug. Let's just say it was a by-product of the values golf carries, not the players."

George Plimpton came to the Masters one year, on a passport issued by *Golf Digest*. He stayed in the finished basement of a large rental house, and he had a roommate, Guy Yocom, a *Golf Digest* writer who, over decades at the magazine, conducted a series of long, entertaining, and revealing interviews with all manner of legends, including Jack Nicklaus and Greg Norman, but also cult figures like Tom Meeks, a rules expert, and Moe Norman, a ball-striking savant whose single-plane swing was a forerunner to DeChambeau's single-plane swing. (Looks mechanical, works great!) Plimpton became fascinated with Yocom's obsessive interest in tornadoes and tornado photography, including the famous 1965 Paul Huffman photo from the Palm Sunday tornadoes near Goshen, Indiana, with its two funnels. Plimpton suggested to Yocom that they meet with Robert Gottlieb, a celebrated editor in New York, about collaborating on a tornado book.

Plimpton's assignment was to write about his experience at Augusta. As part of it, an editor suggested that Plimpton try to apply for membership at the club. Yocom's job was to take Plimpton around and make introductions as needed. They talked late into the night each night, Plimpton absently scratching his stomach through his pajama top as he asked a long series of questions, egging on Yocom with phrases like "My, my—oh my." The basement was dank, but Plimpton, experienced in the ways of the New England boarding school, registered no complaints. Dan Jenkins, a contemporary and a professional Texan, was staying upstairs. The two would meet in the kitchen around a communal ham. They were both titans of sportswriting, with deep ties to *Sports Illustrated*. They got along, but didn't click.

Yocom supplied Plimpton with a greatest-hits stream of Augusta legend and lore. The azaleas on ice, to keep them from blooming too early. The blue dye in the ponds, for aesthetics. The discovery of a lifeless Cliff Roberts by the club's par-3 course, his death ruled a suicide by gunshot to the head, and how the death weapon ended up in a Japanese auction house. Plimpton's curiosity was insatiable, and he talked about arcane things, too, like the piercing sound JFK made when he clapped. Plimpton stayed up late and was out of the house early.

One evening, Plimpton slipped out of the basement in the middle of the night with a 5-iron he borrowed from Dave Anderson and a plan to play Augusta National under the moonlight. No shots were played, and Yocom believes something happened that Plimpton did not want to discuss. On another night, Yocom took Plimpton and others to the chain sports bar Hooters, the one near the club, on Washington Road. By tradition, the Augusta Hooters brings in fresh talent for the Masters, attractive young women known as Hooters Recruiters. Their job is to keep the patrons, largely male and sometimes facing lengthy waits for cold pitchers, happy. These perky women took a liking to George, then in his early seventies. "You're so cute," a Hooter said to him as she planted a kiss on his cheek. George turned beet red.

In his piece, which was published the following April, Plimpton made a lone reference to Hooters. The Augusta National chairman was a somber man named Hootie Johnson, and Plimpton describes how he and Jenkins went to see him: "As we were about to enter the chairman's office Dan urged me to start off by asking Mr. Johnson, 'Now let's get it straight—is it Hootie or Hooters?' I resisted."

In an effort to fulfill the requirements of his assignment, Plimpton asked a green-coated member sitting in a golf cart, "How do you get into this nice club?"

The response, as Plimpton described it: "For an instant he looked into what I believe is called the middle distance. And then he said, 'There are some application blanks up there at the clubhouse,' and he drove off."

After that Masters, Plimpton and Yocom discussed by email the possible tornado book but never saw Gottlieb about it. Plimpton's Augusta story, in mock Q&A format, is wry and subversive. This is how it begins: "Late last winter, the editors of *Golf Digest* asked me if I would like to attend the Masters—a tournament I had never thought I'd see, because it is so difficult to get a ticket." *Ticket.* A one-word protest—the tournament prefers *badge.*

Plimpton died two and a half years after the piece ran, at age seventy-six. Heart attack. The phrase *participatory journalism* "pursued him into his obituaries," the writer Nathaniel Rich noted with regret in an appreciation in *The New York Review of Books.* The phrase made Plimpton uncomfortable. It's such a mouthful.

I have had huge amounts of fun over the years playing in and around Augusta. Once, my name was picked in the media lottery to play Augusta National on the Monday after the tournament, with the holes still in their challenging Sunday pin positions. Pin positions alone can make an easy course difficult, and nobody would call Augusta National a walk in the park, not when you're playing it for a score. I played with an older tennis writer from England who had played maybe twice before—not Augusta National, golf itself. Also in our group was a radio personality from Atlanta who was a slightly more experienced golfer. He wrote up his experience, and somebody sent me the clip. I didn't save it, but it included something like this: "I played with Mike Bamberger from *Sports Illustrated* and he's really good." I might have shot a newspaper 99. There are no easy pitch shots at Augusta National, not for me, anyway.

People who are familiar with Augusta only from watching the Masters on TV might not know there is a lot of good golf in and around Augusta. If you're looking to play golf there, you might consider any of the following courses, though several of them are hard to get on. They are listed here in descending order of accessibility, along with some observations from my visits to them over the years.

Augusta National Golf Club. Wide fairways mowed to crew-cut length. Gruesome grave-deep traps with powdery sand that invited thin shots and fat ones, too. Bring extra balls—water seemingly unavoidable for most of the back. Play generally becomes more difficult as you get closer to the pin. Any hole can be two-chipped and four-putted. The course fools you, as it looks more like a garden or an arboretum, and some of the tee shots seem benign. It's all highly curated and distractingly perfect: the bridges, the benches, the yellow flags with the Augusta National logo; the sturdy tee markers, about the size of a small baguette and made from hickory branches; fairways so pristine you're afraid to take a divot. Unnerving.

Augusta Country Club. On a tract of land similar to that of its neighbor, The National, as Country Club members refer to the course next door. The Country Club is an unadulterated Old South club, with an old-timey course that is playable, scenic, and fun. Sane greens. Fast play, most of it by members (not guests), typically in carts. The club plays a central role in the social life of white affluent Augusta. The list of people who are members at both the Country Club *and* The National gets shorter every year. During the pandemic, the Country Club bought a neighboring Black church, Cumming Grove Baptist, where the first parishioners (1840) were enslaved Augustans. With the church in need of expensive repairs, its members voted to sell the building and move down the street. The club razed the church to expand its parking.

Palmetto Golf Club. In Aiken, South Carolina, a half-hour drive from downtown Augusta. Small and private but open for outside play during Masters week for a hefty price. In heavy rains, hundred-year-old golf balls the color of the harvest moon will rise in the mud. A roller-coaster course that dates to 1892, with undulating fairways and elevated tees. It serves as living proof (nodding to Rees Jones here) that scruffiness is an important and enduring value in course design and maintenance.

West Lake Country Club. Not a memorable or exciting course but a pleasant one. It's in a gated community with serious security, on the outskirts of Augusta, almost in the country. Many of the roads in the development are named for well-known courses. There's Medinah Drive and Medinah Court. Inverness Way and Inverness Place. Pebble Beach Drive and Pebble Beach Court. Before the advent of Google Maps, you could circle West Lake for a half-hour, looking for your Masters-week home. *Sports Illustrated* rented houses in West Lake for years. The houses were typically spotless, with numerous and complicated TV remotes and an inexhaustible supply of supermarket cookies. Driving through West Lake, you might see touring pros or their family members coming in and out of their own rental houses. In the mornings, you'd see housekeepers reporting for work. Augusta schools are closed during the Masters, and the house-rental business, for one week, becomes a cottage industry.

A group of us—*SI* writers evading work—enjoyed the West Lake course, usually on a slip-out basis. It felt like playing hooky from school. The West Lake range was often crowded but not at the odd hours my colleague Gary Van Sickle, always working on something, used it.* Poking around the large clubhouse one morning after a jog, I stumbled upon

---

* For years, *SI* published a Masters preview issue that included a poll where players would respond to questions assembled by the writers. One year, Van Sickle nominated the following question: "Have you ever had sex within the city limits of Augusta or anywhere in Richmond County?" It didn't make the cut.

the community gym. Not at all my thing, but when I entered and made eye contact with Mark Steinberg, Tiger's agent, engaged in a serious workout, I felt compelled to stay and pretend I knew my way around the various machines. Minutes later Rory McIlroy came in with his fiancée at the time, the tennis player Carolyn Wozniacki. She ramped up a treadmill to an insane speed and jumped on and off it repeatedly. Rory watched.

Forest Hills Golf Club. A sturdy public Donald Ross course owned by Augusta University, about five miles from Augusta National. The course has no rough, few water hazards, many tall trees, a good range, and you can carry your own bag. The headquarters for the university's golf teams is in a complex on the course named for Fleming Norvell, a man-about-town in Augusta invited to join The National in 1975. Fleming would sometimes serve as a host to Jack Nicklaus when he wanted to play Augusta National. On more than one occasion, Jack confused Fleming's first and last names, sometimes calling him Fleming and other times Norvell.

"Jack, it's actually J. Fleming Norvell," Fleming said one day, trying to settle the matter.

"Well, what does the *J* stand for?" Jack asked in his matter-of-fact way.

"James," Fleming said.

"Then why don't they just call you Jim?"

Fleming grew up playing Augusta's public courses and caddying at the Country Club, which he later joined. In high school and college, he worked at The National during the tournament. His first job was on one of the giant manual scoreboards. He did well with the green-and-red numbering system and the sliding ladders and in the following year was assigned to work the counter in the club's small pro shop, shocked one day to realize, with some exciting thing happening on the course, that he was the only employee in the place. This was in the early

1950s and Fleming was in high school. Fleming was always aware of what the game had given him, and it's fitting that you can see his name in two public golf settings in Augusta: at Forest Hills and, not even a mile away, at the First Tee of Augusta, where there's a grass range and a pleasant six-hole course, which I would also recommend.

One last note about Fleming: For years, he was a starter at the Masters, announcing contestants on the first tee in an old Augusta brogue you seldom hear anymore: *Fo-ah, pleeze. Now drivin': Seveh BAH-ee-STARE-oss.* You heard Fleming and you knew you were in Augusta.

Aiken Golf Club. A public course that offers memberships, and one of my favorite courses anywhere, with a redbrick pro shop and a small clubhouse built into a hillside, a mile from downtown Aiken, South Carolina. Everything at the Aiken course radiates charm, including its owner-operator, a wiry man named Jim McNair, a lifer in the game. The course plays fast, with short par-5s and long par-3s. You never need to break out your water ball, and the green fees are beyond reasonable. There are double greens and blind tee shots and shallow, crusty bunkers. It's rustic, sensible, and sort of Scottish. There's no real rough, but you do play recovery shots off beds of pine needles, just as you do at The National. That this course, well over a hundred years old, exists at all is a testament to Jim, who lives with his wife in a house on the course, and it's Jim who makes the course the fine experience it is. I was once standing with Jim on the eighth tee, looking down the fairway at a sandy wasteland and a hodgepodge of pine trees and, maybe 340 yards away, a nestled green. "Jim, standing here, you'd think you're at Pine Valley," I said. "You're shitting me," Jim said. In a life around the game, sixty-plus years, he had almost never played outside the South.

The Patch. Formally, the Augusta Municipal Golf Course, but locals always refer to it as The Patch, a reference to a cabbage and vegetable garden that the club's longtime pro and manager Red Douglas had tended near the old tenth tee, which is now part of a runway at Daniel Field, a small airport that abuts the course. The course opened in the late 1920s and eventually became the epicenter for Black golf in Augusta, which is ironic because Black golfers were prohibited from playing the course until 1964 and, even then, were not made to feel welcome. The course is hilly, and some of the holes have a severe tilt. It's often baked out, and the best grass on the property can typically be found on the driving range, where the balls are an odd and interesting assortment of brands and colors. It's a good course, and to play it well, you have to be able to pitch your ball off hardpan lies and be skilled at the bump-and-run. But what really makes the experience at The Patch so rich are the people you see there, including two of its longtime pros: Jim Dent, Jr., whose namesake father played the tour and senior tour for years, and Conan "Flip" Sanders, who got his nickname in 1970, when *The Flip Wilson Show* became a popular national TV show and people began to comment on Conan's resemblance to the comedian. During one round at The Patch, my friend John Garrity and I played through a single golfer in a cart. The man was in his mid-twenties, ordinary in every way, new to golf, dressed to mow the lawn. (At The Patch in summer, you'll see guys playing without shirts at all.) This young man was accompanied by a stunning, beautiful woman dressed to the nines. When we got out of earshot, Garrity, a writer with deep reserves of understated wit and an almost Victorian sensibility, noted the woman's good looks and said in a gleeful burst, "How do you explain *that*?"

If you can play only one of the courses mentioned above, I suggest you go to The Patch.

In the clubhouse at The Patch, there's a bare-bones cardroom where you might see a gathering of Black men of a certain age playing a card game called Barracuda, a cousin to Tonk and other games in the rummy family. Over the course of two hours, a player in that game might make or lose twenty dollars and talk about things not suitable for Sunday dinner after church.

For instance, the fellas paying tribute to one of their own, Charlie Choice, after his death some years ago. Charlie was a native Augustan who grew up in Sand Hills, a Black neighborhood near the Country Club, the same part of Augusta where the senior Jim Dent was raised. Like Dent, Charlie caddied as a kid, and he could make his golf ball sing. Whenever he entered the pro shot at The Patch people said, "Here comes Mr. Golf." He had the short game everybody wanted. Charlie was kin to the Hornsby family, owners of a prominent Black business in Augusta, Pilgrim Insurance, and Charlie was baptized at Cumming Grove, the historic church next to the Country Club. Unlike Dent, Charlie was more interested in cash-on-the-barrel golf than tournament golf.[*] He spent his days on golf courses, and at night he worked as a cook and a driver, eventually doing both in Atlantic City, New Jersey. Before long. Charlie became a cook and a driver for John Gotti, head of the Gambino crime family. Gotti loved Charlie, and the guys at The Patch liked to tell about the time Charlie and one of Gotti's associates went to Pinehurst for some golf and R&R. The two men, the large Black driver from Augusta and his friend-of-the-Don passenger, arrived at their hotel. When they went to register at the front desk, they were told that only one reservation could be found, and it was not for Mr. Choice. Then came the story's kicker, with belly laughs for its final punctuation: *Ten minutes and two calls later, ol' C.C. was in the biggest suite that hotel had!*

---

[*] "C.C. could play," Jim Dent says. "Back in the day, C.C. could play with anybody. But C.C. didn't like the quiet life. He was more interested in partying at night than playing golf during the day."

From the start of the Masters in 1934 through 1982, every player in the field used a club caddie, and all of those caddies were Black. When I made my first visit to Augusta National as a guest in the early 1990s, all the caddies I saw were Black, as was every employee in the locker room and dining room and clubhouse, along with the club's drivers. Most of them were men, and they most commonly lived in either downtown Augusta or in the Sand Hills neighborhood. A lot of them played golf and cards at The Patch. That world is dying out but I've been lucky enough to catch some of it.

Nobody would ever call The Patch uptight. Impossible. You'll see golfers drinking, smoking, cussin', hanging, gambling, needling. On the first tee, you'll hear things like *You want shots? See your doc, bro.* The regulars have games named after animals, including Wolf, Rabbit, and Squirrel. The day's action is set on the first tee, and payout comes next to an open car trunk. Wherever you go—pro shop, grillroom, cardroom, parking lot, driving range, practice green, course—no one is in a rush. Gathering these mental snapshots from over the years, I realize The Patch is coming off here like a haven for men, and I guess it is, but you do see women there, on the course, for sure, but more often working in the grillroom and in the pro shop. I can recall a recent visit when an older man, a regular, arrived at the pro shop counter with a large bag of potato chips and a large bottle of green soda. The young woman working the counter looked at the items, then at the man, and said, "You sure you want all this?"

"I'm hungry," the man said.

Her look said it all: *Too much sugar, too much salt, too many empty calories.* She rang up the man, old enough to be her grandfather. At least she gave him something to think about.

Leon Maben is a buddy of mine who lives in downtown Augusta and has an abiding interest in the city's Black golf culture, even though he is not a golfer himself. A couple days before Bryson DeChambeau became the talk of the Masters with his first-round 65, Leon arranged for me to visit The Patch and interview one of the cardroom regulars. (One of my Golf.com colleagues taped it.) The man was Bobby "Cigarette" Jones, a former Augusta National caddie and chauffeur and an accomplished saxophone player. Cigarette Jones, Marble Eye, Cemetery, Do-Hickey, Do-Funny—there were generations of Black caddies at Augusta National who went by their nicknames wherever they went, outside of their mothers' kitchens. As a kid in the 1950s, Cigarette Jones saw Bob Jones around the club and caddied in groups in which Cliff Roberts and Dwight Eisenhower played. I asked Cigarette about Ike. "He was cool," Cigarette said. He was sitting on a chair outside The Patch clubhouse. "I liked to hear him cuss." He mimicked the sound of an Eisenhower tee shot hitting a tree, followed by a quick "Goddammit."

For some years, Flip Sanders, the former head pro at The Patch, has played cards or golf or both with Jim Dent, Sr., several days a week. Even in retirement from the club, Flip is there most days. Late one afternoon, after seeing my bag filled with Ping beryllium Eye2s, he told me about a Patch regular who had the same clubs. The guy could shoot 80—if everything fell his way. Then one day Flip gave the guy a playing lesson and the man shot 72, his best round ever. The next time he was playing cards at The Patch, the man announced he had sold his Eye2s and bought another set of clubs.

"Now, why in hell would you do that?" Flip asked. "You just shot your best round with those clubs."

"'Cause I got the money to buy some new ones," the man said.

"What, you think you're gonna buy a better game?" Flip asked.

The man shrugged.

Flip shook his head and told everybody, "I can't teach somebody that stupid."

They remained buddies, continued to play cards and golf. But Flip was done trying to help the guy with his game.

Flip grew up as Conan in Texarkana, on the Texas side of the

Arkansas-Texas border. His mother got his name out of a baby book in late 1946. Conan Sanders was a well-known athlete in Texarkana, at least in Black neighborhoods in the vicinity of Oak and Elm streets, near a minor-league ballfield, Lee Park. In high school and college, he was so strong he could lift the back end of a VW, where the motor is. He went to the Black high school in Texarkana, Dunbar High, where he played football, basketball, baseball, ran track, and played golf. After high school, he went to Prairie View A&M, a historically Black university near Houston, on an academic scholarship and through a work-study program. He played on the golf team there for two years, and he and his teammates built a primitive four-hole course and range on the outskirts of the campus. They played their matches at nearby courses. When Conan was at Dunbar, the golf team played on the public nine-hole course in Texarkana, where Black golfers were allowed to play.

At the same time, Conan worked at a course in another part of town, Northridge Country Club. There were no Black golfers at Northridge in the early 1960s, not as members, not as guests. A Black caddie or course worker might sneak in a hole or two, but that was about it. Still, Northridge was like a school for Conan, for golf and way beyond. One day there, a drunk member addressed him with a historically revolting word. Conan lifted the member by his armpits, pinned him to the wall, and got in the man's face. The head pro, Jerry Robison, stepped in. He sent the drunk member home and told him he wasn't coming back without an apology. Jerry Robison was a legend at Northridge.

Every day at the club, Conan would see a kid named Bill, who was a half-decade younger than Conan. The kid was a talented junior golfer. Also an entitled country-club brat who would hang around Northridge all day, chipping, putting, playing, swimming, eating, hanging, cussing. Conan knew Bill's family, including his father, Mr. Rogers, a retired, decorated career Air Force pilot. One day the kid's behavior was particularly bratty, and Mr. Robison, an Air Force veteran himself, had had enough. He called Bill's mother, and Mrs. Rogers came barreling into the club's parking lot, found her son in the pro shop, and let him have it right there, in front of everybody. Bill was maybe twelve. He grew up. At twenty-nine, he won the British Open. Texarkana named the road leading to Northridge for him, Bill Rogers Drive, and you can see his name on the Claret Jug beside the year 1981, with Tom Watson, the winner in '80 and '82, above and below it.

Conan grooved his swing on the driving range at Northridge. On the range itself, not the practice tee. In the field, where the balls land. One of Conan's jobs at the club was to pick the range by hand, earning a dollar every time he filled a plastic five-gallon bucket. A Northridge member gave Conan some golf principles he never abandoned: Get yourself square over the ball at address, play out of the short grass, keep your swing thoughts simple. Conan, with a red-gripped Dunlop 7-iron in hand, would walk to the middle of the range, put down his plastic bucket, and chip ball after ball in its direction. His best shots were announced by the dull thud of the ball striking the plastic bucket. The joy of golf.

Conan spent twenty-two years in the U.S. Army—he played a lot of tournament golf in the service—and retired as a sergeant first class. After his discharge, he became a teaching pro and moved to Augusta, first to run the Boys & Girls Club and later to run The Patch as its pro and general manager.[*]

He met a lot of connected Augustans. In his Boys & Girls Club years, he arranged for hundreds of kids from Augusta to attend the Masters during its practice rounds, on Mondays, Tuesdays, and Wednesdays. He went to the Masters so often he lost his desire to go back. He received invitations to play the course but never accepted. That might seem un-

---

[*] "Holy cow," Bill Rogers says, hearing the name Conan Sanders for the first time in sixty years. "I can picture him, on that range. An absolutely gifted athlete, and Mr. Robison had a knack for bringing in local kids who could handle that country club environment and get a lot out of it. That's just amazing, what Conan went on to do, in the Army and in golf. I'm just floored."

imaginable, but in my reporting experience, a lot of Black golfers in Augusta, Flip Sanders among them, have a deep ambivalence about Augusta National and the Masters. "They have all the money, they have all the power," Flip told me. "They do what they want." He was disgusted by how the club had bought a neighborhood of modest homes and torn them down to build tournament parking fields. "What a waste," he said.

In Augusta, Flip met people from the Tiger Woods Foundation and from Nike, Woods's primary sponsor. For a five-year period beginning in 1997, he was part of a group of golf instructors who would accompany Tiger and his father to foundation exhibitions, where Tiger would put on a clinic for a hundred or more junior golfers. In that period, Tiger would do five of these clinics a year, all over the country, and Flip did twenty-five in all, never missing one. He found Earl to be standoffish, even though they shared golf, the Army, and other things. Tiger was methodical but not a complete robot. He had a nickname for everybody, and his name for Flip was Cody. Flip never knew why. Flip and the other instructors had their own nickname for Tiger, RLB, for Rich Little Brat. They had their reasons. Once a year, if that, Tiger would hang for a bit, have a beer, and talk golf.

Tiger was in and out of town the same day, but for Flip and the other instructors, the clinics were three-day gigs. On the range, Flip took a page from his own experience at Northridge, when he would hit those 7-irons at the bucket without a thought in his head except maybe to be square over the ball. He didn't go much beyond that with the kids. He didn't want them to get bogged down in the technical aspects of the swing. He preferred *See ball, hit ball.* To get started, to get bit by the bug, that was enough. He could see a lot of the kids were intimidated by golf's seemingly complicated rules of etiquette. He didn't think a kid taking up the game needed to be formal or stiff or church-mouse quiet. "Golf etiquette is treating others the way you want to be treated," Flip would say. He knew the kids might not get that immediately, but over time they would. Along those same lines, he would try to boil down golf to a single sentence with the kids, without getting preachy about it: "In golf, you have to be truthful with yourself." That idea had kept him engaged in the game all these years, as Conan became Flip, as a kid on a range in Texarkana became an Army officer and later a golf pro.

Norman left Augusta, DeChambeau faded on the weekend, and Scottie Scheffler won his second Masters title in three years. The first time he had won by three shots, and now he won by four. There was no drama. You couldn't write the loser because there was no loser.

When Scheffler was on the eighteenth green, Verne Lundquist, at eighty-three and with help, was descending a set of steps from the broadcast booth on the par-3 sixteenth hole. He had just finished working his fortieth and final Masters for CBS. His workstation was in the woods, but he had an unobstructed view of the green. Tiger once pitched in his second shot there—maybe you've seen it—on the way to his fourth win at Augusta. It was an unlikely birdie, his ball making one last rotation from the weight of its logo. Verne captured the moment with this impromptu sentence: "In your *life*, have you seen anything like that?" Ten million live viewers: No. The genius of Verne. As he came off the ladder a final time, Verne was greeted by a small group, maybe a half-dozen people, dwarfed by the tall trees above them.

Late on any Masters Sunday, the focus is all uphill, toward the eighteenth green and the clubhouse behind it. You see the last finishers bounding up their final hill, bent at the waist, shoulders and chin leading the way. The eighteenth green is one of the highest points on the course, and the sixteenth hole is one of its lowest. As I waited on Verne, I saw a girl wearing a food worker's uniform walking downhill instead of up, away from Scottie Scheffler and the real action. I introduced myself and we talked briefly. Kyshana was sixteen and a student at Richmond Academy, a large public high school near downtown Augusta with great pride and entrenched economic problems. (Nearly the entire student body qualifies for the school's free lunch program.) She had never been on a golf course before this Masters and had just finished her own final workday, at a concession stand about four hundred yards away. Her pants and shirt were damp in places, as happens when your job involves ice and soft drinks and an end-of-shift washdown. I asked what drew her this way, deeper into the golf course and farther from her exit. She couldn't say, really. She was looking around, something caught her eye, and she followed it.

"I don't mean to be ignorant," she asked, "but what's going on here?"

I pointed out Verne and Verne's wife and mentioned the end of his forty-year run on CBS. Husband and wife hugged, took seats in waiting golf carts, and headed off. Kyshana watched closely—she took in the whole scene, Verne and his wife, the towering trees, everything—and said, "That's true love."

It's such a privilege, to be able to witness a scene like that, in all its familiarity and strangeness, and write it up, as I did that Sunday night for Golf.com. As you get older you only become more aware of life's chance opportunities, the fleeting nature of them. Nicklaus used to talk about something similar, about making every shot count, because you'll never get another crack at it. As is often the case in golf, there's a world in that.

The next day, I played the six-hole course next to The Patch and started the drive home.

8

Jersey Girls

GOLF PARTIES CAN BE NUMBINGLY STODGY, WITH THEIR RUBBERY cheese squares and predictable conversation about the benefits of the claw putting grip. And then there was the pre-tournament pro-am party I attended for an LPGA event in northern New Jersey in mid-May, a few weeks after the Scottie Scheffler show at Augusta. Out*stand*ing golfing get-together.

There was Pat Bradley—LPGA legend, now in her early seventies—doing a little dance move by the charcuterie table, swept away by the piped-in funk. Nobody said, "Are you Keegan's auntie?" Not on this night, not at this party. She was on the covered terrace of the Upper Montclair Country Club at an annual event that pays tribute to the LPGA's founding members while honoring its living legends, two at a time. On this occasion, those legends were Bradley, winner of thirty-one LPGA events; and Beth Daniel, winner of thirty-three. Lee Trevino won twenty-nine times on his tour, on the chance you don't know.

The tournament itself was called the Cognizant Founders Cup, its middle name a nod to the thirteen women who founded the Ladies Professional Golf Association in 1950, Patty Berg and Babe Zaharias among them. Mickey Wright and Kathy Whitworth were second-generation LPGA stars, and Pat Bradley and Beth Daniel came in the next wave. All were first-ballot World Golf Hall of Fame inductees.

Beth was at this Tuesday-night party with her partner, Meg Mallon, one of the most beloved players in LPGA history and hugely accomplished in the game in her own right. (Eighteen LPGA wins, including two U.S. Opens and a British Open.) Nancy Lopez, the Arnold Palmer of women's golf, was there, too. On Thursday morning, Lopez would be the tournament's honorary starter, much as Gene Sarazen was an honorary starter at the Masters all through the 1980s and '90s, connecting present and past. Nelly Korda and Rose Zhang were at a sushi table with its own uniformed, hatted sushi chef. I was invited (got myself invited) to the pro-am party as well as the pro-am the following day. It was some gathering. I tried not to stare.

Korda, a Florida native in her mid-twenties, had won the previous five LPGA events in which she had played, making her the third member of the Five Straight Club, joining Nancy Lopez and Annika Sörenstam in the club. Maybe that threesome should get a lounge jacket with a purple shawl collar, as Tom Hanks and Tina Fey and others have for hosting *Saturday Night Live* on five or more occasions.

The best women tennis players, including Althea Gibson in the 1950s, Billie Jean King in the 1960s, and Martina Navratilova in the 1970s, have always been major, global sporting figures. Women's tennis has had a long series of dynamic stars who oozed personality. Through their play, their interviews, and their chat-show appearances, fans could actually feel like they knew them. Serena Williams is one of the most famous people in the world.

The icons of women's golf deserve a similar place in the international sporting landscape. It has never happened. But now Nelly Korda was coming on. At least, she was knocking on the door.

The night before the pro-am party in the Upper Montclair clubhouse, Korda attended the Met Gala, an annual holy night for divas and other fashionistas, held each spring at the Metropolitan Museum of Art on Fifth Avenue in New York City. Photographers and fashion reporters working the event, plus innumerable guests, wanted to know who Korda was wearing. (Oscar de la Renta.) Her ankle-length dress, patterned with open pink lilies, was practically glowing. Her long hair, which Korda wears up in a bun when she plays, was down for the evening, accentuating her considerable height. Even in modest heels, she was well over six feet tall.

The next night, Korda was wearing Nike. This was at the pro-am party, which she had crashed, searching for sushi on a dinner-to-go plate. Off-white Nike gym pants, off-white Nike gym shirt, Nike running shoes, Nike visor. Hair up. No fluorescent anything. Still, she wasn't exactly blending.

An athlete on a heater gives off a certain vibe. I saw it repeatedly with Tiger over a twenty-five-year period. I saw it with Lenny Dykstra when he was batting over .400 two months into the 1990 baseball season and at other times that summer when he owned pretty much every National League pitcher he faced. I played golf with Lenny a handful of times that spring and summer, and he always looked surprised when his putts didn't fall, even from twenty feet. The zone. It's a real thing. The athlete in the zone is aware of it, and everybody around the athlete is, too. On the range before the Wednesday pro-am, Korda was hitting draw shots, straight shots, and push fades—with a sand wedge. Not something you see every day. She was a study in athletic balance and swing ownership. She was putting on a clinic. She wasn't intending to, but she was. Your eye was drawn right to her.

Everything suggested Korda could win her sixth straight event, but it's much harder to dominate in golf than in tennis, where you only have to beat one player at a time. In golf, you have to beat dozens of others in the final round, on a playing field that is irregular, unpredictable, and exposed. Weird, inexplicable things are more likely to happen in golf than almost any other sport. Just to be contending on Sunday, you have to do so many things correctly, and one bad swing can undo it all. That's why full-field events (typically with more than one hundred golfers) played over four rounds with a mid-tournament cut is a way of life in professional golf. The tension builds and builds; players earn their places on the leaderboard over time. Whether all that makes traditional tournament golf an effective way to sell life insurance and luxury cars in an *I said now* culture, I can't say. I can't say, and I don't care.

By the time the LPGA commissioner, Mollie Marcoux Samaan, got to the mic at the pro-am party, the four World Golf Hall of Famers on hand—Ms. Bradley, Ms. Daniel, Ms. Mallon, Ms. Lopez—were huddled, discussing *whatever* among themselves. (Ms. Korda and Ms. Zhang had left for another room.) The greats in any field share a language and life experiences that the rest of us can never really understand, try as we might.

For decades, Meg Mallon has been one of the most accessible LPGA stars to fans, reporters, caddies, sponsors, pro-am partners, rising players—anybody, really. Her relationship with Beth Daniel was known on the LPGA tour for years but not beyond it, until Mallon talked about it at her Hall of Fame induction in 2017. If you go to Pine Tree Golf Club in South Florida, there's a decent chance that Meg and Beth will be there. Ditto for any U.S. Women's Open or Solheim Cup (the Ryder Cup of women's golf, named for Karsten Solheim). In their long prime, it's hard to imagine any couple who would have been more effective in a better-ball competition, though maybe Laura Baugh and Bobby Cole—to cite a rare LPGA-PGA Tour marriage—could have given them a game, at least for a while. In terms of a long, lean, tall swing, Beth Daniel was Nelly Korda before there was a Nelly Korda. She was Davis Love III before Davis made it on tour. (Beth took lessons from Davis's father.) For a brief while, I was on the World Golf Hall of Fame election committee with Beth. She sat in a swivel chair with her perfect posture and listened so intently that her silence was like a force field. I voted as Beth voted.[*]

Nancy Lopez was a first-ballot Hall of Famer, no debate necessary, even though Lopez never won the tournament that meant the most to her, the U.S. Open. It happens. Kathy Whitworth never won a U.S. Open. Neither did Beth Daniel, neither did Sam Snead. Phil Mickelson had *six* second-place finishes in the U.S. Open without a win. (There's something tender about a superstar not having it all, isn't there?) All through the night, party people were introducing themselves to Nancy Lopez. I was one of them. I was on a mission . . . from Fred. Fred Roos. I don't imagine you would know the name, unless you are a student of behind-the-scenes Hollywood.

For forty years, Roos wanted to make a movie about Lopez. For many years, Roos worked with Francis Ford Coppola. In 1975, as producers of *Godfather II*, they won the Academy Award for Best Picture. Roos produced films made by Coppola's daughter, Sophia, including *Lost in Translation*, starring Bill Murray. He had an astonishing eye for acting talent and was a casting director for *American Graffiti*, which featured, among other rising talents, Ron Howard, Richard Dreyfuss, Cindy Williams, Suzanne Somers, and Harrison Ford. The movie unfolds over the course of one night, California kids on the cusp of college or war or work.

American Graffiti was the seminal movie of my middle-school years,

---

[*] When Love was in college, in the early 1980s, he watched as his father had Daniel practice with one bathroom scale under her right foot and another under her left, to teach getting her weight to the right side at the top of her swing. "That was the first time I considered weight shift in the swing," Love says. "Now they call those bathroom scales force plates and they talk about pushing off the ground."

and it never left me. About thirty years after its release, I wrote a sort of fan letter to Roos, which led to meeting him. Some years after that, I began providing modest help to Roos on his Nancy Lopez movie idea.

In my experience, Fred was exceedingly direct. Not, at all, a schmoozer. But he enjoyed going deep on any number of subjects, including movies, baseball, golf, and sportswriting. In the early 1950s, he had been the sports editor of his student newspaper at Hollywood High, *The Crimson Chronicle*. The paper's editor was Carol Burnett. Once, while Fred and I were having a late breakfast at a diner off Mulholland Drive in Los Angeles, Jon Voight passed by our booth on the way to his own. Voight and his two brothers grew up hanging around Butch Harmon and his three brothers in and around Westchester, New York. Voight's father, Elmer (Whitey) Voight, was the longtime head pro at Sunningdale Country Club, near Winged Foot, where Claude Harmon was the head pro. At the Beverly Glen Deli that day, Voight and Roos gave each other the silent treatment by way of perfunctory nods. Those nods screamed. I left the whole Voight-Harmon golf thing alone. Fred and I had other things to talk about.

I had been assisting Fred with his Lopez movie chiefly by gathering old clips and photos, collecting Nancy Lopez YouTube highlights, talking to people who knew her, and writing a treatment, a sort of synopsis, for a possible script. Fred's father had been a family doctor in rural Southern California in the decades before and after World War II who, often on a pro bono basis, provided medical attention to immigrant Mexican-American families. Fred heard broad similarities in the stories his father told about his Spanish-speaking patients and in Nancy Lopez's family history, which had a lot of Mexico in it, as well as New Mexico, Texas, and Southern California, where Nancy was born. Roos had been following Lopez's career in the sports section of the *Los Angeles Times* going back to her arrival on the national sporting scene.

In 1975, at eighteen and shortly after graduating high school in

Roswell, New Mexico, Lopez finished second in the U.S. Open—as an amateur. At the 1977 Bing Crosby Pro-Am, as a sophomore at the University of Tulsa, Lopez became one of the first two women to play on the amateur side of a modern PGA Tour pro-am. (Marianne Bretton, a UCLA golfer, played that year, too. The idea of women playing in the pro-am, alongside Jerry Ford and Jack Lemmon and the like, was met with resistance at tour headquarters, but they played at Crosby's insistence.) That summer, as a newly minted pro, Lopez again finished second in the U.S. Open. She had two more runner-up finishes in U.S. Opens in 1989 and 1997. Four seconds, in the event that meant the most to her in part because it meant the most to her father.

As a U.S. Army soldier during World War II, Domingo Lopez saw combat and witnessed death. As a returning vet, he was spat upon (literally) by his fellow Americans who were somehow offended by his Mexican heritage. In the face of such bigotry, Domingo's resolve to make it in America exploded. He introduced his daughter to golf at the height of the Arnie's Army golf craze. In her own way, Nancy followed Arnold's path. American sports fans like Fred Roos saw Nancy evolve from teenager and prodigy to icon and middle-aged mother of three daughters she had with her second husband, the baseball lifer Ray Knight. Knight was fired as the manager of the Cincinnati Reds two weeks after Nancy finished second in the '97 U.S. Open.

Fred Roos had a lot of story to tell. For a while, his working title for his project was "Nancy with the Dancing Eyes." It was a play on a headline from a 1978 *Sports Illustrated* cover story by Frank Deford about Lopez and her father that ran under the headline NANCY WITH THE LAUGHING FACE. That headline was a play on a Frank Sinatra song of the same name. Fred and I were calling the project "Play Happy," one of Lopez's pet phrases and keys to good play, which she got from her father. There was something lost-world about the whole thing. A Nancy Lopez *biopic*. I told Fred early on that I had never interviewed or even met Lopez, but I hoped someday I would. And there she was, headlining a country-club LPGA pro-am party. The real-life Nancy Lopez.

She was in her late sixties, with black hair and lively brown eyes bordered by crow's feet. Her third husband, Ed Russell, was with her. Seeing him, you did a double take because of his resemblance to Ray Knight. But Ed never played for the Big Red Machine. He had spent his career in the military.

Long after Lopez stopped playing in LPGA events, she remained connected to the tour. It has kept her current. She has known Nelly Korda going back to Korda's amateur days. When Korda played on her first Solheim Cup team, Lopez, as an assistant U.S. captain, was her minder. (*Pod leader*, in the modern-day management vocab of these events.) On her phone at the Founders event, Korda showed Lopez highlights from the Met Gala, along with photos of the two dresses that didn't make the final cut. They were the only two people on campus who knew what it was like to win five straight, and here was Korda going for her sixth. Over the years, Lopez had a pull-the-string response when people asked what it was like for her when she ran the tables: *When you're going good like that, the fairways are as wide as a turnpike, the hole is as big as a manhole cover, and the game seems easy.*

You wouldn't know it by looking at her that night at the pro-am party, but Lopez was recovering from rotator cuff surgery, and for the first time in her life, she was not playing golf on a near-daily basis. (Nancy Lopez and Gary Player never tired of playing golf. Bernhard Langer and JoAnne Carner never lost their desire to play tournament golf.[*] Ben Hogan and Mickey Wright never stopped hitting balls.) Lopez was nervous about the star turn she would be making in a couple

---

[*] "It's the love I have for the game and the love I have to compete at the highest possible level," Langer says, explaining his fifty-year infatuation with tournament golf. *Highest possible level* is a telling phrase. Approaching seventy, he could not make cuts on the PGA Tour. But he could contend on the senior tour.

of days as the honorary starter, which required one swing off the first tee with a driver in hand at seven in the morning, no mulligans allowed. There would be nothing easy about it.

A half-decade earlier, before the first round at the inaugural Augusta National Women's Amateur, Lopez had served as an honorary starter. She did so alongside three other LPGA legends, Annika Sörenstam, Se Ri Pak, and Lorena Ochoa. It was a big moment and a big stage.

For starters, the setting: Augusta National, a gated bastion of male golfing excellence, from Bobby Jones to Arnold Palmer to Tiger Woods. Also, Lopez was the oldest of the four (thirteen years older than Sörenstam) and much longer removed from her playing prime than the other three women. And Lopez, in any public forum—this is a legacy she inherited from her father—feels a responsibility to represent the United States. A small American flag is stitched into her golf bag, right above and far more prominent than her name. If there's a playoff in an LPGA event and one of the players is American, Lopez roots for the American. If somebody was going to win six straight LPGA events, she wanted it to be an American. Lopez had one shot that morning at Augusta and a lot riding on it. She could barely breathe.

Before heading to the tee, Sörenstam helped Lopez remove the windbreaker she was wearing in the early-morning cool. The club chairman, Fred Ridley, introduced Lopez, and Se Ri Pak applauded enthusiastically, palm to palm and fingers out, Korean body language for joy. Condoleezza Rice and Bubba Watson, in their green club coats, watched from behind the tee. Ed Russell did, too. Lopez took an extra practice swing (smart) and, with a long, flowing swing, hit her shot right down Broadway and deep into an oval created by spectators. She returned to her place in the lineup with the other three women. Ochoa high-fived her, hugged her, put her arm around her. Lopez could breathe again.

A few years later, when a rule change made Ochoa eligible for membership in the World Golf Hall of Fame, Lopez was asked to call her with the news. Ochoa had quit tournament golf after a stunning, fast eight-year career, citing her desire to have children and be a full-time mother. She was in Valle de Bravo, the lakeside resort town in Mexico, in the backyard at the family home with her dog. Ochoa's husband, the CEO of Aeroméxico, was at work. Lopez called without advance notice, and Ochoa answered and learned she was going to be a Hall of Famer after all. (Ochoa had won twenty-seven times in those eight years, including two majors, but per earlier house rules, an LPGA player was required to have played at least ten years.) Ochoa laughed, cried, walked in happy circles with the family dog, got in her car, and picked up the kids from school.

It was surprisingly easy to introduce myself to Ms. Lopez and her husband, as he stood beside his famous wife. I told them about Fred Roos and how he wanted to make a movie about Nancy's life and times. I'm sure I was too excited and that I was singing a song Nancy knew all too well from other suitors with silver-screen dreams. But she said all the things you might expect a legend to say. (*That's very flattering. I don't know Fred, but I certainly know those movies you're talking about.*) We talked about an autobiography Lopez had been writing with the help of Rhonda Glenn, a golf historian and writer out of the Herb Wind tradition, and how Glenn's death, years earlier, had stalled the project. I didn't want to hog Nancy Lopez's time. There were paying guests in the room.

At the end of our brief conversation, with his wife's attention elsewhere, Ed Russell returned to the subject of Fred Roos and his movie about Ed's wife: "How can we make this happen?"

I talked that night to Meg Mallon and Beth Daniel, to some tournament sponsors and other guests, and to Mollie Marcoux Samaan, the LPGA commissioner. One of the things on her to-do list as commissioner (though nobody would word it this way) was to make Nelly Korda and other top players—Lydia Ko, Rose Zhang, Charley Hull, Jin Young Ko—global stars. To do that, she would have to figure out a way to raise the LPGA's entire profile. Others have tried to do the same with limited success. Viewed that way, the job is impossible. Still, the commissioner was having a good night, and the LPGA was having a good year. The LPGA's best player had won five straight events and had been a star at the Met Gala. The U.S. Open was in June, the British Open was in July, the Olympic golf in Paris was in August, the Solheim Cup was in September. Some lineup. It was all happening.

As I left the Upper Montclair Country Club, I saw Stacy Lewis, the captain of the U.S. Solheim Cup team, on her phone, behind the wheel of a big Chevy Suburban parked near the clubhouse. During the pro-am party, Lewis had hosted a dinner meeting for prospective members of her Solheim Cup team. Rose Zhang and Nelly Korda attended, bringing in their own dinner, their freshly prepared sushi plates from the pro-am party. You could see all these little scenes unfolding in front of you. Pat Bradley, dancing. The commissioner in a chic black leather jacket, so unlike anything a PGA Tour commissioner would ever wear. I haven't been to loads of LPGA events, but whenever I do go, I leave thinking the same thing: They feel like PGA Tour events did in the 1980s, when you could talk to star golfers—a Hubert Green, a John Mahaffey, an Andy North—by the practice putting green, maybe see them in the lobby of a nearby Holiday Inn, or at a salad bar at a nearby steak house. LPGA events remain intimate. The stars are still *right* there.

When I received an email from Fred Roos in early May about his Nancy Lopez movie—he had been thinking about the actor Eva Longoria for the role of adult Nancy—neither of us could have known I'd be chatting up the actual Nany Lopez at a pro-am cocktail party just a few days later. I looked forward to calling Fred and telling him all about my evening with Nancy, or those five minutes, anyway. I waited to call. Why, I don't know.

Nancy started the Founders tournament with her honorary tee shot. Rose Zhang won. Nelly Korda was never in it. Six days later, Fred Roos died. He was eighty-nine. The last paragraph of his *New York Times* obituary quoted a statement from the Roos family: "Fred Roos was determined to never retire from the film business and to go with his boots on. He got his wish."

The LPGA had four consecutive events in the Northeast, three of which had pro-ams, and I was invited (got myself invited) to play in each one, all in New Jersey: the Cognizant Founders Cup at the old-timey Upper Montclair Country Club in Clifton; the Mizuho Americas Open at Liberty National, a new-age course built on a landfill in Jersey City; and the ShopRite LPGA Classic on two resort courses, one on a bay, one in the pine barrens, about five miles as the gull flies from Atlantic City. After Jersey City and before Atlantic City, the LPGA had its biggest event of the year, the U.S. Open at the Lancaster Country Club in Lancaster, Pennsylvania, run by the USGA. USGA events never have pro-ams.

Pro-am participants have said forever that LPGA players are far more engaging pro-am partners than their brethren on the PGA Tour. I might have picked up on that when I caddied in Lori Garbacz's pro-am group at a tournament on Long Island way back when. I definitely did while reporting a story about Betsy King at the 1987 McDonald's Championship. I caddied for her in the pro-am there, and at the end of the round, she shared her tournament strategy: Assess the course, look at the forecast, predict a winning score, try to shoot it. She said on that Wednesday afternoon that the DuPont Country Club course would yield a winning four-round total of six under par. She made a birdie on the final hole on Sunday to get to six under and win by two. It was her tenth win on tour. She won thirty-four LPGA events, including two U.S. Opens, in addition to winning a British Open and three times in Japan. An astounding career that made her a first-ballot World Golf Hall of Famer and, no surprise, a Cognizant Founders Cup honoree. After retirement from golf, Betsy started making regular trips to Africa, dozens of them over the years, working to bring drinking water and basic medical care to poor, remote African villages. (Betsy's father, like Fred Roos's father, was a family doctor.) Betsy King has raised millions of dollars, in country-club settings, in the name of digging water wells in remote African villages where nobody has ever seen a McDonald's take-out bag and likely never will.

In Betsy's era, the pros played full pro-am rounds with their amateur partners. On the PGA Tour, that was the practice for decades. But over time, the players on both tours lost their patience for these rounds that often took more than five hours to play. It became more common for them to play only nine holes, with a changing of the guard at the turn. For the ams, it's a loss. Had we played only nine holes with Jake Knapp in the Arizona desert, the whole experience would have been different, less meaningful. At the ShopRite pro-am—an extravagant two-day affair involving hundreds of pros and amateurs on three courses—I played an eighteen-hole round with a retired LPGA player, Vicki Goetze-Ackerman, who was the president of the LPGA players union. She was hugely fun, and so was the day. At the end of the day, you feel like you actually know, at least a little, the pro and your playing partners, too.

In general, I don't see a bright future for pro-ams, especially on the PGA Tour, as fields become smaller and the tours become more star-driven. Ideal conditions for player revolt. Maybe they'll dump nine and nine and go to six, six, and six before they call the whole thing off.

At the Cognizant Founders Cup pro-am at Upper Montclair, every foursome of ams had one pro for the front and another for the back. I played in a foursome of reporters (or maybe I should say multiplatform content providers). I played with my Golf.com colleagues Alan Bastable and Zephyr Melton, and Addie Parker, a young freelance style writer for GolfDigest.com, among other publications. Zephyr, a Texan, describes Alan's swing as an oil derrick in action. (It does have an up-and-down, piston-at-work quality.) Zephyr's swing, per Alan, is a Gatsby-era move best imagined on a black-and-white newsreel. We'll give my own a break for now. As for Addie's swing, it's a sight—long, flowing, rhythmic, *powerful*. Addie's father started her in golf as a toddler, and by seven she was playing in junior tournaments in Richmond, Virginia, and beyond. She took to golf and golf took to her. She was in her mid-twenties and had been around golf all her life.

On the front nine, we scribblers played with Yealimi Noh, a promising young pro from the San Francisco Bay area. Yealimi (*YUH-lee-me*) was homeschooled after her sophomore year of high school and had planned to go to UCLA on a full-ride athletic scholarship. But she had a hot run of amateur golf in the summer she turned seventeen and told UCLA she had changed her mind about college. She was still seventeen when she turned pro and was twenty-two when we met on the first tee. (It only seemed like she was twenty-three by the time we holed out on nine. Funeral processions move at a better clip.) Her parents were out there the whole time, walking along the rope line for close to three hours on an unusually warm afternoon in May. Somehow Yealimi was able to look fresh all through this nine-hole slog. Grant Boone, the Golf Channel broadcaster, touring the course in a cart, stopped to say hi to Yealimi and complimented her on her red-

and-black Air Jordan golf shoes and her overall strong fashion sense. Once he said it, I could see it. It was obvious. Every article was well considered.

Addie, a testament to style herself, had a lot to talk to Yealimi about. Addie was probably the only person who had a Tumi golf bag on her shoulder as she boarded the C train that morning at the Ralph Avenue station in the Bedford-Stuyvesant section of Brooklyn, the first leg of her long trip to the Upper Montclair Country Club. She traveled (and played) wearing Jayebird navy-and-white gingham pants, a sleeveless A. Putnam polo, pink adidas Samba all-day golf shoes, and a visor from the Quail Hollow Club in Charlotte. When Yealimi told Addie about her move from Malbon Golf (didn't like the fit) to Anew Golf (liked the fit), Addie was all ears. The insight was central to her beat and right in her wheelhouse. She was wearing her Ralph Lauren sunglasses by then, in the afternoon glare. Yes, there's a lot of fashion and attire here, as we have crossed the border into women's golf. That's because women's golf fashion is actually inventive and interesting.

On the back nine, Yealimi was out, and Lucy Li came in. This may sound familiar, but it's a coincidence: Lucy Li grew up in the San Francisco Bay area, turned pro at seventeen, and was now twenty-one. She was fighting with her own golf game throughout her race-against-sunset nine-hole pro-am round with us. We gave her a wide berth so she could do her work. Two shots off some tees, multiple chips and putts, switching clubs in her indecision, long discussions with her caddie. It was hard to watch.

Deep within the culture of golf, Lucy Li was best known for one thing: qualifying for a U.S. Open as an eleven-year-old. Her driver shaft at that Open was about as long as she was tall. She had a strawberry ice-cream cone in hand when she talked to reporters after a long day at Pinehurst No. 2 and a first-round 78. No player had a bigger gallery that Thursday.

From left: Alan Bastable; Zephyr Melton; Yealimi Noh; Lucy Li; Addie Parker; author with banana. At the turn, Upper Montclair Country Club.

Ten years after that U.S. Open, there was Lucy at Upper Montclair, playing in a nine-hole LPGA pro-am. In the middle of it, Addie made a conversational breakthrough with her. While walking down a fairway, they talked about their shared interest in the NBA, the Golden State Warriors, and Steph Curry, a break-70 golfer. In our three hours with Lucy, that was when she was most animated, talking about basketball with Addie. Addie is good at finding common ground, a useful skill for any reporter. "I can talk to a tree," she told me.

Yealimi and Lucy both wondered where Addie had played college golf. Addie had given up competitive golf by then, but she had the swing, and she had the vocabulary. She can talk stack and tilt through the stroke of midnight. She can talk right-knee position at impact to a tree.

Addie's father, Flotilla Parker, was a huge and athletic man, built like a long-retired NFL lineman in a tastes-great beer commercial. In high school in Roanoke, Virginia, he played football, basketball, and baseball. He fell into golf in his thirties, when Tiger turned pro and set fire to the game. A decade or so later, Flotilla and his wife, Tracy, were in the throes of young parenthood when Tracy was diagnosed with stage IV breast cancer. Flotilla left his job as a BMW car salesman to focus on his wife's needs and those of their two kids. Tracy continued to work as a pharmacist at a university hospital. In this new arrangement, Flotilla got a crash course in modern parenting. He managed the house and the family's meals, the kids' schoolwork and athletic pursuits, starting with golf. He cut down a set of irons and painted them pink for Addie. He got Addie and her older brother, Gavin, to their golf tournaments, their lessons, their range sessions at two First Tee programs, one in suburban Richmond, near their home, the other in the city itself, which Flotilla and the kids preferred. They especially liked one of the teachers there, and they enjoyed seeing kids from a wide array of backgrounds at the city First Tee. Flotilla Parker had a dream about seeing more Black kids find a place in golf, beginning with his son and daughter.

Tracy Parker got through her cancer scare. She would need yearly checkups, but she had received an all-clear report. The joy was short-lived. On a June day when he was sixty-two, shortly after Addie had finished her sophomore year at Virginia Tech, Flotilla Parker died from a heart attack. It happened on a golf course the day before Father's Day. It was a chaotic scene and a numbing day.

On Father's Day, Addie and Gavin, looking to gather themselves and find a measure of peace, went to the range at their First Tee, the one in Richmond, and hit balls for hours. In the years since then, a half-decade and counting, they have continued down the path their father set them on. Gavin became a teaching pro. Addie became a golf writer.

Soon after our round at Upper Montclair, Addie was recruited and hired by Skratch, a golf media company, as an editor and writer with a focus on style, travel, and women's golf. Skratch is based at the PGA Tour Studio in Ponte Vedra Beach, Florida, about a half-mile from the notorious seventeenth hole of the PGA Tour's Stadium Course. There's some kind of new-media connection there, between Skratch and the PGA Tour. (Publishing without fear or favor is so legacy media, so *New York Times* in its 1896 mission statement.) But Addie was not moving to North Florida. She was staying in her brownstone in Bed-Stuy. She was where she wanted and needed to be. "New York City," she said, "is the fashion capital of the world."

When our long day of pro-am golf was over, Addie treated herself to a car ride home. She put her Tumi golf bag in the trunk of her Lyft ride, placed herself in its backseat, propped her head against the window, and watched the day turn into night as she crossed one bridge from New Jersey into Staten Island and then another into Brooklyn.

The Solheim Cup was first played in Orlando in 1990, the year before the War-by-the-Shore Ryder Cup. Like the Ryder Cup, the Solheim Cup features an American all-star team playing a European all-star team. Kathy Whitworth was the American captain that first year, and her team included Pat Bradley, Beth Daniel, Betsy King, Nancy Lopez, Dottie Pepper Mochrie, and Patty Sheehan. The European team had Laura Davies, Helen Alfredsson, and other accomplished players, but it was not a fair fight from the opening bell. In the ensuing years, women's golf across Europe became much stronger, as it did in Japan, Korea, Australia, New Zealand, Thailand, and China. In recent years, the captain's picks for the American team typically had been rookies or other young players. The pool of veteran American stars still playing at the highest levels had been almost drained.

When Stacy Lewis convened a meeting of prospective members of her Solheim Cup team on the night of the Cognizant Founders Cup pro-am party, Lucy Li was invited, chiefly on the basis of hope and promise. Four months into the season, her highlights had been a pair of top-ten finishes. Bailey Tardy, an Epson Tour alumna, was invited, too; the Founders Cup event would be her seventh of the year. In those first six tournaments, Bailey went missed cut, win, missed cut, missed cut, missed cut, withdrawal after a first-round 79. It almost doesn't seem possible.

Bailey went to Lewis's Solheim Cup dinner, played nine holes in the pro-am, missed the cut at the Founders Cup, and headed to Jersey City for the next tournament, which was where I met her. I got paired with Bailey at the Mizuho Americas Open pro-am at Liberty National.

Growing up in suburban Atlanta, Bailey was a country-club kid (the sprawling Atlanta Athletic Club) who played every sport in season. She liked soccer best, but when she hit a growth spurt, she lost the speed that had made her good. She had a knack for swimming but "hated the smell of chlorine," she told me. She played tennis, volleyball, basketball, lacrosse, and golf. Golf had two big things going for it: "You can talk while you're playing, and you can listen to music," she said.

Bailey took her golf talents to the University of Georgia. She majored in family financial planning and turned pro as a senior, taking one class in her final year called Chickenology. The class required Bailey to rank chicken fast-food franchises near the Georgia campus. Her top four were Champy's, Chick-fil-A, Zaxbys, and Popeyes Louisiana Kitchen. She never claimed to be a fried-chicken connoisseur. She was just trying to graduate on time, and she did.

In her first year as a pro, on the Epson Tour, Bailey played twenty-one events, made seven cuts, earned thirteen thousand dollars—and spent five times that. She didn't need a degree in family financial planning to know she was amassing debt. The next year, the Epson season was canceled because of the pandemic. In 2021, with the top ten players on the Epson money list earning LPGA playing privileges, Bailey finished twelfth. In '22, she finished eleventh. She had had enough.

She was ready to take a job with a club manufacturer as an LPGA equipment rep. Knowing nothing technical about golf clubs was an issue, but she was loaded with personality, so that was a positive. Her future boss had one final question for Bailey before sending her to HR: "Are you ready to work with the girls who succeeded at the dream you failed at?"

It stung. She didn't take the job.

Meanwhile, Bailey's mother had secretly signed her up for the LPGA qualifying tournament. Bailey finished second, earned LPGA playing privileges for 2023, and finished fifty-first on the money list, earning almost $600,000. She missed her first cut in 2024, flew to rural China for her second event, had severe jet lag, never played a full practice round, suffered through a terrible case of food poisoning all through the second and third rounds—and found herself making every putt she looked at. She was barely thinking about her place on the leaderboard. Her main concern was the location of the next (her phrase) *squatty potty*. (Her description: "There's one spot for your left foot, one for your right, and a hole in the ground.") She won by four and doesn't know how she did it. First place paid $330,000. She had a job on tour for at least another two years. Two months later, she was at a Solheim Cup dinner with Nelly Korda.

Nelly Korda had a strange run of golf in her tour of the Northeast in May and June. At the Founders Cup, on the old-fashioned Upper Montclair Country Club course, she was in position to contend after two rounds, then crashed on the weekend, 73-73. She tied for seventh, but that sounds better than it was. She was seventeen shots behind Rose Zhang's winning score. The following week, down the road at modern Liberty National, with its views of the Statue of Liberty, Korda won. So six wins in seven starts, with the grandest of all women's golf events, the U.S. Open, on deck. She had played in nine of them and never contended. Kind of strange, really.

The U.S. Open was being played on a course designed by William Flynn, a Golden Age architect who never had a publicity machine behind his name. Any budding architect who wants to make a study of how to turn farmland into a world-class golf course would do well to tour the Lancaster Country Club course.

A good golf course, like the game itself, turns on intimate moments. Where a pin is located. The depth of a bunker and the steepness of its face. The banks of a creek and how they are mowed. The elevation change from fairway to green and the green's slope and size. It's a shame that huge numbers of golfers—male and female, professional and amateur—can drive a ball more than 250 yards now. Golf's governing bodies lost control of equipment standards around the time Tiger Woods turned pro. At Lancaster, you're reminded that a good golf course is always close to being tournament-ready. At Lancaster, for the Open, the fairway grass had a tight, unforgiving weave, the rough was punishing, and the greens were firm and fast. Without doing anything extreme, an enjoyable, playable country-club course was turned into a classic, par-70 U.S. Open test, and it wasn't even 6,700 yards long. *So* sane. Ben Hogan and Mickey Wright would have loved it. Loved it, understood it, recognized it, and picked it apart, to see what it would yield. Put your tee shot on this side of the fairway. If you're going to miss a green, miss it here. Pitch your ball below the hole and never above it. These are the shot-making qualities that make a U.S. Open a U.S. Open. In my opinion, when setting up courses for U.S. Opens, the authorities at the USGA should do all they can to take driver out of the players' hands. For anybody with good coordination and strength, the humongous modern driver is way too easy to hit, with a rock-hard, low-spin golf ball sitting high on a tee. You want to impress your friends with your driving game? Lift more in the gym; move the ball forward in your stance; tee the ball ridiculously high; turn your grip (you righties) clockwise, and hit it as hard as you can. Doesn't require much talent. Want to bring back the driver as a skill club? Start a movement to eliminate the golf tee.

In the first round at Lancaster, Nelly Korda started on the back nine, on the tenth tee, a longish par-4. She opened with a bogey, after flubbing her second off a tight fairway lie. (Golf can make anybody nervous.) She then made a par on the short par-4 eleventh. She arrived at the twelfth hole, a par-3, playing 160 yards. One-sixty, with a narrow green with plenty of back-to-front tilt, bunkers over it, a narrow creek in front of it, a hole that brings to mind the twelfth at Augusta National. Korda made a beautiful swing off the tee but hit the shot too far, and the ball finished in a back bunker. Her shot from the trap never stopped rolling and died in the creek in front of the green.

Korda chose to play her next shot from the other side of the creek, closer to the tee, off tight fairway grass and a slight downhill lie. The swing was tentative, the contact was poor, and she watched her ball land on a slope and tumble down the hill. It, too, finished in the creek. Her next shot was pure *Groundhog Day*. Lancaster to Punxsutawney, Pennsylvania, by the way, is two hundred miles.

Korda deposited three balls in the creek and made a 10. Tiger Woods once made a 10 on the twelfth at Augusta, when he was the defending champion. He hit three in the creek, too. That was in the final round, and as the defending champion that year, he stuck around to help Dustin Johnson into his winner's coat. He played the last six holes in five under par. Korda played the next thirty-three holes in two over par, missed the cut by two, and went home.

Wei-Ling Hsu, an LPGA player in her late twenties from Taiwan, played all four events of the LPGA's swing through the Northeast. In the second week, at the pro-am at Liberty National, I played the back nine with her, after going around the front nine with Bailey Tardy, the former chicken-studies student. They were some contrast. Wei-Ling was as still and contemplative as Bailey was energetic and loose. I got to talk to Wei-Ling several times, in Jersey City, in Lancaster, and at the Jersey Shore event. There's an otherness about her.

I asked Wei-Ling if she saw Tiger as a blend of Eastern and Western cultures. "Yes, definitely," she said. We talked some about how angry Tiger could get on a course and how quickly he could let it go. In watching Tiger, often at close range and all through his professional career, I have seen that one-two punch often. His anger-and-release program seemed to add to his focus. Wei-Ling told me she had a lot of that in her, too.

"I might look like this sweet girl," she told me. "But I could come off the course and want to punch something." So, not a Zen golfer. "I worked on that. Now I try not to go crazy. But you don't let go of all of that." Wei-Ling saw golf as a constant effort to balance internal feeling and external expression, what anybody could see. I wish I could rewatch Tiger's entire career through those two lenses. We all saw the external. But were there clues available about what he was thinking and feeling before he played his shots and while he played them? Were there questions that could have been asked in post-round interviews that would have elicited insights? Wei-Ling's mother is a Buddhist and used to caddie for her, and Wei-Ling said she applies Buddhist principles to every shot she plays, which she defined this way: "You don't take too much, but you don't take too little." You take what's there to be taken. You could say that a lot of Tiger's career shots looked audacious. But at his skill level, they weren't. They weren't greedy and they weren't modest. They were correct for the situation. "They were right in the middle," Wei-Ling said. "It's hard to explain."

For Wei-Ling, plying her trade in the United States and in other countries far from home, she has lived a life where nothing is second nature to her. The menus in restaurants, the beds in hotels, the grass on the greens—it was all different from what she knew as a kid. In her LPGA career, she has always been navigating something. She has found that the easiest thing is to be alone or in a small group. Her closest friend on tour was Minjee Lee, an Australian of Korean descent. "We can go out for dinner and not talk," Wei-Ling said. She didn't mean total silence. She meant that neither felt the need to fill every minute with jabber. At the U.S. Open, they went out for dinner one night to celebrate Minjee's birthday. Dessert was a shared serving of crème brûlée lighted by a single candle. There was no Mariachi band.

Wei-Ling had a moment of insight while driving from Upper Montclair to Jersey City that settled deep within her. She was in an unfamiliar car on an unfamiliar highway. She had missed the cut in Upper Montclair after a second-round 79. Home was a sixteen-hour flight away. So was her mother. She was not feeling good about her game. She was as alone as she could be, and she was happy. *I got myself here.* That was the thought that ran through her head, and she meant it in the most positive way imaginable. Her skill, her drive, her *everything*, got her where she was, southbound on the Jersey Turnpike, full playing status on the LPGA tour, a place in the field in the Liberty National event, a place in the U.S. Open field after that. The whole journey was bringing her joy. It was hers.

You can see Jack Nicklaus's famously legible signature on Wei-Ling's clothes, boldly embroidered on her shirts and pants. Her belt buckle is a large metal gold-painted bear, the Nicklaus logo. She wore the Nicklaus clothing line as part of an endorsement deal. I asked Wei-Ling if she had ever met Nicklaus. "Oh, no," she said. As if that could never happen unless she did something to make it happen, to earn it.

Wei-Ling missed the cut at Liberty National, but she played well the second day, when she shot 69. It gave her something to build on as she headed to the U.S. Open at Lancaster. Her play there was spectacular. I'm not saying that just because I am a new member of the Wei-Ling Hsu fan club, although I am. I'm saying it because she was in control of her golf ball for four straight days on a demanding golf course. She finished in a tie for twenty-fourth with rounds of 72, 69, 74, and a Sunday 72, playing the final round with an LPGA star, Anna Nordqvist of Sweden, a nine-time member of the European Solheim Cup team, capable of driving it fifty yards past Wei-Ling. In Wei-Ling's thirty-eight major championships, she had missed fifteen cuts and had one top-ten finish. I saw her play some pitches and chips, and hole some curling par putts, that were mind-boggling in their excellence. She made ninety-nine thousand dollars, a huge step toward keeping her LPGA playing privileges for the following year. That week at Lancaster, she got everything out of her game that was there to get. That's some feeling.

U.S. Opens are intense. You finish and you let your hair down. That's what Wei-Ling did. She finished her Sunday round and went into a grillroom to watch the leaders play in. Many others did the same. On a TV above the bar, there was her friend Minjee Lee, in the middle of her back nine. Minjee had been in a three-way tie for the lead through three rounds. On Sunday, she made a birdie on the first hole. Then her ship began to list, and she could not find a way to get it upright again. That's golf, too.

It was a warm Sunday afternoon in early June, but this grillroom— above a gym, next to the driving range, across a parking lot from the main clubhouse—felt more like a ski lodge after the lifts have closed. Caddies and players and their family members were bopping around, bottles of beer and cocktail glasses in hand, going from table to table congratulating one another for playing, and surviving, a U.S. Open. The next tournament for those playing it, the ShopRite Classic near Atlantic City, was two hours away by car, and the hotel was on the property. You could fall out of bed and find yourself on the driving range. Two easy courses (relatively speaking) and a purse one-seventh the size of the

U.S. Open purse. A holiday with prize money, really. Wei-Ling would be heading there soon enough. Mike Whan, a well-liked former commissioner of the LPGA tour and now the CEO of the USGA, was making the rounds in the grillroom, chatting up the spent players. It was intimate. Golf is meant to be intimate. A course is big, the hole is small, the clubs are odd, the terminology is strange. Golf could not possibly be for everyone. But it does promote intimacy. That is one of its great attributes. Wei-Ling was taking it all in. Every person in that room, in various ways, knew how the others felt. If that's not intimacy, I don't know what is.

Wei-Ling Hsu, left; her caddie, Nicolas Pereira; Anna Nordqvist, putting.

9

Summertime

A COUPLE WEEKS AFTER THE WOMEN HAD THEIR U.S. OPEN AT THE Lancaster Country Club, the men had theirs at a Donald Ross resort course, Pinehurst No. 2, in a remote village in the North Carolina sandhills. Greater Pinehurst has more courses than you have clubs in your bag and is, by marketing slogan and actual fact, the cradle of American golf. The U.S. Open, per Ben Hogan, Arnold Palmer, Jack Nicklaus, Tom Watson, and other reliable sources, is the most important championship in golf. There's something alchemic about the meeting of tournament and course. The British Open celebrates primitive, humps-and-hollows golf on an annual basis. But every five years, when the British Open is at St. Andrews, golf's ancient mecca, a multiplier kicks in. A U.S. Open at Pinehurst is its American cousin. A U.S. Open at Pebble Beach or Shinnecock Hills is, too.

Part of Pinehurst's appeal is that it feels sort of Scottish. Not in summer weather but in other ways. Donald Ross was born and raised in Scotland, in Dornoch, in the far north. He apprenticed as a young man under Old Tom Morris in St. Andrews. He brought all that spirit-of-haggis purity to New England at the start of his American life and later to Pinehurst. There's something plain, frugal, and Scottish about the Ross courses in Pinehurst. There's no wow factor. They're more like a long, long loop of kiddie roller coasters, a nearly endless series of humps and hollows on firm, sandy turf. The village feels closer to Dornoch than a spiffy American resort town. It's a small, early-to-bed town with a one-track mind. That's okay. People come to Pinehurst for the golf.

There was a lot of preamble to this U.S. Open at Pinehurst. The USGA had recently moved its headquarters to Pinehurst from Far Hills, in the New Jersey horse country. The World Golf Hall of Fame had recently moved to Pinehurst from unincorporated St. Augustine off I-95 in North Florida. Pinehurst had been recently named as one of the USGA's three "anchor sites" for the U.S. Open, with Pinehurst on the docket for the 2045 edition. Pinehurst, both the resort and the village, couldn't market itself with crashing surf (Pebble) or ancient cathedrals (St. Andrews). But it did have Donald Ross and the four courses he designed in Pinehurst: Pinehurst No. 1, Pinehurst No. 2, Pinehurst No. 3, Pinehurst No. 4. (Who needs names when numbers do the same thing with such efficiency?) The Pinehurst message was Donald Ross Slept Here. It was Arnold Palmer did this here and Payne Stewart did that. *Pinehurst.* Just hearing the name gets you in the mood.

Payne Stewart won the 1999 U.S. Open at Pinehurst over Phil Mickelson. Mickelson's wife, Amy, was home in San Diego and the couple was on baby alert, their first. In Pinehurst that Father's Day, it was misting. Stewart was wearing a sleeveless rain jacket (he had cut the arms off). He holed a long putt on the last to win, grabbed Mickelson's head like it was a bowling ball, and said, "You're going to be a father!" The moment was unscripted, aware, alive. It was everything you could want from golf. When Stewart died five months later—he was in a private plane that crashed into a South Dakota farm field, killing all six people on board—that joyful moment took on a deeper poignancy. On that Father's Day in 1999, Payne Stewart gave golf a picture of itself, golf's true heart, that will last forever. The caption will always include the name Pinehurst.

Arnold at Pinehurst gets only a passing mention when the story of his life and times is told, but in a manner of speaking, he was launched there. He went to college at Wake Forest, in Winston-Salem, ninety back-road miles from Pinehurst. It was a small Baptist college, and Arnold knew almost nothing about it before he arrived. He knew nothing about it at all until one of his golf pals, Bud Worsham, told him about it in the summer of '46, when Arnold was a rising senior at Latrobe High. Bud, a senior at Bethesda–Chevy Chase High School, in suburban Washington, D.C., was set to go there himself. When Arnold arrived at Wake in September '47, it was the first time he saw the place.

At the end of his freshman year in May '48, the Wake team went to Pinehurst for the Southern Conference championship. Duke was in the conference, as were Washington and Lee, Virginia Tech, Davidson, and some other old, mannerly Southern schools. Arnold was eighteen, a Presbyterian unfamiliar with Southern Baptist traditions, a working-class kid with a western Pennsylvania down-in-the-holler accent and a slashing homemade swing. His opponents, at least some of them, were golfers with syrupy swings and matching brogues: E. Harvie Ward, for instance, from the University of North Carolina, almost four years older than Arnold, with the grace and ease of a movie star. But Arnold slashed his way to the individual title there ahead of E. Harvie and all the other fellas. People started talking about him. Later that summer, he played in his first U.S. Amateur. Arnold was off and running.

Arnold told me that as a kid he liked to go to the small airport in Latrobe to watch planes land and take off—and to hear radio broadcasts of distant sporting events. The reception was better there. I don't know if he heard any of the radio broadcast of the 1947 U.S. Open at the St. Louis Country Club, but his interest in it had to be intense—he knew the eventual winner's kid brother! The '47 Open was settled in an eighteen-hole Father's Day playoff when Lew Worsham defeated Sam Snead by a shot. Whenever the conversation turned to great U.S. Opens, Arnold would cite Lew Worsham and the '47 playoff. Lew Worsham, older brother of Bud. Arnold had a connection to a winner of the national Open.

One week after the '47 Open, Arnold graduated from Latrobe High. He didn't know where he'd go to college or even if he would. But he was already telling people in town that he wanted to become a pro golfer, just like Lew Worsham. Worsham had made $2,000 for his U.S. Open win, plus a $500 bonus for the playoff. It must have sounded like a dream. Play golf on great courses and get paid for it.

Later that summer, the sports section of the *Latrobe Bulletin* ran a three-paragraph story about Arnold's more immediate plans, and this was the lede: "Arnold 'Arnie' Palmer, Latrobe's golfing king, left yesterday for Wake Forest, North Carolina, where he will matriculate at Wake Forest College." That was on September 11. The "golfing king" bit had legs.

Arnold took an overnight bus to Wake Forest. He arrived on campus and walked to the athletic department office with his suitcase in hand and his golf bag on his shoulder. As Arnold later recalled it in his autobiography, the first person to see him offered this welcome: "Who the hell are you?"

The trip the Wake Forest golf team made to Pinehurst at the end of his freshman year left a permanent stamp on Arnold. Pinehurst suited him. As a young pro, Arnold became a pilot. He owned prop planes first and jet planes later. He liked the walk-the-tarmac single-runway airport at Pinehurst. He flew different planes there, to Moore County Airport, dozens of times, and his photo is on a wall there alongside one of Amelia Earhart. He liked the easy ten-minute drive from the airport to the Manor Inn, the modest hotel in the heart of the village of Pinehurst where Arnold preferred to stay. (His father, Deacon, first stayed there in the 1930s.) Arnold designed a course in Pinehurst called Mid South Club, located on Palmer Drive. Deacon Palmer Place is down the road. In 1994, Arnold and Jack Nicklaus played a made-for-TV match at Pinehurst No. 2, part of the *Shell's Wonderful World of Golf* series. (Orchestral music playing during the closing credits, Arnold using a wooden driver, Jack winning handily, Arnold sounding gracious but looking annoyed.) When Arnold was creating Bay Hill, just outside Orlando, he had Pinehurst in mind. He wanted Bay Hill to be what Pinehurst had been from its start: a demanding resort course beside a comfortable, commodious hotel. But he also wanted Bay Hill to have, as Pinehurst did, its own club, with member tee times and club competitions and the rest. And he wanted the course, as Pinehurst was, to be at the center of a community of well-built, unpretentious homes. People say there's a lot of Arnold in Bay Hill, and there is. But there's a lot of Pinehurst, too.

Arnold Palmer, left, of Wake Forest, and E. Harvie Ward,
of the University of North Carolina, Pinehurst, 1948.

Arnold and Winnie had two children: Peg, born in 1956, and Amy, born two years later. For years, Amy Palmer Saunders and her husband, Roy, have held key positions at Bay Hill, where they raised their four children. The youngest of the four children, Sam Saunders, is a professional golfer. Peg Palmer Wears lives in Durham, North Carolina, where her son and daughter were born. For years, Peg owned a gift shop (artworks, home goods, women's clothes) in a redbrick building on Main Street in Durham and has been active in Durham's annual documentary film festival.

I have written a lot about Arnold over the years and some about Peg, and we became friends along the way. One useful thing I have done in my life is get Peg and Dan Jenkins together at the 2018 Masters, during an annual golf writers' dinner, eighteen months after Arnold's death. Jenkins and Palmer were both born in 1929, and Jenkins covered Arnold's entire career. That Masters was Dan's last. He died shortly before the 2019 Masters.

Peg owns two homes in Pinehurst. The main one, where she stays, is in the village, a short walk to the No. 2 course, and near the cottage where Donald Ross stayed when he was in Pinehurst. The second is a couple miles away, a friends-and-family vacation house that Peg invited me to use for the Open at Pinehurst. In my road life, I am much more of a hotel guy than a private-house one, but the hotel prices in Pinehurst were obscene—Arnold would have been outraged and Deacon might have had a heart attack—and how often can you stay in a house owned by Arnold Palmer's daughter during a U.S. Open? I was happy to say yes.

Deacon Palmer called the U.S. Open the National Open. So did the Latrobe papers when Arnold was growing up. So did Ray Watson (Tom's father) and Charlie Nicklaus (Jack's father). Ben Hogan and Sam Snead did, too. I have had the opportunity to get U.S. Open tutorials from all manner of tenured teachers. Please forgive me as I do some serious name-dropping here: Sandy Tatum, an erudite, make-'em-suffer

USGA president; David Fay, a witty former USGA executive director; Mike Donald, runner-up in the 1990 U.S. Open; Hale Irwin, winner of the 1974, 1979, and 1990 U.S. Opens; Snead, Palmer, Nicklaus, and Watson; Johnny Miller, Curtis Strange, and Ernie Els; Ken Venturi; Dave Anderson and Herb Wind; Mark Loomis, the TV producer; Jim (Bones) Mackay, the caddie; Rees Jones, the course architect; Mickey Wright, a four-time Open winner. I could go on. Can I slip in Larry Rentz here? I caddied for Larry at the 1985 Open at Oakland Hills, where Andy North of Madison, Wisconsin, defeated T. C. Chen of Taiwan. Afterward, Herb Wind wrote in *The New Yorker* how excited he had been at the prospect of seeing an Asian golfer winning a U.S. Open for the first time. Herb was looking at the big picture. The view from the caddie yard was more microscopic. It didn't take long for T.C. to become Two-Chip Chen for hitting his ball while it was in the air when chipping from over the fifth green in the Sunday round. Chen and North played a combined thirty-one majors after that '85 Open. Neither ever had a top-ten finish again. Majors weigh on you.[*]

Arnold once told me he wasn't the same after his win at the 1960 U.S. Open. That's the year he shot a final-round 65 at Cherry Hills in Denver and leapfrogged everybody, including Hogan, getting near his end, and Nicklaus, still an amateur. Arnold's most thrilling one. But after it, Arnold said, "I lost the edge." He told me that in an interview at the Latrobe Country Club in 2012. Mike Donald was there, and I'm certain that elevated the conversation. They could talk pro-to-pro. Mike knew what it was like to come close in a U.S. Open.

---

[*] Andy North and T. C. Chen saw each other often, for years to come, after that 1985 U.S. Open. They never discussed any aspect of North's win. Rocco Mediate and Tiger Woods never discussed Woods's playoff win over Mediate at the 2008 U.S. Open. Arnold Palmer and Billy Casper never discussed their 1966 U.S. Open playoff, won by Casper. Jack Fleck and Ben Hogan never discussed their 1956 U.S. Open playoff, won by Fleck. The winner won, and the other guy can't change a thing. Greg Norman and Nick Faldo never discussed Norman's collapse, and Faldo's victory, at the 1996 Masters.

Arnold Palmer didn't do psychobabble. But it was a baffling observation, and I have puzzled over it for years. He won bunches of tournaments after that 1960 U.S. Open, so he didn't lose his golf game. But he was saying he had lost *something*. He had reached a mountaintop and found that his desire was marginally less intense. In this new state, he couldn't count on shifting his game into fifth gear on a Sunday afternoon when he most needed it. That's how I understood it. Curtis Strange once told me, "Arnold didn't say a whole lot." He didn't. Arnold wasn't one to waste money or energy or words. But there was a lot in those four words, in *I lost the edge.*

The first time I saw Arnold in person was in 1979 at the U.S. Open sectional qualifier at the Charlotte Country Club. I was there as a caddie, and Arnold was in the group in front of us. He was four months shy of his fiftieth birthday, well past his prime, and trying to play his way into the Open in a thirty-six-hole, one-day qualifier. I can see it today like a movie in my head: arriving in his Cadillac, fetching his clubs from the trunk without help, his silver hair.

Arnold owned a Cadillac dealership in Charlotte, where he was close to a prominent businessman in the city, James Harris, and Johnny Harris, James's son. Father and son paved wide paths for Arnold in Charlotte. The Harris family was instrumental in the building of the Quail Hollow Club in Charlotte and, along the way, in Arnold getting a house on the course. The Kemper Open was played at Quail eleven times, through 1979, and Arnold played in all of them. He made the cut at that final Kemper, and the next day he played in the two-round U.S. Open sectional qualifier at the Charlotte Country Club. There might have been a hundred people following him. Maybe more for the second round, after lunch.

There was a column in *The Charlotte Observer* wondering why Arnold, at age forty-nine and with all he had done for golf, didn't receive a special exemption from the USGA to play in the U.S. Open. Arnold rejected even the idea. He didn't want a special exemption, he said. He wanted to play his way in like everybody else, and he did. He played that Monday, and he made it.

Sam Saunders, youngest child of Roy and Amy and a longtime touring pro, had hopes of playing in the U.S. Open at Pinehurst. (Any touring pro would say the same.) To do so, he would need to get through two stages of qualifying, an eighteen-hole local qualifier followed by the thirty-six-hole final. Many established players qualify for the U.S. Open by virtue of their Official World Golf Ranking, among other pathways, but what makes the Open unique is that any golfer, in theory and in practice, can play his way (or her way) into a U.S. Open field. This qualifying grindfest sets the mood for the U.S. Open on an annual basis. The U.S. Open, any U.S. Open, is stern. The U.S. Open is your father after you borrow his car for a road trip and burn the engine's oil to nothing on the trip home. And we like it that way.

At Sam's local qualifier, ninety-six golfers played for three spots. He made it. That advanced him to the final qualifier, where you play two rounds in one day, as Arnold did in Charlotte in '79, as U.S. Open aspirants have done forever. Sam had a chance, a chance to play in the U.S. Open at Pinehurst No. 2, where his grandfather had been the medalist in the 1948 Southern Conference Championship.

In his first eight Korn Ferry events of the year, Sam had made two cuts. His ninth event was in Raleigh, North Carolina. He made the cut. He'd be playing for a check on the weekend. That was the good news. But he had committed to the U.S. Open final qualifier in Columbus, Ohio, on the day after the Raleigh tournament ended. He needed to be in Columbus early that Monday morning. The drive was eight hours, nothing for a young bachelor pro starting out, but Sam wasn't. He was a husband and a father and in his mid-thirties. On Friday at the Raleigh event, he withdrew from the Monday final qualifier. (It was the responsible thing to do, so a player on the alternate list could get in.) He tied for fourteenth in Raleigh. He now had three Korn Ferry checks for the year: $4,050, $4,800, and $17,000.

The week after Raleigh, Sam played the Korn Ferry event in Greer, South Carolina. He missed the cut. The following week, the week of the U.S. Open at Pinehurst, Sam played in the Korn Ferry event in Wichita, Kansas. He missed the cut. He then missed the cut, often by one shot or two and in consecutive weeks, at Korn Ferry events in Norman, Oklahoma; Springfield, Illinois; Berthoud, Colorado; Springfield, Missouri; and Glenview, Illinois. The following week in Farmington, Utah, Sam made the cut and finished sixty-first. He missed the cut the next week in Omaha, Nebraska. He played the following week in Jackson Township, New Jersey. He shot a second-round 71, missed the cut, and announced (on his Instagram account) that he had played his last round of tournament golf. He said he would always be involved in golf, and he thanked the people who had helped him along the way. But after fifteen years, he was moving on. "It was never easy for me, and I never reached my playing goals, but I wouldn't trade it for anything," he said.

How beautiful is that sentence? The candor of it, the poignancy. Sam Saunders earned the right to write it over the course of fifteen years. Fifteen years and one last summer.

I don't know anybody, pro or am, who will tell you golf is easy.

I realize you've logged a lot of miles riding shotgun in the Mini by now, and I have spared you a bunch of cross-state trips on the Jersey Turnpike, the Pennsylvania Turnpike, up and down the Garden State Parkway. For real road-trip insight—the lure of the road, your tour guide looking for something beyond improved golf—I'd point you to *Blue Highways* by William Least Heat-Moon. My friend Jim Kelly and I devoured it, years ago. We were both newly out of college and reporters for the *Vineyard Gazette* on Martha's Vineyard, an island off mainland southern Massachusetts, no connecting bridge to anything. In winter, things could get, I don't know, closed. And there we were, living through Heat-Moon as he got behind the wheel of his boxy Ford Econoline and went wherever. What Jim and I took from him—and surely others would say the same— was . . . *freedom.*

But not boundless, ridiculous, no-rules freedom, where there are no consequences. Not so free that (as Kris Kristofferson wrote) you've got nothing left to lose. Heat-Moon could go where he wanted to go, but he still needed gas and paved roads and, come nightfall, places to park his sleeper van. Freedom of a kind and to a point.

The corridors of a golf course, from the first tee to the bottom of the hole on eighteen, call to me as those blue highways must have called to Heat-Moon. Golf really is (and I'll recycle this bit from Updike till the sheep come home) *freedom, of a wild and windy sort.* Freedom with boundaries created by the rule book, by white O.B. stakes, by the social contract of playing-partner propriety.

If I didn't think this search for improved golf had some personal and communal value, you'd be doing something else now. But I do. The golf ball sits there doing nothing, and we get it to do something. The psychic rewards are immeasurable. They can be.

And for those of you out there who can make money from your golfing ability: Good for you. But don't get carried away with yourselves.

No matter our level of play, golf gives us the freedom to make our own crappy decisions, along with some good ones. In one of my St. Martins Spring Championship matches, on the second hole of sudden death, I drove it hole-high in the weeds on a short par-4. I took an unplayable, dropped in an adjoining fairway, stiffed the pitch shot, made a 4. Game over. That was good. In another match, on the par-4 first, I drove it crazily left, hit a solid recovery shot that went to the back of the green, and lagged from seventy-five feet to maybe four. Thrilling. I was lingering on the back of the green. My opponent was playing his third from off the green, so I didn't need to mark. (My ball could only help him.) I was in a dream state, in a reverie of solitude and focus. And then my opponent said, "C'mon in here, we're in this together." He woke me up, brought me in, chipped it dead, saved par. I missed my par putt and went to the second tee one down.

We're in this together.

What, like this is some kind of group activity? I don't even get it.

I could have said, *Leave me the fuck alone.* But that would not be golf. So I walked in, closer to the action and to my opponent. I had a close-up view of his chip that nearly went in for a birdie 3. He got me to move. Maybe it was a power thing, I really don't know. Whatever it was, I couldn't let it go, and I couldn't figure out some productive way to use my annoyance. I let the words and their speaker sag deeper into my head.

Crappy thinking, before and after my putt for par. Crappy thinking and a lousy stroke. You can't separate one from the other, the crappy thinking and the lousy stroke.

I lost, of course. I was out of the St. Martins Spring Championship.

A long drive gives you the chance to listen to music as you wish, call whom you wish, stop as you wish. A long drive gives you a chance to let your mind drift.

I've driven Philadelphia to Pinehurst (and back) a half-dozen or more times over the past forty years. Philadelphia to Baltimore, Baltimore to Richmond, Richmond to Raleigh, Raleigh to Pinehurst, the roads becoming more rustic on that last stretch.

Grayson Murray, the winner in Hawaii, grew up in Raleigh and played at the Raleigh Country Club as a kid. He was living in Palm Beach Gardens when Robert Garrigus saw him at the Cognizant event at PGA National, but Raleigh was home. You may recall that Garrigus had Monday-qualified his way into the Cognizant, and Grayson was there not for the tournament but to have his clubs tweaked. That was in late February, almost two months after Grayson's victory at the Sony Open, née the Hawaiian Open. They had lunched and bro-hugged, and Garrigus said goodbye the way he always did: *One day at time, brother.* Grayson went back to his townhouse in Palm Beach Gardens, his legal Florida residence, his IRS residence, his PGA Tour mail and Masters invitation residence.

In mid-May, around the time the women were going from New Jersey to Lancaster, Grayson made the cut in the PGA Championship at Valhalla in Louisville, Kentucky. On Sunday, he shot one of the day's best rounds, a four-under 67, and tied for forty-third place. The next day, the Official World Golf Ranking was published, as it is every Monday, to incorporate the Sunday results. The top sixty on the new list would be exempt into the U.S. Open at Pinehurst. Grayson was number fifty-eight on the World Ranking list. No need to go to the two-round final qualifier. He was in. In three weeks, he would be playing in a U.S. Open on a course he'd known all his life, seventy-five miles from his boyhood home.

The week after the PGA Championship, Grayson played at the Charles Schwab Challenge, at Colonial Country Club in Fort Worth, Texas. He walked off the course with two holes remaining in his Friday round. That night, he flew from Dallas to Atlanta and Atlanta to West Palm Beach.

Grayson's struggles with alcohol, depression, and anxiety were not a secret. He was open about them with Garrigus, with his parents, with his caddie, with PGA Tour officials. He was open about his struggles with others in need. For many, being open is a start and a path to better health. He was working on his life like he was working on his golf. He was a huge golf talent with a big heart and, on any given day, more pain than anybody could know. *One day at a time, brother.*

Grayson ran out of days on that last Saturday in May, the Saturday of Colonial. He was found in his townhouse in Palm Beach Gardens. It rips your heart out. Nobody can explain the dark mystery of suicide. But we *saw* this man—this burly, bearded thirty-year-old man—win the first full-field tournament of the year, the old Hawaiian Open, not even six months earlier! We *saw* him bury a forty-footer on the first hole of a playoff, and jab his drumstick right arm through the warm ocean air. He said that night the win would change his career—he was in his first Masters—but not his life. The wisdom and insight in that comment was striking.

The Open at Pinehurst would go on without him. Somebody would play in Grayson Murray's place. But there was a hole on the tee sheet, and it could not be filled.

It's hard for a sportswriter not to have a rooting interest. I'm speaking for myself, of course, but I suspect for others, too. I've done a lot of deadline typing next to my colleague Alan Shipnuck who likes to say, "Always root for the story." That is, may the best story win. Down the stretch, Augusta, 2018: Patrick Reed or Rickie Fowler? That's not even a question, really. In a World Series, I root for the city that needs the win more, and the longer the series goes, the better, in the name of economic benefit. On that basis,

I was rooting for the Detroit Tigers to defeat the San Francisco Giants in seven games in 2012. They lost in four.

On Sunday of the U.S. Open at Pinehurst, Rory McIlroy and Bryson DeChambeau were trading shots and the lead all through the back nine. DeChambeau, wearing a shirt and hat bearing the emblem of his LIV team (the Crushers), was in the final twosome. McIlroy, wearing the shirt and hat of his main sponsor (Nike), was one group ahead. I went back and forth between the two groups, with a special inside-the-ropes lanyard that actually allowed me to see something. Yes, this is considered work, and yes, you can get paid for it. That tournaments draw any paying fans at all is half a miracle. You miss so much more than you see. But what you see in person can leave a lasting imprint.

McIlroy's playing partner was Patrick Cantlay, and DeChambeau's was the Frenchman Matthieu Pavon. If I could have waved a wand and picked a winner, I'd have chosen Pavon. For one thing, French golf was overdue for a booster shot. The only Frenchman to win a major was Arnaud Massy at the 1907 British Open. French golfers—and Jean van de Velde, the French golfer who had one hand on the Claret Jug in the 1999 British Open, is emblematic of this—do have that je na sais quoi. In his 1922 book *Golf,* Massy wrote, "The golfer's head must be inclined at a perfectly natural angle, without any exaggerated droop." What other great player is talking about a drooping head? But when you think about it, a drooping head is a speed killer and bad body language, too. When Pavon won at Torrey Pines at the start of the 2024 season, he was a study in grace under pressure. So: Pavon, first; McIlroy, second. McIlroy, at thirty-five, seemed to need a victory the most. For almost ten years, he had been stuck on four major wins.

He was nineteen when I first met him during a brown-bag outdoor lunch at a Titleist testing center in Southern California. He had traveled the world as an amateur but had not yet made his pro debut in the

United States. His broad worldview was a breath of fresh air. Most golf prodigies suffer from where's-the-range myopia.

As for DeChambeau, I admire (and how can you not?) his commitment to thinking for himself, the one-plane swing, the single-length irons, his theories about tee height and other important matters. His extreme bulking up during the start of the pandemic, when the PGA Tour suspended play for six weeks, I found to be unsettling. His six-stroke win at the pandemic-delayed 2020 U.S. Open at Winged Foot was built on the hardest swings I have ever seen anybody make with both a driver and (more tellingly) various wedges from deep rough. It was not his fault, but the way DeChambeau won that Open was like a kick in the teeth to Winged Foot and how A. W. Tillinghast designed it to be played. Seeing golf and golfers make steady progress, one generation to the next, is thrilling. But DeChambeau had turned Winged Foot into a drive-it-anywhere, pitch-it-on course. He figured something out, and you could say good for him. But you could also say golf's governing bodies and governors, in charge of monitoring equipment standards, had let the game down. For elite golfers, the par-5 died on their watch, and the seven-thousand-yard course, as a meaningful test for male pros, did, too.

Golf becomes slower and more expensive when courses become longer. When golf courses get crazy long, the finesse game gets killed, and charm is out the window. Imagine a baseball game at Fenway Park where every batter is Aaron Judge, swinging from his heels with a metal bat at an oversize Wham-O Superball. That was DeChambeau at Winged Foot. With a slightly slimmed-down physique, that was DeChambeau at Pinehurst.

In the fourth round, standing on the tee of the par-3 fifteenth hole, McIlroy had a one-shot lead. If he could play the last four holes in even par, he'd probably win or, at worst, be in a playoff. Unfortunately for him, he hit the wrong tee shot with the wrong club and made bogey. It happens. He's a golfer, not a robot. Even Hogan, Nicklaus, and Woods were not robots. Arnold, Seve, Phil—most definitely not robots.

But the death knell for McIlroy was not that bogey on fifteen; it was his three-putt bogey on sixteen. He stroked his downhill birdie putt from twenty-five feet too hard. When he missed his uphill thirty-inch putt for par, I gasped. I was right on the edge of the green and couldn't help myself. (I do get too attached to these proceedings.) It wasn't over for McIlroy but close to it. He was running out of holes, chances, mojo. He made another bogey on eighteen when he missed from inside four feet. A Sunday 69, and it was not good enough. Miss begets miss. It always has. At every level.

DeChambeau made a ridiculous up-and-down on eighteen. A fifty-five-yard bunker shot, a four-foot putt, a par to win by one. He did what he needed to do, and he showed finesse and style and a grace under pressure that was all his own. He became the second LIV golfer to win a major championship. The Open at Pinehurst was McIlroy's sixty-second major championship and his eighteenth top-five finish. He'd get his prize money, $2.3 million, by direct deposit. The USGA gives you a silver medal, too. It's not nothing. It's the opposite. Being in it, trying your hardest, playing your heart out? It's actually everything, not that you can see that in the heat of the day and the moment.

DeChambeau, now a two-time U.S. Open champion, did the traditional winner's press conference in a crowded tent built for the occasion. In the nearly four years since his Open win at Winged Foot, he had embarked on a complete, public makeover. The trophy was by his right elbow. He pulled out a blue British driving cap, the kind Payne Stewart wore when he won his Open at Pinehurst, and placed it on the outstretched wings of the Lady Victory finial that stands atop the trophy's lid. DeChambeau went to SMU because Payne Stewart did. Stewart is one of DeChambeau's golfing heroes. Hogan, who wore a similar cap, is, too. DeChambeau said, "All I want to do is entertain, do my best for the game of golf, execute, and provide some awesome entertainment for the fans." Hogan could have edited that down to one word—execute—but that's okay. It would be a dull world if we all did the same thing the same way.

Anna Wears, Peg Palmer's daughter, stayed at her mother's house in Pinehurst during the Open. She was visiting from Pittsburgh, where she was living with her soon-to-be fiancé and studying for her master's degree in public health at Pitt. Mother and daughter went to the Hall of Fame induction ceremony together, walked the course, took in the sights. There was a chance I would get a roommate in my otherwise empty house. Johnny Harris from Charlotte, maybe. Or Peg's son, Will Wears, an assistant golf coach at Loyola in Baltimore, where he played college golf. (His golf mentor was his maternal grandfather, Arnold Palmer.) But in the end, I had the place to myself. There were tea bags in a cupboard and lemonade in the fridge, and I made a tall pitcher of Arnold Palmers. People seem to think the recipe calls for a fifty-fifty mix, because that's how AriZona Beverages makes and markets the drink, with Arnold's photo on every can, bottle, and jug. But the man himself told me the main ingredient is tea. The rest is up to you.

Golf has been a lifelong thing for Anna, who, as a freshman and sophomore, was a walk-on member of the Wake Forest women's team. She knows a lot about her grandfather's standing in the game, and how her brother's team at Loyola is faring. She's interested in the modern, changing pro game. She's interested in everything related to golf, really.

I took Anna to the tournament's media center, where I introduced her to some writer pals and a few USGA officials. Anna would never, *ever* drop her maternal grandfather's name, but she was comfortable listening to others tell their Arnold Palmer stories. Her running shoes were covered with dirt and dust from all her golf-course hiking. She liked all the golfy parts of the week and the circus-comes-to-town element, too.

On Thursday, looking for a quick in-and-out story, I was thinking about writing up Willie Mack III, who had made the turn at 1 under par. Mack was thirty-five years old and playing in his first U.S. Open, earning his spot by way of local and final qualifying. He was one of two Black golfers in the field of 156, and he was a mini-tour legend. He had won more than seventy minor-league, small-purse events and, in the early going, had spent a lot of nights in his car, sleeping in parking lots near tournament venues. The story writes itself, right? I asked Anna if she wanted to tag along as I chased down Willie, and she did.

Willie, along with half the field, had started the Thursday round on the back nine. That meant he would finish on the ninth green, which was far from the clubhouse. Players who finished on nine signed their scorecards in a temporary air-conditioned scoring room constructed in the woods a few hundred yards from the ninth green. If there were media requests to talk to those players, the interviews were done nearby. There were maybe three writers looking to talk to Willie Mack. I asked a USGA press liaison if Anna could keep close. She was welcome.

Out came Willie Mack, with a (fake) diamond stud in each ear, wearing red, white, and blue FootJoys. He wore a brilliant color-splattered shirt that looked like a Jackson Pollock painting and hung on his slender frame like it was tailor-made. He wore his charisma as if it were his cologne. Some guys just have it.

Mack described a 235-yard downhill 4-iron shot he played: "I told my brother, 'That's probably the best 4-iron I've ever hit.' It went over the green."

Golf will make you an expert in irony. Anna was hanging on his every word. Willie Mack had a force field. He made a bogey on the last for 71, one over. A closing bogey can be a post-round rally killer. Not here. Everybody was having a good time.

Willie had his brother, Alex, caddying for him, taking a slide for a week from his regular job as a financial adviser in Orlando. Alex was standing near Anna and beside Willie's tour bag, stamped with its brand name, Wilson, in the thick-penned cursive lettering that has been around forever. When Arnold got on tour in 1955, he played Wilson clubs in a Wilson bag. The font has not changed.

"Who is the brains of this operation?" I asked Willie, nodding to his caddie brother.

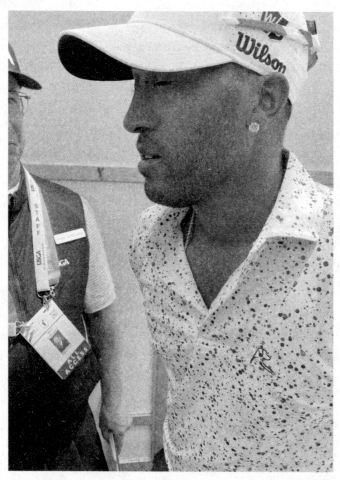

Willie Mack III, interview area, after his first round
in his first U.S. Open, Pinehurst No. 2, Pinehurst, N.C.

"He would say he is, but it's probably me," Mack said without hesitation.

The interview ended. Willie and Alex got in a van for the ride back to the clubhouse. Anna and I, along with another reporter, climbed in, too.

The afternoon was hot and the van was cold. The dirt road was windy, narrow, and dusty. The van did a lot of starting and stopping to make way for the many fans on the course and in our path. Willie, riding shotgun, said he wanted to head to the range and work on his driver. Anna, in the second row, was listening intently and also talking to Willie's brother about their day and week. I've been in a lot of these shuttle vans. The rides are never this lively.

We arrived near the clubhouse, and Willie and Alex and their Wilson bag went their way. When they were gone, Anna said, "I feel kind of nauseous."

"I know," I said. "That ride was sort of rough."

"It's not that," Anna said. She was practically trembling. "It was being so close to Willie Mack!"

Pádraig Harrington was at Pinehurst. As a full-package golfer—playing, thinking, talking—you could say he's a once-a-generation talent. As it happens, Phil Mickelson and Colin Montgomerie overlapped with him, and they could play and think and talk, too. But the point is, Paddy's in an exclusive club. Nick Price, a generation ahead of Harrington, is in that club. Lee Trevino, a generation ahead of Price, is in that club. Everybody mentioned here is in the World Golf Hall of Fame, Harrington as the newest member. He was in Pinehurst not to play in the Open but for his induction ceremony. Peg and Anna, in attendance for it, were charmed by him.

The week after the Open, I saw Harrington at a senior event in Endicott, New York. I went around with him as he played in a pro-am and watched him hit a 3-wood out of the rough.

"Do you move the ball up in your stance when you do that?" I asked.

"It depends," Harrington said. "It's trial and error. It could be right. And it could be terribly wrong."

Three days had passed since McIlroy's second-place finish at Pinehurst. When I asked Harrington about Rory's short miss on sixteen, he sounded like he was still stunned. "I couldn't *believe* he missed it," he said.

You may know that Harrington often sounds stunned. It goes hand in hand with how engaged he is. That same day, he said to one of the ams in his group, "Ya look *incredibly* unathletic." This was not meant as an insult. Harrington was trying to get the man to incorporate his baseball swing (he had described his college days) into his golf swing. He tells Bill Murray to do the same thing. Bill Murray's warm-up move looks like a baseball swing.

Harrington and McIlroy are not close, but they both count Shane Lowry as a good friend. All three have represented Ireland at the Olympics. They have eight major titles between them, and dozens of top-five finishes in golf's four majors. Harrington will tell you that losing close ones is an elemental part of tournament golf. In the aftermath of a loss, particularly in a major, the only useful thing to do was to try to learn something from it, and take stock of the things you did well.

Regarding McIlroy's putt on sixteen, Harrington said, "The player has to sit down and ask, 'What actually happened? Was I focused? Was I not?' It really has to be personal. Rory is the only person who is going to know where his head was when he was over the ball. But I would also say that if you're going to be a good player, and not just a swinger of the golf club, when you miss any shot, you're better off examining your routine rather than your swing." In this regard, and in every regard, a putt is a swing. It really is, every which way you look at it. Every swing has some kind of pre-shot ritual. A routine, if you must. And the most important part of any pre-shot routine, Harrington said, comes at the *end* of it, not its beginning.

Viewed that way, it's not a routine at all. It's preparing yourself for ready-set-go. A routine cannot be mechanical. It requires engagement. Harrington's point is that you go when you're ready to go.

It was impossible not to feel for McIlroy, on the green at sixteen, after that miss. The first putt was an unforced error, too. You're not looking to make that putt, but you would love to tap in without marking, and take a breath. But that didn't happen, and instead he found himself with a thirty-inch par putt. You really have to bury your frustration by the time you pull back the putter head on that second putt. Easy to say.

Golf is slow, except when it's not. There are moments in a tournament round that unfold at breakneck speed, when the player's club is vibrating like the steering wheel of a floored stock car. On TV, even in person, we don't see much. A sagging, drooping head, maybe. But we know. In our own way, we've been there, too.

In late May, when the women were at the Lancaster Country Club for the U.S. Open, there was a second USGA tourney in Pennsylvania, the U.S. Amateur Four-Ball, played on the two eighteen-hole courses of the Philadelphia Cricket Club. It's a newish annual team event that takes its cues from American golf's most common Sunday-morning game and a popular component of the Ryder Cup: the two-man better ball.

If the terms are unfamiliar, maybe this will help: Chris and Will are partners, playing Jack and Arnold. (Four balls in play, two players per team.) On the par-4 first hole, Chris makes 3 and Will makes 4, while Jack makes 5 and Arnold makes 2. For the Chris-'n'-Will team, their better-ball score is 3. For the Jack-'n'-Arnold team, their better-ball score is 2. The eagle 2 beats the birdie 3. Jack and Arnold go to the second tee one up. To win the match, you have to win more holes than your opponent.

Better-ball golf is so much fun, it almost doesn't sound USGA-ish. The format promotes pedal-down play from start to finish, as a team par will almost never win a hole. It also promotes intense bonding between teammates. Will Wears (Anna's older brother, Peg Palmer's son) was in the field for the USGA Four-Ball at the Cricket Club, playing with another good amateur from Baltimore, Chris Baloga, the head coach at Loyola. They got through a stroke-play local qualifier to get to the Cricket Club and, once there, had to play in a two-round stroke-play qualifier to advance to the match-play portion. That is, a knock-out bracket-style competition, with thirty-two seeded teams. Will and Chris shot 64 and 69 for 133, which got them into match play, but even that impressive score was seven strokes behind the leaders. Tough crowd.

On the second day of the stroke-play qualifier, they played the Cricket Club's old Wissahickon course, named for the wide, dark creek that runs through it. A. W. Tillinghast designed the course, and his ashes were scattered in the creek. Eighteen is a long downhill par-4 that swoops left. The creek bisects the fairway about a hundred yards in front of a green that is suitable for kiddie sledding. The green sits in front of a farmhouse clubhouse. The main dining room in that converted farmhouse has a walk-in fireplace and exposed beams and is named for Tillinghast. An idyllic setting for a special hole where a lot can go wrong. I have played it hundreds of times, and it's basically a short par-5 for me. In that second round, Will made 3 there: driver, wedge, putt from ten feet. The Chris-'n'-Will team birdie guaranteed them a spot in match play. Peg was on hand, discreetly cheering them on. A couple days later, Christine and I had a home-cooked dinner with

Peg and friends. Worlds collide in golf all the time, and generally speaking, nobody gets hurt.

In 1963, Arnold played in a new tour event down the street from the Cricket Club, held at another old-school course, Whitemarsh Valley, designed by George Thomas. (Philadelphia, New York, and Chicago are the three great American capitals of Golden Age architecture.) But Arnold Palmer, Julius Boros, Sam Snead, and the others weren't drawn to the Whitemarsh Valley Country Club on Thomas Road in October to sample Thomas's design charms. They came for the money. Nicklaus flew in from Japan for the tournament, which offered the biggest purse of the year, $125,000. Arnold won. His check for winning, $26,000, was then the biggest of his career.

When Arnold played the tour, he often stayed in motels—he was hardwired to save money. Arnold's parents, going back to the Depression, ate deer and rabbit that Deacon shot and Doris baked. Deacon *despised* debt, and Arnold did, too, though he borrowed money to buy the Latrobe Country Club, the course Deacon helped build, digging ditches and laying sod. As a younger man, Arnold, borrowing a memorable phrase from his father, liked to say that if golf didn't work out, "I can always dig ditch." Deacon advised Arnold not to buy the course, but it worked out.

Except for the planes he owned and flew, Arnold lived modestly. He and Winnie spent their wedding night at a motel off the Breezewood exit of the Pennsylvania Turnpike. Frugal living (relatively speaking) is in the family DNA. During the Four-Ball event at the Philadelphia Cricket Club, Peg stayed at a Holiday Inn Express and Suites off the turnpike's Fort Washington exit. Will did, too.

In 1996, Arnold, with Winnie, came to Philadelphia to speak at a ballroom black-tie dinner at the Pennsylvania Convention Center on the occasion of the Golf Association of Philadelphia turning one hundred years old. Arnold was the gala's guest of honor, and Jack Whitaker, legendary pocket-square sportscaster from Philadelphia, was its host. William C. Campbell of West Virginia, a former winner of the U.S. Amateur and a former president of the USGA, spoke.

The next day Campbell was leaving town from 30th Street Station, Philadelphia's limestone monument to train travel. He made a telephone call from a pay phone to a woman he had known briefly in the early 1950s, when she was a young and beautiful amateur golfer with an elegant swing. The decades passed and Campbell never saw her again, until that dinner. The young amateur was now a mother and grandmother, a wife with an ailing husband, a club champion many times over. She was in her mid-seventies. Campbell was a man so proper as to be austere. He said, "I saw you from across the room." The rest he left unsaid.

Arnold Palmer, Jack Whitaker, Bill Campbell, the woman he called, scores of other guests that night in their sixties and seventies and eighties knew American golf in the 1950s, when the game assumed its place in the upper reaches of the postwar high life. The country club became a proving ground for relationships of all kinds, offering business and social opportunity in its dependable rhythms: the Friday-night cocktail hour, Tuesday-afternoon bridge, the standing Sunday-morning four-ball. It was all so beautifully inefficient, days and nights away from home, in the name of escape and connection. As a way of life, it lasted close to fifty years, until it was subsumed by the lure of little machines with magic screens, able to provide escape and connection with hyper-efficiency wherever you happened to be. By the night of the centennial dinner, a way of life was coming to an end. Not that anybody knew.

Two years later, in 1998, George Plimpton came to Philadelphia and gave a talk about the literary life at the Union League on Broad Street, near City Hall, in the heart of our downtown. The Heritage Club in *Trading Places* was modeled on the Union League, but the club's overlords, staying right on brand, didn't allow the filmmakers to use the club. Plimpton was droll and witty. He mentioned in his casual way that for his next writing gig, he might become a TV wrestler. He was in his early seventies.

I know the man who had arranged for Plimpton to speak that night, a Cricket Club member named Matthew Dupee. He had picked up Plimpton in New York City that day and driven him to the Union League. After his talk, Plimpton could have spent the night in Philadelphia—the club had rooms—but he wanted to get back to New York. Dupee, then in his late thirties, drove Plimpton home. It was past midnight when they arrived at Plimpton's residence on the Upper East Side, but the man behind *The Bogey Man* was still raring to go. He invited Dupee in for a nightcap and to shoot pool. Many years later, Dupee could vaguely recall the ring names Plimpton was considering for his nascent wrestling career. The Dangling Participle, maybe. Or The Masked Marauder.

Plimpton died in 2003 at age seventy-six, some months after he fainted, fell, and blacked out in the dining room of one of his New York clubs, The Brook, ten blocks from Grand Central Station.

In the spring of my junior year in college, I wrote to Plimpton and asked if there were any summer jobs at *The Paris Review,* a literary publication he edited. I picked up a ringing phone in my apartment one sunny afternoon, and much to my surprise, Plimpton's voice was on the other end.

There was a brief preamble and then he asked, "Regarding this summer position—are you seeking gainful employment?"

I admit with shame that I had never heard *gainful* used that way. I used my context clues. "Yes?" I said.

"Mmmmm," Plimpton said, or some similar murmur. Whatever it was, it was Plimpton. "We haven't any of that." He wished me well and off he went.

I spoke to him on a couple other occasions in the years to come. He was always polite and gracious, but you could tell he had a lot on his plate.

Chapter 42 of *The Bogey Man*, about Plimpton's efforts to interview Arnold Palmer at the 1966 Bob Hope Desert Classic, is a locker room squirm-fest. It tickled me as a teenager and still does. Plimpton wanted to ask Palmer, at the peak of his powers, about his dreams. Just as Plimpton got started, Palmer became distracted by the arrival of the locker room attendant.

Palmer concluded his business with the attendant and said to Plimpton, "You wanted to tell me about some dream you had."

"No, not exactly," Plimpton replied.

Plimpton's other subjects with Palmer went even less well. When Palmer started to wrap things up, Plimpton knew the clock had already struck twelve. There's always an imbalance of power in these sessions, but it is the writer who gets last licks. How the writer uses those final swings is telling.

> *"Well, how's that for you?" he asked. "That enough?"*
>
> *I looked up from my notes. I wanted to say that I had just a question or so more, if he didn't mind, but I didn't.*
>
> *"Oh, sure," I said. "You've been very kind." I stood up and shuffled my notes together. "Absolutely great." I began backing away. I wanted to shake his hand in gratitude for his time, but Palmer was staring down between his feet. "Great," I said. "Thanks." I backed away around the corner of the locker.*
>
> *I had the quick sense of failure—that I had been accorded valuable time and had not made the best of it.*

It's so good. For starters, you feel like you're there. Also, the writer is vulnerable, as a writer should be (don't you think?). Then the last part, about not making the best use of your time: That just screams at you. It screams at me, I should say.

The U.S. Amateur Four-Ball at the Cricket Club was Will's third USGA event. *Will Wears.* The USGA gives you a money clip with your name engraved on it each time you play. Will's first time in it was at the 2017 Four-Ball, held at Pinehurst. To get in, Will and his partner had to play in a local qualifier, which they did on an Arnold Palmer resort course in Wheeling, West Virginia, right before Labor Day in 2016. More than sixty teams were playing for two spots, and they secured the second one with a 61. Tough, *tough* crowd. On his way back to Baltimore, Will called his grandfather to tell him the news. Arnold was getting near his end but still home in Latrobe. He heard *USGA.* He heard *Pinehurst.* He might have heard *61.* As best as Will could tell, his grandfather said, "That means something." It was the last time they spoke.

In the summer of 2009, Will Wears was about to become a freshman in high school, Anna was a rising seventh-grader, and Peg's marriage to Peter Wears was coming to an end. Peg's mother, Winnie, had died ten years earlier, and Peg had always wished her kids could have known her better. Her father, closing in on eighty, was slowing down but remained active. Arnold was playing golf almost every day, though in a cart. He was still flying his own plane but would not be for much longer. That summer, Peg and the kids moved from Durham to Latrobe, into a house just down the street from her father's. Anna and Will were enrolled in the Latrobe public schools. Will was now a Wildcat, as his mother and grandfather had been. The Wildcats' home course was the Latrobe Country Club. Golf has always been a fall sport in Latrobe—spring is too cold in western Pennsylvania for golf. Will made the starting squad as a freshman. He was already well over six feet. Arnold was often around observing, hands in pockets, wearing a cardigan, offering commentary here and there. Will was jumping right in.

Will played four years of varsity golf and two years of varsity basketball at Latrobe. From there he went to Loyola in Baltimore and played golf all four years there. He spent his college summers in Latrobe, and they turned out to be the final summers of Arnold's life. They talked about everything. Arnold encouraged Will to get himself over to the Tin Lizzy, a taproom in nearby Youngstown. Also a restaurant but, for the purposes of this discussion, a taproom.

"Bumpy, the Tin Lizzy hasn't been that kind of place for thirty years," Will said, using the family nickname for Arnold.

Arnold heard what he wanted to hear. "You should get over there."

On the driving range at Latrobe, Will kept hoping his grandfather would someday unlock the chest and retrieve the secrets. He wondered if Arnold was keeping something from him, even when Will got to the point where he could break 70 at Latrobe as often as not. Over the years, Will realized something: His grandfather *was* giving him his secrets. Arnold was giving him everything he knew and everything he believed. Will got it down to eight principles and three statements.

The Principles

1. The V formed by the left index finger and thumb should be pointing to the right shoulder. The V on the right hand, the same. The grip makes or breaks the golfer.
2. Play the ball back in your stance. Never position the ball ahead of the inside left heel with driver, and play it almost off the right foot with the most lofted clubs.
3. Regarding ball flight: Low is better than high, from driver to

putter. Chip with a putter every time you can. If you can't, hood the face of whatever club you use to chip.

4. Be completely still when over a putt. Lock your eyes on the ball.
5. Do not fan the clubface open on the backswing with any club.
6. Make a slow-motion backswing. The first foot of the backswing cannot be too slow. Build speed gradually. At impact, you should be swinging as hard as you can.
7. When the pressure is on, slow down everything. Feel like you are moving in slow motion.
8. Never make a one-handed finish. It tells your opponents you're off your game.

The Statements

1. "Be completely committed to your shot. Don't let *anything* distract you."
2. "You've got to *make* that golf ball do what you want it to do."
3. "You have to have a system. *Your* system. You have to have a personal style. *Your* style. Once you've got it, don't change anything."

Swing your swing, to use an Arnold phrase. You can take its first cousin anywhere: You do you. Two superpower mantras. They can be.

10

Tradition-*Tradition!*

I HAD ONE MORE PRESS-CREDENTIALED TRIP BEFORE THIS YEAR among the pros wrapped, and that was to the season's last major, the British Open. After that, I went to the Senior British Open, where one of the greats of the game shared wedge-shot insights that had eluded your duffer-at-large for fifty years. I had one more caddie stint, at the City Open in Alpena, Michigan, won by a man who can fish the Upper Peninsula like Hemingway, cook dinner for thirty like Clemenza in *The Godfather*, and shoot 60-something with an endearing smile and an outstretched arm. I gathered twelve pros and twelve ams for one last Shivas, golf on the Cricket Club's Tillinghast course, dinner in front of the walk-in fireplace.

I also had one final teacher willing to go deep with me, on the range and on the course, and one final playing lesson. I'm hopeful it will have staying power, from here to sunset. You're always hoping in this game, and as best as I can tell, the whole thing is one long lesson. If there's one thing I've learned, with sixty-five creeping in, it's that.

I didn't intend to give you so much Arnold, here on these finishing holes. It just happened. Early on—high school years, the 1970s; Grand Funk Railroad and *these fine ladies*, their plan, the rest of it—

Big Jack was my guiding light, and Tom Watson was the thrilling new next thing. Arnie could have been some guy driving past our house in a brown Oldsmobile, waving to my brother and me while we played catch on West Lakewood Street.

Then I saw him—Arnold Palmer, in person!—at that U.S. Open qualifier at the Charlotte Country Club. Eight years later, I interviewed him for the first time, on a driving range at a tournament in suburban Philadelphia. In the ensuing years, he gave me a tour of his plane, Bay Hill inside and out, Latrobe the same. I showed Arnold a chipping club I had invented, and he gave it a thorough tryout on a course out the back door of his casita in the California desert. "I like your club," Arnold said. "There's only one problem with it: What club are you going to take out of the bag to put your club in?" Believe me, I'm not taking *any* of this for granted, Arnold with my club in his hand or anything else. I'm sure I hemmed and hawed and stumbled my way through that first driving-range interview. But it was a start. It's the reporter's job to get the subject in the mood.

That afternoon, I drove—back roads to the Pennsylvania Turnpike to the Jersey Turnpike to the Lincoln Tunnel—from the Chester Valley golf course to the Lion's Rock, a restaurant on the Upper East Side of Manhattan, where Christine and I had our first date. I know what I wore to dinner that night because somebody (Arnold's dentist) kindly sent me a photo of the driving-range interview. Button-down shirt, graduation-gift watch, bright linen tie practically dangling into my reporter's notebook. That first dinner figures in the Arnold pages here in ways that elude logic as life at its loveliest eludes logic.

I have the driving-range photo with Arnold on my desk—and a matchbook from the Lion's Rock. Christine and I have a nonsensical name for it, *Rock de Lion*. Just one of those little secret-language things. The restaurant is long gone but in our minds we can walk in any time and to our table, in the garden, in the back.

I have made the overnight flight to Scotland, England, Ireland, and Northern Ireland dozens of times. My beat-the-jet-lag move is to go straight to a golf course in a rental car. *Hire car*, when I first started going over there.

On this occasion, with the Open at Royal Troon on the West Coast of Scotland, I went straight from Edinburgh International to the wee coastal town of Girvan and its course. (In Scotland, towns and courses share names, and every course has tee times reserved for public play.) On the shoulder of a narrow lane near the Girvan harbor was a beautiful wooden sloop on wooden stilts, and odd bits of fishing net were being pushed by the wind against seawalls. The Girvan course is way off the tourist golf trail. Clubhouse maintenance was casual, and the bunker rakes looked like plastic toys. These are not cited as negatives. (I don't think courses should have bunker rakes at all. While we're at it, let's eliminate the yardage book, too.) The course, per the scorecard, is barely 5,100 yards long. Okay, a short course. But if the yards are good, who cares? Plus, wind. Wind can render any yardage meaningless. Eight of the holes at Girvan are on the Firth of Clyde, a flat body of water leading to the Irish Sea, and those holes will put air in your lungs. On a clear day, you can imagine sailing straight across from Girvan to Ballycastle, in Northern Ireland, sixty miles from Rory McIlroy's boyhood home. A golf course doesn't need eighteen great holes. You remember the holes you play well. If Girvan were an eight-hole course, it would likely be the greatest eight-hole course in the world.

Going up the sixth hole at Girvan with the sea on my right, I saw a man walking with two dogs, no leashes, through wispy beach grass. *Rough*, to golfers, but wispy beach grass to the course walkers. There are always course walkers in Scotland. We nodded hello. The man was wearing running shorts and a T-shirt on a cool afternoon. When I came in, done for the day, we crossed paths again. Without any sort of pre-lude, he said, "Did you want these?" He handed me a green plastic bag with maybe ten gently used golf balls in it.

The first time I went to Israel was in 1968, with my brother and our parents. As we walked across the tarmac from the plane to the ter-minal, several men, black-coated and bearded, dropped to their knees and kissed the ground beneath them. Ben Crenshaw did the same after Justin Leonard holed a bomb on the seventeenth green at the Country Club outside Boston to clinch an American win at the 1999 Ryder Cup. I have never felt a similar urge, in Israel or the British Isles or anywhere else, but there is something extra for me in Scotland. I'm drawn to the country, her people, the simplicity of the golf there. I'm trying to bring that simplicity into every aspect of my golfing life (and my *life* life). My bag, the clubs in it; my downswing, its finish; my scorecard, the num-bers on it; my matches, travel, swing thoughts. There's a whole world in Arnold's Statement No. 3: "Once you've got it, don't change anything." Golf in Scotland, and Scottish golfers, resist change.

The final major Arnold watched was the British Open in 2016, when Henrik Stenson of Sweden pounded away at Royal Troon in Scotland for four straight days. Arnold was home in Latrobe, watching the golf with Will and Tom Ridge, former Army officer in Vietnam, for-mer lower-the-debt governor of Pennsylvania. "I like the way he plays," Arnold said of Stenson. Arnold won the 1962 Open at Troon by six. Stenson won by three. He had it. The next trick is to hold on to it.

The most useful thing I did at the Open at Troon (selfishly speaking) in-volved a visit I made to the Rolex suite along the sixteenth hole. I was try-ing to get myself invited to the pro-am at the Senior Open at Carnoustie, being played the following week, per scheduling custom. Rolex sponsors the event, and a Rolex executive named Arnaud Laborde runs it. I know the gent. To say M. Laborde has savoir faire would be a grand understatement. He motioned for me to join him at his table. Some distance away, Mark Steinberg, the super-agent, was waiting on a plush white leather sofa to see Arnaud. They had, I imagined, actual business to attend. I could have tried to move things along, but it would have been pointless, as M. Laborde is not a man to rush anything.

I had once been down a similar road with Steinberg. Years before Donald Trump was a presidential candidate for the first time, I was interviewing him at Mar-a-Lago, over breakfast. He was hosting an LPGA event at his West Palm Beach course. Steinberg represented Annika Sörenstam then and must have had an appointment to see Trump. He approached our table and Trump said to him, "Mark, you know Michael Bamberger, the publisher of *Sports Illustrated*, the most powerful person in sports." "Yeah, I know Mike," Steinberg said, not joyfully. He had earned his nickname, Dr. No, at least among the *SI* writers I knew. Our interests and his did not align. But he has served his clients well. His players all say that.

Back to the Rolex tent at Royal Troon: It was midafternoon, but Arnaud insisted I eat. No menu was needed. He ordered wine for both of us. It was all delicious. As we visited, Arnaud had short chats with various passersby in various languages. He and I talked about golf in the Olympics, the Ryder Cup, Tom Watson's long association with Rolex. There was a photograph of Watson on a nearby wall, among other Open winners.

The first of Watson's five Open victories came at Carnoustie in 1975, in an eighteen-hole playoff. I was watching at home. It's embedded: Watson in the rain, wearing a wool plaid cap; his beautiful black-haired wife embracing him in victory; the bleak course he had just played for five straight days; the antiquity of the tournament and its traditions. I was smitten by the whole thing. The Open has always been my favorite tournament.

Its winner gets a title from the R&A along with one-year custody of the Claret Jug: the Champion Golfer of the Year. All over the Rolex tent were photos of Open winners cradling the jug.

I must have done okay with Arnaud. Soon after our midafternoon meeting, he invited me to play in the Senior Open pro-am. I knew the drill, having been to the event as a spectator and reporter. I knew the day as one of the special ones on the pro-am circuit.

"You know Gary Player, don't you?" Arnaud asked. He held his wineglass with a casualness I would never attempt.

I have interviewed Player often, played golf with him twice, watched him hold a long plank once, his elbows exposed to a cement walkway.

"I do." I didn't ask why he was asking, although I could guess.

I saw Arnaud a couple more times before the Open concluded. Xander Schauffele won on a dank Sunday night. Two months earlier, he had won the PGA Championship. He had it.

The next morning, I went to the Marks & Spencer in downtown Glasgow and bought a blazer. You can't go to a Rolex event without a blazer. Even I know that.

I arrived at the official tournament digs, the Carnoustie Golf Hotel & Spa. A man eyed me, I thought suspiciously, as I carried my golf bag and suitcase from the car park, through the lobby, and to my second-floor room. But that night I found myself seated next to the fellow at a tournament dinner and learned more. His name (on his engraved calling card) was Sir Rocco Forte. He was an accomplished triathlete (eighty, looked sixty), had the posh accent of a visiting aristocrat on *Downton Abbey*, and owned a string of five-star hotels across Europe. He was watching my arrival, he said, as a student of hotel culture. Getting deeper into the subject, he said the most important employee at a hotel is its housekeeping manager, because a hotel's housekeeping staff has by far the most intimate relationship with its guests, and the manager sets the tone. When a finance executive at our table said in an offhanded way that San Francisco had no good hotels, Sir Rocco looked offended. Not because he owned properties in San Francisco—he didn't—but because the comment was so pretentious.

Jerry Tarde, the longtime editor of *Golf Digest*, sat on the other side of Rocco, and Jerry and I compared notes about our biz in a more glamorous era. (It was Jerry who persuaded George Plimpton to attend the Masters the year Plimpton attempted to join Augusta National—a bit for the ages.) "Well, the hotel business was once glamorous," Sir Rocco said. It was a charming thing to say, even if Rocco's presence alone suggested it could not be true. The people you meet in this game.

Nobody would call Carnoustie glamorous. Not the hotel, not the course, not the town. The hotel is solid and comfortable, decorated in Early, Middle, and Late Old Tom Morris (1821–1908). The town is gray and cramped, with a working high street where you can buy lighting fixtures, pick up a boxed pizza, and get a haircut from a Turkish barber. The course is famously demanding, its reputation cemented by the quality of the winners of the first Opens there: Tommy Armour in 1931, Henry Cotton in '37, Ben Hogan in '53, Gary Player in '68, and Tom Watson in '75. In every photo and write-up from those Opens, the course looks gnarly and the winner seems to have marched through pea-soup haar (Scottish coastal fog) on his way to immortality. My room was above the putting green. Late into the evening, there were senior pros, not ones you might immediately recognize, practicing on it, some of them with their wives beside them. The Senior Open has always been a magnet for dreamers. Bernhard Langer has won it four times and Tom

Watson three, but it's also been won by Bruce Vaughn, a former fire-fighter, and Tom Wargo, a former ironworker.

Across Great Britain and Ireland, many of the big-name courses have multiple clubs attached to them. The Carnoustie Golf Club is connected to the Carnoustie links, as are the Caledonia Golf Club and the Carnoustie Ladies Golf Club. (Caledonia is the Roman Empire name for Scotland.) There is golf for everybody in Carnoustie. There are three eighteen-hole courses in town and a five-hole course that is free to all.

There is nothing snobbish about golf in Carnoustie. My caddie at Carnoustie, Martin, a firefighter from Dundee, was a member of the Carnoustie Golf Club. If you were looking to join, he said, all you had to do was go on the website and fill out an application. Other clubs in town include the Carnoustie Ladies Golf Club, with a charming clubhouse that resembles a cottage, and the Caledonia Golf Club, with a stone clubhouse where anybody can walk in, get lunch, watch golf, and talk golf. There's a wall there filled with caricatures of Open winners, their feet often reduced to little nubs and chins that look like bricks. You can hear the artist winking. There's a club down the road from Carnoustie called Panmure. It does have a reputation for being posh but I played there with a local member who was a retired plumber. The course is surrounded by working farms and, at one end, a caravan park. I hit a drive into the rough in the vicinity of two locals out for a casual evening walk on the course. They marked the location of my ball with a wee stick.

When Updike wrote the short story "Farrell's Caddie," he had his American banker playing the Royal Caledonian Links. I believe Updike was combining elements of Carnoustie and Panmure when he invented the course and its name and when he wrote this: *Farrell would never have walked thirty-six holes a day in America, but here in Scotland golf was not an accessory to life, drawing upon one's marginal energy; it was life, played out of the center of one's being.*

On the taproom wall at the Caledonia Golf Club is a framed letter from Bobby Jones to a Mr. Martin Johnston. The letter's date is rendered thusly:

July
12th,
1933.

The writing is loaded with style, too:

My dear Mr. Johnston:
   I am very grateful indeed to you for sending me the proof of your etching of the Royal & Ancient Golf Club. I think it is a very excellent piece of work. It now occupies a place of honor alongside maps of Old St. Andrews and of my new course in Augusta.

I didn't even know you could use *very* with *excellent* that way.

I looked up Martin Johnston later. He was a working artist in Dundee. One of his etchings of the R&A clubhouse sold at auction in the United States in 2019 for $580. Another one is on display at the Caledonia Golf Club, underneath Jones's letter. Jones's "new course in Augusta" had not yet hosted a Masters tournament. The view Mr. Johnston depicts, across the eighteenth green of the Old Course and to its first tee with the clubhouse behind it, has barely changed. Jack Nicklaus likes to say that Jones had the Old Course in mind when he conceived Augusta National. Most people can't see the connection all these years later. To Nicklaus, it's obvious.

Arnaud from Rolex was the matchmaker for all the pros and their ams at the Senior Open pro-am at Carnoustie, and he put me with . . . Mr. Gary Player. Eighty-eight years old and clear-eyed, dressed impeccably and all in black, the oldest living member of the first generation of global golf stars. Also the most global golf star ever, by far, including Seve Ballesteros and Greg Norman. A man dripping with style in every way. In his speech. (Every sentence is a pronouncement.) In his dress. (Every item is expertly tailored). In his golf swing. (Every swing, in basic shape, looks the same. Draw shot, draw shot, draw shot.) His fitness announces itself with his handshake, the right hand coming at you like a punch. Also, the man has the happy gene. Even when he's railing about something—juiced athletes, hot golf balls, fast-food diets—Gary Player always seems to be having a good time. His life, you could say, is a type of performance art.

Arnold Palmer was drawn to him. He and Winnie traveled to South Africa with Player and his wife, Vivienne, to see their ranch and to see their lives. (The Players had been married for sixty-four years when Vivienne died in 2021.) The Big Three was a real thing, Arnold and Player and Jack Nicklaus attached at the hip in the name of business and in the name of friendship. Barbara and Jack Nicklaus named the fourth of their five children for Gary. As public personalities, the so-called Black Knight and Golden Bear could not be more different. Nicklaus is as contained as Gary Player is gregarious. You can't imagine Jack Nicklaus beginning a pro-am round with this:

"Mike! How are you, man!"

How can you not like being greeted by one of the best golfers ever with *that*?

The other pro in our group was Colin Montgomerie. If Colin Montgomerie devoted himself to broadcast booth commentary, he'd combine the best of both worlds, a color commentator with Peter Alliss's wit and Johnny Miller's insights. But he prefers to play. His am was Neil Donaldson, the captain of the Royal & Ancient Golf Club, a Scotsman and scion of a Scottish timber family going back forever, not that you'd know it. The previous week, during the Open at Royal Troon, he had an intimate view of all the proceedings. He found the winner, Xander Schauffele, to be humble and unassuming, and was struck by how gutted Justin Rose was after finishing two shots behind the winner. Deep on the back nine, Neil saw a focus in Rose's eyes that made him think of a matador in the ring with a bull, ready to kill or be killed. He attempted to console Rose in the players' lounge. Colin told me later that he was struck by Neil's unassuming manner, given his status in business and in golf, and the depth of his insights.

We were on the first tee of one of the great championship courses in the world on a day with the wind down and the sun out. This was not the bleak Carnoustie of yore—the opposite.

"I'll take care of the pars, you take care of the net birdies," Colin said to Neil before the first shot was played. Colin then made a bogey on the first and a bogey on the second. Nobody seemed too worried, not about Monty's golf or anything else.

There was a lot of chat. Player asked Colin, "How many times did you win the Order of Merit?" That is, the European Tour's money list.

"Seven in a row, eight total," Colin said.

"Eight times!" Player said. "That's about how many wives you've had!"

Pros poking at one another—once it was part of the culture. Colin seemed fine with it. Besides, Sarah is only Colin's third wife. She was also Colin's long-standing manager. At Carnoustie, wherever you saw Colin, there was Sarah, a portrait in new-marriage bliss.

Neil asked Gary how many times he had shot his age or better.

"Three thousand seven hundred and twenty-one times!" he said.

That was a new one on me. Other items from the Gary Player set list I knew. The sixteen million air miles he had flown—"a record for an athlete that will never be broken!"—for instance. Later in the round, we heard about the eighteen majors he had won, counting his nine senior majors along with his three British Opens, three wins at Augusta, two PGA Championships, and his victory at the 1965 U.S. Open in a playoff, where he completed his career grand slam before turning thirty. (The next day, Colin Montgomerie, as witty as anybody in golf, said to me, "Usually you hear about the eighteen majors before you get to the first tee.") Player made a familiar claim, that one day all pro golfers will be the size of LeBron James, and they will all be able to drive the first green at Augusta. It's some picture.

This, too, came out of Player's regular rotation, but I think it's important—I think it gets to the core of the man: "I envy the ease with which Tiger Woods has been able to travel the world. His equipment. The science available to him about nutrition and exercise. But I wouldn't trade what he has for what we had for all the money in the world."

We. The Big Three, along with Billy Casper, Lee Trevino, Raymond Floyd, Tom Weiskopf, Tom Watson, Hale Irwin, Hubert Green, Tony Jacklin, and other greatest-generation golfers from the 1960s and '70s he didn't need to name. Gary Player was part of a wandering tribe, golfers traveling the world and especially the United States, trying to bash in one another's heads for money and glory, going to the bar together when it was all over. I was lucky to catch some of that era, and to get to know many of its stars.

The length and reach of Player's life in golf is staggering. He sought swing advice from Ben Hogan, who was born in 1912. At his first Open Championship, in 1956, he and Henry Cotton, born in 1907, both finished in the top ten. At Augusta each April, he visited with Bobby Jones, who was born in 1902. When he cites any of those three legends in conversation, he's not name-dropping. He's telling you about people he knew well.

Gary Player, eighty-eight, scorer's tent, Senior Open pro-am, Carnoustie Golf Links.

Player's admiration for Jones was profound. Hogan once asked Player how much he was practicing. "Constantly," Player said. (Probably the only answer that could land with Hogan.) Sir Henry Cotton, winner of three Opens, told Player that a golfer's hands cannot be too strong. Player spent the rest of his career trying to improve his hand strength.

Player brought up the subject of hand strength as we were walking down the fifteenth hole. He told Martin, my firefighter caddie and a strong young man, that he would pay him two hundred pounds if he could hold two golf clubs shoulder-high horizontally while weaving the shafts through three fingers of one hand. Martin did not collect. Player did it with ease. All the while, three kids from Carnoustie, all golfers, had casually attached themselves to our group without any sort of parental involvement. Colin Montgomerie was struck by the depth of the questions they were asking Player, but also how unusually engaged Player was with the kids.

Gary Player won all those majors—I'll say nine but you say whatever you wish—hitting pretty much all draw shots. At the pro-am at Carnoustie, Player hit every last shot with a hook stance, hook path, and hook spin. Every drive, every putt, every everything. I had seen it before but had never paid so much attention to it.

On the fourteenth hole, a short and very excellent par-5, Gary had about forty yards for his third shot from the right side of the fairway. He couldn't see much of the flagstick from where he was because of a bunker protecting the front right of the green. Colin was standing on it. Player asked Monty for the distance from the bunker to the pin. "Ten paces," Monty said. Gary Player then hit a low, hooded, drawing wedge to a firm green that I would consider one of the most memorable shots I have ever seen. It finished hole-high. It was beautiful. Gary Player has spent his life playing similar shots.

In my own ridiculous golf (if you can stand this again), I try to hit fades with the long clubs and draws with the short ones. Gary Player, taking an active interest in my golf, wanted *every swing* with *every club* to *come from the inside*. I have been told this before. Mike Donald has said it to me many times. But on some level, I must not have accepted it. For a reason I cannot articulate, the wedge shot Player hit into fourteen was a trip switch for me.

On eighteen, I hit a tee shot with a driver that was a low, running from-the-inside draw shot that went forever. I almost made my short putt for par.

The next morning, as Player was leaving, I saw him at the front door of the hotel. A couple came over to talk to him and he asked, "How long have you been married?"

"Fifteen years," the husband said.

"It's a record!" Player said.

He turned to me and said, "Mike, man, that was so much fun yesterday! The way you hit those shots the last few holes—you rotated, your hands followed. It was like a mirage!"

During our round, Gary talked some about his girlfriend, his first since his wife had died. He described his lady friend most vividly. She was in her eighties, Jewish, from New York, a person who loved to golf, fish, read, work, and travel. "And she has her own money!" Gary said. You could imagine them as a couple. Making his exit from Carnoustie, Gary Player looked like a movie star, right down to his black slip-on boots, the kind the young people in lower Manhattan wear, and his sharp black suit.

I thanked him for the lesson he had given me and said, "Not that you need it, but good luck with your new lady friend."

Gary Player laughed, shook my hand, and said, "Mazel tov!"

Later, on my way back to Edinburgh for the flight home, I stopped in St. Andrews on the off chance that I could find a slot to play. There was a four o'clock tee time on the Eden Course. I played with two local kids named Apostolos and Comhghall, an Irish name pronounced "Cole." They were in high school and new to golf. Comhghall's mother writes for a Dundee newspaper, *The Courier*. Comhghall's father works at the University of St. Andrews. Apostolos's parents both work at the university, too.

"How far do you guys live from here?"

"Forty-five minutes," Apostolos said.

He was born in Belfast and his parents were born in Greece. He speaks fluent Greek and English.

If you go forty-five minutes from St. Andrews in any direction, you are either far at sea or deep in rural Fife.

"Forty-five minutes—who does the driving?" They were too young to drive.

"No, walking," Apostolos said.

Eden is a joyride, especially the front nine. I was playing beyond well until my tee shot on fourteen, which I hit into the weeds. I was using one of the balls given to me by the dog walker at Girvan. The boys were insistent that the ball could not be left behind. They got on their stomachs and fished it out. When I told them I couldn't imagine American kids making such an effort, they had no idea what I was talking about. They played every hole into the bottom of the cup, nothing ever given. There was no casual anything. When Apostolos hit a ball O.B. late in the round, he hiked back to the tee to play the shot again. The boys were playing a stroke-play match and painstakingly counted up their shots when they were done: Apostolos 103, Comhghall 102.

Apostolos, left; Comhghall, right. Eden Golf Course, St. Andrews, Scotland.

My friend Ryan French invited me to caddie for him at the fifty-seventh playing of the City Open in Alpena, Michigan. He has lived in Alpena all his life (with a few notable gaps) and he and his wife, Stephanie, are raising their daughter and son there. He grew up in a house on the public course in Alpena, and you could say he grew up on the course, period. Alpena is a remote town on Lake Huron on the Upper Peninsula, and it's hockey country. A lot of the big strong kids in Alpena, like Ryan, were raised on hockey in winter and golf in summer. With the bounce off the lake, the reflected light, you can play golf in July and August past nine p.m. It's almost like being in Scotland.

My plan was to fly from Philadelphia to Detroit and then make the four-hour drive to Alpena. But on the day I was booked to fly out, there were thunderstorms across the East Coast and the Midwest, and both airports were a mess of delayed and canceled flights. I talked myself into making the drive instead. It's twelve hours by car if you don't stop. I wouldn't recommend doing it in a day, but I had no choice. Caddie duty called.

I arrived at the Holiday Inn in downtown Alpena the night before the first round and to a care package. There were all manner of treats, including a bag of caramel popcorn and assorted teas, delivered by Ryan and Stephanie. My arrival package included a field guide to animal tracks in the Midwest—Ryan's maternal grandfather was an Upper Peninsula outdoorsman and an outdoor writer who livened up his stew with squirrel brain.

The following morning, Ryan and I were raring to go. The City Open is a two-day event, one round on the city course, one round at the country club, as the Alpena golfers described the two venues. Ryan is a big fella with a fast, hefty swing and a lot of athleticism.

I believe I helped save him one shot over the course of two days. On the par-4 second hole at the city course, the public Alpena Golf Club, Ryan had driven it into a dense grove of trees (and in the general direction of his childhood home). For his second shot, he saw an escape window out of this forest and to the green. I didn't see even a letter slot. I suggested he punch out, pitch on, try to make a putt for par, and that was what he did. Ryan did the work. I just helped him see another path to the bottom of the hole.

When Ryan was young, the best golfer in town was a man named Bill Peterson, owner of a restaurant near the Alpena course called Twin Acres by nongolfers and the Nineteenth Hole by those who played. On Mondays, kids in town could use the range and play a four-hole loop without charge. Mr. Peterson was often on the real-grass practice tee offering free lessons. He stressed one thing: Come from the inside, come from the inside, come from the inside. For the hockey players in town, that move came naturally. Bill Peterson—a hockey player, a cook, and an outdoorsman—won the City Open nineteen times. At the fifty-seventh City Open, his son Erik—a hockey player, a cook, and an outdoorsman—was the first-round leader.

That night, Ryan, Stephanie, their kids, and a few others went for dinner at the Nineteenth Hole. Ryan's mother was there, as was Ryan's friend Mark Baldwin, a touring pro who has spent years trying to make it to the PGA Tour. Between them, Ryan and his mother knew half the people eating in the restaurant on a busy Saturday night. Bill Peterson sat with us. Erik was the cook. When Erik and his older brother were young, their father would flood the backyard to create a hockey rink. They lived on seven acres. Erik, a left-handed golfer (as many hockey players are), created an informal backyard driving range. As a teenager, he could drive a golf ball 320 yards and onto a neighbor's property. He learned early to swing fast and cook fast. On Friday nights during Lent, the restaurant serves a hundred pounds of walleye. You can't get the dinners out too fast.

The day after our dinner, Erik won the City Open for the third time. He had his wife, daughters, and the City Open trophy in his burly arms and a beaming smile on his bearded face.

There's something about this Erik Peterson. He exudes a certain ease about who he is and how he lives. Erik briefly played minor-league pro hockey after high school and in every amateur league there was to play in on the Upper Peninsula. "You'd skate by the other team's bench and scream at 'em, 'Hey, so-and-so did your sister last night.' And they'd get so mad and come out hacking, and some guy would wind up in the penalty box, and then you'd score on the power play. Scored a bunch of goals that way." He was laughing at the memory.

Erik's wife, Heather, was a few years behind him in school. One summer night when they were both in their twenties, Heather, with friends, went out to a 170-acre hunting and fishing camp on the Thunder Bay River that the Peterson family had owned for decades, in the country and far from town. On this Cinco de Mayo evening, a friend of Erik's was playing an acoustic guitar. There was a bonfire. There was tequila. Erik hopped on a Yamaha four-wheeler, about to go out for an evening ride.

"You wanna come?" he asked Heather.

Heather climbed into the saddle behind him, put her arms around his waist, and, before the night was out, told him, "You're the one."

Erik's life goes by the seasons. Golf is a summer game. In spring and fall, he's a fly-rod-fishing guide in Michigan, Arkansas, and Alaska. Erik cooks what the clients catch. In his phone he has numbers for a network of camps, lodges, boats, and launches. He owns tackle for every occasion. He's a master of the outdoor grill, the indoor fireplace, and the top shelf of the bar, with its Scotch bottles and other brown spirits. He can tell fishing stories late into the night and have the gang up predawn for a cooked breakfast. This is not a hobby. "We're on the water," Erik told me, "a hundred and fifty days a year." That still leaves a lot of days for golf, and a lot of nights over the stove at the Twin Acres–Nineteenth Hole. It's a half-mile from the restaurant's kitchen to the first tee at the Alpena course.

Ryan French and I first met when we were working for a noble and short-lived experiment in golf journalism called the Fire Pit Collective. We both have a long-standing interest in golfers who are looking for a tour they can call their own, looking for a way to stay in the game. We're interested in the game's lifers, regardless of age. My friend Mike Donald. His friend Mark Baldwin. A tall, lean young man we both know named Rasmey Kong, whom I have seen often over the years hitting off a mat and under the lights at a range in South Florida, his diminutive father, Soweth, born in Cambodia, crouched beside him. They learned the swing by going to a Barnes & Noble and reading the instruction books there. Buying them was out of the question. Ryan and I both find these kinds of lives, rooted in the American dream, endlessly inspiring.

At the Fire Pit Collective, Ryan and I worked with a former club pro named Laz Versalles. Laz's uncle was Zorro Versalles, born in Cuba as Zoilo, the first non-American to win an MVP award in baseball, which he did in 1965 as a shortstop for the Minnesota Twins. Laz grew up in Minneapolis, and his surname was like a passport to the city and its suburbs, its golf course and its baseball temples, first the Met and, after its demise, the Metrodome. Laz has had a lifelong interest in immigration, migration, race relations, and the intersection of race and sports. Aided and abetted by Fire Pit money and people, Laz made a series of documentaries called *Migrations*, about Black men and women leaving the South for Philadelphia, Los Angeles, and other cities and discovering golf. Laz shared with me a rough cut of an episode about the Black golf experience in Detroit.

Early on, you see and hear a man, maybe in his seventies, with a Southern accent, and he's talking to himself as he gets into a golf cart: "What day is great for golf? Every day that ends in *y*!" The man was identified as Mr. J. B. Brown, formerly of unincorporated Birmingham, Alabama, later a winner of the Detroit Open in its senior division. He cackled to himself at his little joke as if he had never told it before. He jumped off the screen at me, everything about him, starting with the tee behind his right ear.

Laz had his number, and I called Mr. Brown, told him about *Tour '24: Do the Loco-Motion.*

Do you do any teaching?

"Yeah, man."

Could I come see you?

"Sure."

Do you have a regular range?

"I've got a bunch of 'em."

After Alpena, I drove to Detroit on a hazy August night and got a hotel room. I figured I'd see Mr. Brown in the morning, have my lesson, drive on home.

He had one range in mind, and then he switched it to another. I was early and he was already in the parking lot. He said, "I like somebody who's early. Sometimes I'll go to teach a friend's kid or something, and they're late. But if you want to be there, why would you be late?"

Can I leave it at that for now, like a ball sitting on a tee, waiting to be hit? For now, just remember the name, please: Mr. J. B. Brown.

If *Tour '24* had a calendar, it would have shown two final events after Alpena, both pro-ams, one in September after Labor Day, the other in November after Election Day. I was invited to the September event, a Champions Tour event at Pebble Beach. (Yes, actually invited, and yes, at Pebble Beach!) The other was the Shivas, my little fall golfing get-together at my home course, Philadelphia Cricket. Over the years, various pros have played in it, but never in a pro-am format until Shivas '24.

I would say the September event at Pebble, the PURE Insurance Championship, is one of the best pro-ams in golf. You're promised one round at Pebble Beach and another at Spyglass Hill. If you make the cut, you play in the tournament's third and final round, on a Sunday at Pebble. A serious incentive. Almost every pro in the field is a name you know.

On my way to the first tee of the first round at Pebble, I saw Billy Andrade. I have known Billy a long time. After I helped him with a speech some years ago, he put me on his All-Time Favorite Jews list, south of Sandy Koufax and Larry David but safely in the top ten. (Billy is a baseball guy. Baseball fans love lists.) We were going in opposite directions. Billy stopped and I stopped and he offered me some advice: *Breathe.*

As a one-word swing tip, it's now in my top ten. It's in my top one. You can take it to your grave, if you like. I plan to.

No other tournament has a format like this PURE event. Every amateur has an amateur partner. The tournament director, Steve John, does the matchmaking. My partner was a retired beer distributor named Geoff Couch, excellent guy, good stick. Steve knows us both, but I did not know Geoff. We met at an outdoor pre-tournament pro-am party where there was a woodburning pizza oven. Vijay Singh was nearby.

I know Vijay, at least a little.

"Vijay, can I ask you one swing question?"

"Not now," he said in his dismissive way.

I've been playing cat and mouse with Vijay for more than thirty years. He has no use for reporters but sometimes half tolerates me because when I first met him, I was a caddie on the European tour for Peter Teravainen, an American who lived in Singapore. Vijay and Peter played practice rounds together. They were friends and their wives were friends.

I said, "Vijay, if not now, when?"

He half-nodded his assent.

I mentioned his evening session on the range at Carnoustie during the British Senior Open two months earlier. He seemed to know immediately what evening I meant, which is amazing, because he's had so many evening sessions on so many ranges.

"My transition," he said.

Maybe that's what he always says in response to that question. Anyway, it was a useful answer. Among my swing problems, my own transition is high on the list, and I'm sure I don't focus on it enough.

Geoff Couch and I compared golf and life notes at this pro-am party.* We had one senior pro assigned to us for the first round (Steve Flesch), another for the second (Kirk Triplett), and we would get a third if we made the cut. Each foursome comprised a senior pro, two ams, and a young golfer from one of the 150 First Tee programs across the United States. Geoff and I had one First Tee golfer assigned to us for the first round, another for the second, and we would get a third if we made the cut. There were seventy-eight First Tee golfers in the field, seventy-eight senior pros, and seventy-eight two-person amateur teams. (The kids paid for nothing and earned their way to Pebble by way of essay writing, their play, and interviews.) Ten teams, from the seventy-eight two-player am teams, would make the cut and get back to Pebble on Sunday. Ties for tenth would play off by a match of cards. Such a creative way to put on a tournament.

As I did in February when I caddied for Fred Perpall in the AT&T Pro-Am, I stayed with Sam and Betsy Reeves in their house off 17-Mile Drive. Sam was now ninety and still working on . . . everything, including his putting. Sam and Betsy had a raft of people at the house for the tournament—ams, pros, spouses, Fred Couples's caddie—and the general consensus was that your two-person team had to be at least 18 under for the two rounds to make it to the third. That score might sound absurdly low, but the event was designed for absurdly low. Each day, your foursome was a team producing one score per hole. The amateurs had handicaps.

---

* At the party, Mark O'Meara announced his retirement from professional golf. He won the 1979 California State Amateur at Pebble Beach and five Bing Crosby/AT&T tournaments—six if you count the Pebble pro-am title he won with his father. Later, I mentioned to Mark that Chuck Will, the CBS golf director, told his wife he wanted his ashes distributed at Pebble Beach. "I've told my wife the same thing!" Mark said, with notable good cheer.

(I was getting twelve strokes, and Geoff was getting one.) Any stroke hole where an am made a par was a birdie on the team scorecard. The pros would make a lot of birdies. The First Tee kids didn't get shots, but they were good golfers—they'd probably make some birdies. If, as a foursome, you made nine pars and nine birdies in one round, you were nine under. You weren't out of it. Do it a second day and you'd be eighteen under and you'd have a chance, a chance to play on Sunday at Pebble.

You might be tempted to say: *Yo, Mike, suddenly you're all excited about the competition part in one of these pro-ams?*

Well, that was then. In the PURE, you were playing for something. You were playing for your partner, and for you and your partner to get to Sunday and back to Pebble. This felt like real golf to me from the get-go. Real golf to me is when your golf matters, when you're playing for keeps, when someone sees you walking to the first tee, stops you, and reminds you to breathe.

You might recall Jason Snow, the kid I met in February at the Pacific Grove muni during the AT&T pro-am. We played the eighteenth hole almost at night, with an unexpected third, Chris Wagenseller, the Pebble Beach caddie. Jason told Wags about his dream to become a Pebble Beach caddie. Maybe it was only psychic help, but Wags opened a door for Jason in some manner. Now, a half-year later, Jason was a Pebble Beach caddie. I asked Jason if he wanted to caddie for me in this pro-am, and he did. He was still sleeping in his car. He was still taking classes at Chico State.

As a caddie, Jason was unpredictable. He left one of my clubs on the range, for instance. He talked incessantly. (I prefer quiet and all twelve of my clubs accounted for.) But he knows golf. He breathes golf. The game is at the core of his life. He understood what I was trying to do with each shot. He cared as much as I did. He was skillful not only at reading putts but reading chip shots, pitch shots, bunker shots, wind strength and direction, my mood. The off moments were the off moments. When I asked Jason if I needed to reload after I shoved one wide and right at Pebble, he said, "No, that's fine." The ball was deep in some guy's backyard. But it really didn't matter. My job was to make pars on my stroke holes, and Jason was helping me do it. You're not making par from some guy's backyard.

Annesley MacFarlane, Sam and Betsy's daughter, was staying at her parents' house and playing in the tournament. (She and her father, as partners, won it on one occasion.) Fred Couples and his wife, Suzanne, were staying in the house. Fred's caddie, George. Jay Haas and his wife, Jan. Other people were coming and going. Sam showed me to my room off the kitchen with twin beds in it and said, "It's a little dodgy, but it should do."

Fred is a listener. He'll talk, but he'd rather listen, and he can listen in more than one direction at the same time. If the conversation to his left is about modern art and scoring at Spyglass is to his right, he can stay engaged in both. Conversation comes to him.

One night I was across the table from Fred, and not directly across, talking to Betsy Reeves about the Bon Marché department store in downtown Asheville, North Carolina, a store she knew going back to the late 1930s through the '40s and into the '50s. Betsy said playfully that she sometimes had the thought that if things did not work out for Sam as a cotton merchant, she could get a job at the Bon Marché. *The Bon.* Sam and Betsy were married in Asheville in 1958 and before long had four children, all girls. Private cooks and the rest all came much later.

"What department?" I asked. People always remember their childhood department stores. We had one in Patchogue called the Bee Hive, the only store on Main Street with an escalator.

"Oh, let me think," Mrs. Reeves said. "Maybe women's gloves."

"The Bon Marché," Fred said out of nowhere. "We had one in Seattle."

That's how it went, for five straight nights.

Billy Andrade and his one-word (*breathe*) swing tip: I used it on the first at Pebble and made a . . . tap-in par! A birdie on the card. We were off and running. Geoff and I were playing with Steve Flesch, a feisty left-hander, newly remarried and on his honeymoon. Our First Tee player, Olivia Braun, was a high school sophomore from Aberdeen, South Dakota, pushing her bag on a trolley (all the kids were), making athletic swings and playing some beautiful ready golf. She made a mess of one hole, started to cry, saw her mother and grandparents in the gallery, collected herself, and made a bounce-back natural birdie. Geoff, in his early sixties, could hit it forever. He grew up in St. Louis. His father worked for Anheuser-Busch and died when Geoff was eleven. Dow Finsterwald, winner of the 1958 PGA Championship, knew Geoff's father and arranged for Geoff to come to Cherry Hills in Denver to join him for nine holes with Arnold Palmer. This was in the summer of 1973, a few months after Arnold had won the Bob Hope pro-am. Cherry Hills was where Arnold won his U.S. Open. Geoff was smitten by Arnold. We both knew the feeling.

We were playing loose, fun golf. The whole foursome was. We were having a ball. Geoff made a 4-for-3 on 14, a par-5 and the only hole all day where he stroked. He hit a beautiful third shot on the par-5 eighteenth and made the putt for a closing birdie. Olivia made a mile of putts. Steve shot a honeymoon 70. We had a best-ball score of . . . 60! There were lower scores, but not many. Par at Pebble is 72. We were twelve under and looking good.

Spyglass the next day was long, wet, and difficult. Our pro, Kirk Triplett, was terrific. Our First Tee kid had a lot of skill and clubhead speed and a lot of as-seen-on-TV mannerisms. We could get nothing going (as tournament golfers in distress have said forever). Geoff had some errant shots on our last hole. Kirk made a bogey 5 and so did the kid. I had a four-footer for 5, with a stroke. If I could make it, we would finish our thirty-six holes at nineteen under. We thought that was a good number. Jason read my putt. It was a hook putt if I went lefty with my two-way putter. I went for the hook putt, made the stroke of my life, and in it went. We had finished early. We looked at the scores. We assessed the weather. At nineteen, we had a chance. The waiting game began.

We knew before the soup course was served: nineteen under wasn't under enough. There were twelve scores at twenty under or better, so two of the twenty-under teams didn't make it to Sunday at Pebble, losing out on a match of cards.

Honestly-honestly-honestly: I was not disappointed. First of all, we had absolutely tried our best. What more *can* you do? Of course there were shots thrown away, just wasted. But what can you do? Those chances are gone. When Geoff and I compared notes, we said the same thing: We had been lucky in every aspect of our golfing lives, right up to and including the days we had just spent together. The pro-am party on Tuesday. A round at Cypress Point on Wednesday. A practice round at Pebble on Thursday. The incredible round at Pebble in the sunshine with Steve and Olivia on Friday. And then we tried our best at Spyglass on Saturday and it wasn't enough. That's golf. You get one chance to pick the right club, choose the right line, make the right swing. But what we had experienced was an embarrassment of riches, in a long line of them.

"There are gonna be guys playing Pebble on Sunday who need it more than we do," I said to Geoff by phone on Saturday night.

"Absolutely," Geoff said.

By tradition, a full field for the Shivas, my little fall golfing get-together, was eighteen players in six threesomes, with gross and net winners duly feted. We also had something called the striped-ball competition. (Pronounced *stry*-pid, nodding to the way old fishermen on Martha's Vineyard pronounced *striped bass*.) Each threesome, as a team, was given a ball with a stripe on it. Each player in each threesome was to use the striped ball on any six holes but on not more than six. At the end of the round, your threesome would turn in an eighteen-hole striped-ball score to the committee, provided the ball made it home. For prizes, each player on the winning threesome would receive a striped tie or a pair of striped socks. The striped-ball competition created a lot of intra-threesome camaraderie and some tsuris. There was always a lively discussion at dinner about striped-ball strategy and errant shots with "the striper." I note, should this write-up ever serve as an official history of the Shivas, that in its first year, 1990, we had the concept but striped balls came later. The ball that first year was an X-out orange Top Flite, the official ball of duffers around the world. Some consider any orange golf ball to be déclassé. The thrift implied by using an X-out—a factory reject typically due to paint imperfections—as a tournament ball speaks for itself. There were complaints to the committee. I was the committee. I was shamed into upgrading to a ball with higher status. (Well, that would be any ball.) We switched to out-of-the-box white Titleists with a decidedly imperfect hand-drawn stripe around each ball's equator.

I decided to make Shivas '24 the event's finale. "I've heard that before," my friend Bob Warner said. Bob is a retired newspaper reporter and he played in them all. Bob's wife, Jeannie, played one year. Their daughter, Annie, was the flower girl when Christine and I got married a week after the inaugural Shivas, and now she is a trauma surgeon. (Also an obsessive golfer.) I understood Bob's inference, but I was sure. It had been a good run. It was time.

Over the years, a lot of pros have been invited to the Shivas, Arnold Palmer among them, and a good number have played. We've had after-dinner remarks offered by various golf-to-the-bone people, including writer friends, Michael M. Thomas, James W. Finegan, and Joseph O'Neill among them. For this swan-song Shivas—nodding to George Plimpton's *The Bogey Man* and his pro-am struggles—I decided to make the event a pro-am. My plan was to get twelve teams, with one pro and one am per team. For the striped-ball competition, the pro would use the striper for nine holes and the am for nine. I invited Mike Donald to play as my partner. He had won the event, the gross portion, before. I invited Jim Herman, a longtime tour player and a former gross winner. Both said yes. Jim's am was the Cricket Club's director of grounds. We had two pros from the Philadelphia Cricket Club and pros from other clubs in greater Philadelphia, the golf capital of the world.

Getting a dozen pros and a dozen ams to commit to golf in the Northeast in mid-November is about as easy as herding goldfish, but it all worked out. On the am side, and in the event's tradition, a half-dozen of us came out of the typing trades. The Shivas pays homage to the Scottish golf teacher Shivas Irons and his creator, the writer-philosopher Michael Murphy, alive and well and in his early nineties, living in Northern California and engaged in the world. I consider it a privilege that I can call Mike and ask him most anything. I once asked him if playing golf was a waste of time. "Absolutely not," he said. That was good enough for me.

When I was thinking about and later planning Shivas '24, the presidential campaigns were in full swing. In their late-June debate, Joe Biden claimed he played to a 6-handicap when he was vice president, and Donald Trump claimed to have won two recent club championships. (Memo to both: Oh, please.) Three weeks before the election, Trump went to the Arnold Palmer Regional Airport in Latrobe, near Pittsburgh, for a rally. Trump began his remarks with a twelve-minute riff on Arnold, starting with the Palmer family's hardscrabble life in Latrobe when Arnold was a boy and ending with why Arnold was called The King, relating it to Arnold's emergence from various club-house showers. "This is a guy who was all man," Trump told the crowd. On *The Daily Show* on Comedy Central, Jon Stewart fact-checked the claim: "He was actually half man, half lemonade."

Later, I asked Will Wears what he thought it meant when people called his grandfather The King.

"The king of golf," Will said. "He helped put the British Open on the map for American golfers. He helped make the Masters the Masters. He put the Masters on TV. He put *golf* on TV. He built dozens of courses, encouraged so many people to play. So to hear him be reduced to a drink, or to be known for supposedly having a big dick, that's not Arnold at all. He was all about golf and people enjoying golf."

We played the Shivas on a Thursday in mid-November. The day was cool, still, and gray. The course was firm, and we had the leaf rule in effect, but nobody needed it. We went off in six foursomes at fifteen-minute intervals, all walkers, playing no-wait golf. The day was all about golf and people enjoying golf.

Mike Donald and I played in the last foursome, off at high noon. We have had many great experiences together. Mike and I were once in Arnold's office at Bay Hill, and Arnold introduced Mike to Amy, the younger of his two daughters. Arnold said, "Mike and I played the tour together." It was a stretch—in the 1980s, Mike was trying to find a secure home on the PGA Tour, often driving from one event to the next, and Arnold was a legend in his fifties who dropped in now and again, arriving in his own plane. It was a comment designed to make Mike feel good, and it did.

I was the captain of our striped-ball usage. My ninth and last hole with the striper came on the fourteenth. The Tillinghast course at Philadelphia Cricket wraps up with four demanding holes, and there is O.B. right on each of them. I was relieved to be done.

"You're striping from here to the house," I said to Mike on our way to the fifteenth tee, handing him the striped Titleist. I was borrowing one of his phrases. A pro is always trying to get to the house. Get to the house at a certain number. There is something thrilling about an am playing this-counts golf with a pro, especially one as accomplished as Mike. In select company, Mike sometimes say, "Do you know how good you have to be to miss two hundred and fifty-one cuts?"

Striping all the way, Mike played the final four holes in one over, and we shot a striped-ball 79. Given that I shot 90 on my own ball (with a three-putt on the last), I thought our score was pretty good. But of the twelve teams, six shot better than 79, and one shot a striped-ball 70. Steve the am and Mark the pro collected their striped socks at dinner.

Christine dropped in briefly to help with prize distribution. We didn't always have a clubhouse dinner. There were years when the Shivas after-party was at our home, sometimes as a stag event, sometimes as a coed night. Christine was game for all of it. She doesn't play, but she has walked many courses with me, and in some of our books on Scotland I have uncovered dried wildflowers that she placed between pages.

Sunset in Philadelphia in mid-November is well before five, and the night was cold when Christine arrived at the Cricket Club and joined us in the Tillinghast Room. We had one long table in front of a wood-burning fireplace, the table set for twenty-four men. Christine liked the room. I announced the winners and Christine handed out the prizes, curtsied in response to a round of applause for her role in Shivas nights present and past, and went off to a dinner of her own.

Jim Herman shot the low score of the day, 72. Jim is in his late forties and has made an excellent living as a touring pro by driving it in the fairway and playing to the center of greens with a long series of baby draws. He had a stock-in-trade shot, and he was smart enough to stick with it. He won three times on the PGA Tour, each time by a shot. One of his wins came on a Donald Ross course in Greensboro, North Carolina. Jim loves old golf courses and has a genuine appreciation for the Cricket Club and for Tillinghast. His Shivas title did not come with a payday, but it did get him stewardship of the Shivas artwork, the framed 1930 black-and-white photograph of one of golf's great clubhouses, the R&A fortress behind the first tee of the Old Course.

Jim made a few brief remarks about his day, the course, the challenges of the striped-ball competition. Many touring pros, understandably, would not be drawn to a day of golf with no prize money, where the only rewards are golf, dinner, and camaraderie. Jim (of course) would not be among them. He told me later, "At every level I have played, golf has given me joy. Amateur golf and college golf. Working as an assistant pro, competing as a touring pro. Playing in the Shivas. The stakes don't matter: Golf brings you moments of pure joy." The Shivas artwork is above a bookshelf in his office at his home in Telford, Pennsylvania, beyond the Philadelphia suburbs, where there are still plenty of Mennonite farmers. Jim's wife, Carolyn, grew up there and went to a Mennonite school that the two Herman children attend. The school has a coed golf team and Jim is its coach.

The Shivas Trophy is the night's grand prize, and yes, feel free to insert air quotes. Choosing its winner weighs on the committee all through the day and into the night. Per the rule sheet, it is awarded to the golfer who shoots the lowest score after his UGH (usual game handicap) is subtracted from his gross score. The relationship between a player's normal handicap and his UGH is willfully vague. In the end, the Shivas Trophy goes to the golfer who, *all things considered*, got the most out of his game on that day. At Shivas '24, one of the pros in the field, David Clark from Pine Valley, shot 74. Like a lot of club pros, David doesn't get to play nearly as much golf as he wishes, and he had never played in the Shivas or at the Cricket Club. When he fell into golf, he was an eighth-grader in Middletown, Rhode Island, picking the range and cleaning clubs at a Seth Raynor course, and he approaches the sport with a no-fuss manner that typifies Rhodey golf. There were other worthy contenders, both amateur and professional, but David's 74, all things considered, carried the day. Christine handed him his trophy and David beamed. It's always a good feeling, to get a lot out of your game.

David knew and admired two golf people—the writer Jim Finegan and Fred Anton, a coffee-shop golf-and-life philosopher—who shaped my life immeasurably. After the Shivas, David told me how, whenever he saw either of them, he was almost bowled over by their love of golf. He could see it in their eyes. He talked about his Shivas foursome and how they all encouraged each other. "An encouraging word goes a long way," David said. How true is that? Everybody needs encouragement.

Over the course of our dinner, some of the participants spoke. They talked about how they got started in golf, the people who shaped them, what golf meant to them. It was moving to hear the club pros at the table express appreciation for their careers, helping people enjoy the game, despite the struggle that golf imposes on every last person who plays. They were, these gathered club pros, a band of brothers. They teach. They run tournaments. They get the right club in the hands of the right golfer. They explain golf's rules and customs. They're there when you break 90 for the first time, should you ever be so fortunate. I'm always describing the touring pros as high priests, because they do a difficult thing at such a high level, and we are understandably mesmerized by their skill. But the club pro *serves* the game and the people who play it. The club pro, the golf teacher, perpetuates the game. I'm thinking now of what Jerry Robison at the Texarkana course did for Bill Rogers (British Open winner, later a club pro) and Conan Sanders (Army officer, later the head pro at the Augusta muni) and what those two did for others.

The youngest Shivas contestant was my colleague James Colgan, age twenty-seven. James is a talented writer, podcaster, and video personality for Golf.com. (These young media people wear so many visors.) He's a big, strong kid, half-goofy, half-earnest, often sporting a fresh haircut straight out of 1958. James stood, as some others did, when he made his remarks at dinner. He told the group about the Masters tradition by which reporters covering the tournament can put their name in a lottery to play the course on the Monday after the tournament, and how, on his fourth attempt, he was chosen. He described the experience with detectable awe: the locker room, his caddie, the second shot over the pond at fifteen, getting up and down for a birdie. The room was so silent you could hear the pops from the burning logs. You could also see thought balloons rising above some of his fellow Shivas contestants: *Holy shit, kid got to play Augusta.* When the night was over, the writer Jaime Diaz said to James, "Keep going." I've heard Tiger Woods say the same thing to young players: Keep going, keep at it. What else is there to do? If you love it, you will.

Jaime, in his early seventies, was the oldest person at the table. Jaime (*HI*-me) and I were colleagues at *Sports Illustrated*, and a few weeks before the Shivas we had played in the same group at a seventy-fifth-anniversary celebration for the magazine. Our former boss Mark Mulvoy arranged the golf and joined us for a few holes. It was Mulvoy (you may recall) who helped Plimpton set up his West Coast pro-am golf in 1966. Jaime grew up in San Francisco and saw Plimpton's Pebble Beach pro—mournful Bob Bruno—in person in the 1960s. Jaime devoured *The Bogey Man* as a young reader and met Plimpton a few times as a grown man. Jaime was drawn to Plimpton's playful spirit and enduring curiosity. Jaime, as golfer and person, is loaded with those same qualities. He's always on the prowl for something new and useful while never losing track of how he got where he is. He wears these old FootJoy street shoes, a split-toe model the company no longer makes, and maintains them beautifully.

Jaime loves *Golf in the Kingdom* for the same reason so many of us do. It captures the game's elusive smells and sounds, inanity, and hard-earned pleasures. It captures our romantic attachment to the game and its playfields and most especially its people.

Jaime, at our Shivas dinner, had a copy of *Golf in the Kingdom* next to his dessert plate, and he described an especially lovely moment in it. In his coat and tie and horn-rimmed glasses, with the book in hand, he looked like a university professor. He described how Mrs. Agatha McNaughton, good-looking Scotswoman and hostess, is at a tableful of golf kooks, Shivas Irons and a golfing pilgrim named Michael Murphy among them. They're singing the praises of the game. They're pontificating. Then Agatha cuts to the bone: "*All those gentlemanly rools, why they're the proper rools of affection—and all the waitin' and oohin' and ahin' o'er yer shots, all the talk o' this one's drive and that one's putt and the other one's gorgeous swing—what is it all but love?*"

That has to be it. *What is it all but love?* Nothing else could explain the endless, illogical devotion so many of us have to this mad pursuit. Agnes had identified the starting point, the turning point, and the finishing point.

"And that's what is going on in this room right now," Jaime said. "All of us together, connected by golf."

The fireplace glowed. The room was still. Nobody was counting shots, not at this point in the proceedings. Numbers had given way to words. It's always this way. On a long table against a paneled wall, under a portrait of Tillinghast, there was a table filled with desserts, cookies and little cheesecakes and brownies. Jaime finished and we rose from our chairs, all twenty-four of us, in the name of Agatha McNaughton, this game of golf, and the siren song of dessert.

Over these past fifty years, I have gone down the rabbit hole of golf with a thousand people and maybe far more. I have played with hundreds. Over the course of *Tour '24: Do the Loco-Motion*, I crossed paths with scores of golf people on this fairway or that one, this driving range or that one, this press tent or that one. Jake Knapp in Phoenix and his caddie, Mike Stephens. Jason Snow at the Pacific Grove muni and Chris Wagenseller sitting on the bench beside its eighteenth tee. Swing Liu from the Epson Tour and Wei-Ling Hsu of the LPGA tour. David Feherty in Las Vegas. Greg Norman in Miami. Pádraig Harrington in upstate New York. Gary Player in Scotland. Erik Peterson, fishing guide/cook and three-time winner of the City Open in Alpena, Michigan. Renee Powell, the owner-operator of Clearview Golf Club, a public course in East Canton, Ohio.

I stopped there in the dog days of summer to play Clearview and get a lesson from Dr. Powell. (She has an honorary doctorate from the University of St. Andrews.) Powell was the second Black woman, after Althea Gibson, to play the LPGA tour, and her father, Bill, was the first Black builder, owner, and operator of an American golf course. O.B. right on Clearview's seventh hole is a wall of cornstalks; the greens are hand-watered, and the August fairways were almost a khaki color. The course had been baking all summer long. An elderly couple was playing in front of me, but Clearview was otherwise quiet on this August afternoon. Renee had had a long day made longer by a flat tire. She sat on a folding chair at the informal Clearview driving range, watched me hit some good shots and some poor ones, and said, "So what's going on with you? You've been playing all these years."

It was earlier on that same drive home that I had stopped in Detroit to see J. B. Brown, the man who jumped off the screen in *Migrations*, the documentary about the Black golf experience. You may recall: I was drawn to the backdrop (a public course), his accent (Old South), and his cackling, casual way. He had that tee behind his right ear.

We met at the Royal Oak Golf Center, a massive driving range not far from the Detroit Zoo. When I arrived, J.B. was sitting in his spotless convertible, a sleek black Mercedes, top up. He popped out of it with effortless zeal. He was skinny-legged and slender, not tall, wearing roomy shorts and a golf shirt with the tails out. By manner, you might have guessed he was seventeen. He was seventy-seven.

"Beryllium Eye2s," J.B. said, checking out my clubs. "Lemme see the color." He examined the tiny dot on the back of the clubhead. "Black dot. That's a handsome club." Black dot on a Ping iron is standard loft and lie. Ping has many other colors. No matter what brand you play, you need a loft and lie that's correct for you. I've known that forever, but my stop in the Ping trailer at Bay Hill, in March, reconfirmed it.

I figured I'd go to the range with the man, hear what he had to say, and then get back in my car bound for Ohio, Pennsylvania, home. We did go to the range, but I didn't get right back on the road. J. B. Brown was an original. It didn't take me an hour to figure that out. I stayed.

He first held a golf club in the 1950s in a field behind the Hooper City School, the all-Black school he attended, first grade through twelfth, five miles and a world away from City Hall in Birmingham, Alabama. One kid had a club and a few balls. He and the other kids dug a hole.

One night in 1962, when J.B. was in high school, he took a white girl to a white party in a white neighborhood. The Brown home was a thirty-four-acre family farm in rural Sayreton beyond the Birmingham city limits. Police came to the party. A scene unfolded. Somehow J.B.'s father heard about it. When he arrived, his son was half in a squad car, in a choke hold, an officer's handgun pointed at his head, for the crime of being a Black teenager at a white party. The senior Mr. Brown came racing in, bellowing at the cops, "You are *not* gonna kill my son tonight."

Two years later, J.B. graduated from Hooper City and got on a bus bound for Detroit. One suitcase, eighteen dollars. Talk about the warmth of other suns. At the Brown farm in Sayreton, J.B. killed the hogs his family ate. Everything they ate came off their land. In Detroit, J.B. got an assembly-line job at (as he calls it) Ford's, bought groceries in a supermarket, and sometimes went out for dinner. The Ford Motor Company paid a living wage and then some.

J.B. had friends, three brothers, who took him out for golf at a city course in Detroit called Palmer Park. Jimmy, Freddie, and Slick Goodman. The first time J.B. played a full nine holes, he shot 52 with a lost ball on the fourth. Slick was the best of the bunch. He could shoot 36. "Man, you play pretty good," Slick said. "You should come out with us more." J.B. was recounting the round to me as if it had happened that morning.

"What I felt that day," J.B. said, "was freedom."

He got good. He represented Michigan several times in a Michigan versus Indiana amateur event. ("You must have been one of the few Black players," I said. "I was the *only* Black player," J.B. said.) He won the Ben Davis Detroit Open, the senior division, twice, as an amateur. An amateur, but not the kind you'd ever see promoting the USGA in a publicity campaign. In his prime, J.B. played a lot of big-money games with low-level mobsters at a course called Wolverine. More than once, he saw golf days there end with drawn guns, when the losers wouldn't pay. He played a lot of money games for whatever was in the pot at Palmer Park. "You'd have drug dealers and judges in the same foursome, and guys so broke we'd say they were playing on their ass, 'cause there wasn't no wallet in their back pocket."

He knew a lot of people at the Royal Oak range, and if there was someone he didn't know, like the attractive woman hitting balls next to us, he figured out a way to introduce himself. She was a beginner, and

J.B. talked to her about rotating her shoulders. She was charmed, and whenever she got one in the air, she'd look over at J.B. to see if he saw it. J.B. and I were taking turns in our stall. J.B. was hitting punch shots and hooks and fades and on command, not long but right on the face, and every shot had shape. We talked about ball position. He's a right-handed golfer (and a lefty putter, like his newest student) with a strong grip and a low right shoulder, and he keeps his weight on his back foot longer than most golfers do. He reminded me, in swing and body type, of a decorated amateur from Chicago named Joel Hirsch. I know and have played with Mr. Hirsch. He's in his early eighties and he breaks 80 every time he plays. J.B.'s on that same path.

We went through several tall buckets, talking about golf and trying different things. I was hitting it well but off a mat you never really know. (You can't hit it fat off a mat, and thin shots launch better than they ever would off grass.) We got lunch. We went to a nine-hole course also called Royal Oak. We paid our twelve-dollar green fee and putted on the practice green that was country-club perfect. A storm blew in, and we waited it out in the pro shop. I started with two pars. Then my game fell apart. By the end, I was morose.

"I feel sick," I told J.B. in the parking lot when we were in.

"Why?" he said.

"Because you worked so hard with me at the range, I was hitting good shots there, and I just couldn't make it work on the course, and I feel like I've wasted your time and let you down."

"No, man," J.B. said.

The next day was better, and the day after that better yet. I asked J.B. if he could explain the difference.

He said, "You got comfortable, is all."

What follows is a list of people who knew or know, golfing souls who (you might say) took the lid off the game:

- *Michael Murphy, creator of the original List of People Who Knew (which I am stealing here), a golfing swami;*
- *Adolphus "Golf Ball" Hull, a tour caddie who understood you had to read the golfer before the green;*
- *Arnold Palmer, golf promoter;*
- *Chuck Will, a longtime golf director for CBS Sports who saw golf as one, long continuous-loop story;*
- *John Stark, a Scottish golf teacher who taught breathing, among other things;*
- *Mike Donald, a touring pro who would rather give than take (rare!);*
- *Sam Reeves, my Pebble Beach landlord, a living link to Bob Jones, and a model of Do unto others.*

I'd like to go on, but I won't. Golf teaches restraint. There's a lot to be said for it. For years, this was the preamble to golf's rule book: "All players should conduct themselves in a disciplined manner, demonstrating courtesy and sportsmanship at all times, irrespective of how competitive they may be. This is the spirit of the game of golf." But please stay with me as I slip in one more name here:

- *J. B. Brown of Detroit, golfing freedom fighter.*

Mr. J. B. Brown. A man with an encyclopedic knowledge of how the golfing greats—Bobby Jones, Ben Hogan, Payne Stewart—did their thing. He has studied scores of players, courtesy of YouTube magic. Lydia Ko. He raves about Lydia Ko.

"People talk about the swing, the golf swing, the swing's the thing, all that," J.B. told me. We had played the Royal Oak nine-holer, and now we were eating ice cream at a place called Ray's in Royal Oak. (Let me make this easy for you: 4233 Coolidge Highway, eleven in the morning to nine at night, seven days a week. They've been in business since 1958, and I've got a feeling they're not going anywhere.) After we were done eating and talking, J.B. got two scoops of mint chocolate chip in a to-go cup for the counter woman at the Royal Oak course.

"I don't think about the golf swing," J.B. said. "I think about how a body moves through the ball. When I watch Hogan, I'm trying to see his body movements. Golf to me is dancing. The swing is a dance. You're doing a dance with that golf club."

In the late 1970s and the early '80s, J.B. would make regular trips in the dusk light to a sprawling grass-covered field at the Detroit Armory on East Eight Mile Drive. He'd bring his clubs and his shag bag and hit hundreds of balls. Other guys would do the same. Security never chased them off. They weren't bothering anybody. J.B. would roll down the car windows and turn on the radio as loud as it would go and hit balls while listening to whatever songs Martha Jean the Queen and other Detroit DJs were playing that night.

Now it was many years later, and J.B. was singing to me the final two lines of the chorus of an old disco hit he remembered from those nights at the armory.

Ain't no stopping us now!
We've got the groove.

There was a sweetness in his voice, and it caught the cadence of the original recording. I don't think he did any singing in those money games at Wolverine, but he was singing now.

"At *Ain't no*, I'm waggling," J.B. said. I was getting a lesson as we held our cups of melting ice cream, a crying baby within earshot. "On *stopping us*, I'm taking it back. On *now*, I'm coming down. Then, *We've got the groove*. I'm following through. That's what it is."

"Ain't No Stopping Us Now." It's an anthem, really. "It's got a good beat, and you can dance to it," the kids on *American Bandstand* used to say about songs that fired on all cylinders. "No Stopping Us" qualifies. A good beat, and you can dance to it.

We went back to Royal Oak, the nine-hole course, and J.B. made his ice-cream delivery. The lady behind the counter was overjoyed. It was late on a languid afternoon with lots of light in the sky. There was nowhere I had to be.

I went to the Royal Oak Golf Center, the nearby driving range, and set myself up in a remote sloping corner of the property (not exactly legal) where there was grass to play from. The early-evening air was warm and heavy, and it carried the scent of every summer night you ever knew when time crawled just because it could. The grass was damp and thick, and your feet left imprints in it. I pulled out a sand wedge. Somehow, as if on shuffle, the old David Bowie hit "Let's Dance" began playing in my head, and then it got lodged there. I took the club back on *let's* and down on *dance*.

Let's . . . DANCE.

When I flushed it, I knew. My whole body knew.

Illustration Credits

About the Author

Michael Bamberger was born in Patchogue, New York, in 1960. After graduating from the University of Pennsylvania in 1982, he worked as a newspaper reporter, first for the (Martha's) *Vineyard Gazette*, later for *The Philadelphia Inquirer*. After twenty-two years at *Sports Illustrated*, he is now a senior writer at Golf.com. He lives in Philadelphia with his wife, Christine.

Author email:
mfbamberger@aol.com

Avid Reader Press, an imprint of Simon & Schuster, is built on the idea that the most rewarding publishing has three common denominators: great books, published with intense focus, in true partnership. Thank you to the Avid Reader Press colleagues who collaborated on *The Playing Lesson*, as well as to the hundreds of professionals in the Simon & Schuster advertising, audio, communications, design, ebook, finance, human resources, legal, marketing, operations, production, sales, supply chain, subsidiary rights, and warehouse departments whose invaluable support and expertise benefit every one of our titles.

Editorial
Jofie Ferrari-Adler, *VP and Co-Publisher*
Carolyn Kelly, *Editor*

Jacket Design
Alison Forner, *Senior Art Director*
Clay Smith, *Senior Designer*
Sydney Newman, *Art Associate*

Marketing
Meredith Vilarello, *VP and Associate Publisher*
Katya Wiegmann, *Marketing and Publishing Assistant*

Production
Allison Green, *Managing Editor*
Benjamin Holmes, *Senior Production Editor*
Alicia Brancato, *Production Manager*
Cait Lamborne, *Ebook Developer*

Publicity
David Kass, *Senior Director of Publicity*
Eva Kerins, *Publicity Assistant*

Subsidiary Rights
Paul O'Halloran, *VP and Director of Subsidiary Rights*
Fiona Sharp, *Subsidiary Rights Coordinator*

The author wishes to express his thanks to everybody at Avid Reader Press; to two editors with whom he has worked for decades, Beth Thomas and Mark Godich; and to Lady Kris Dahl, avid reader and advocate.

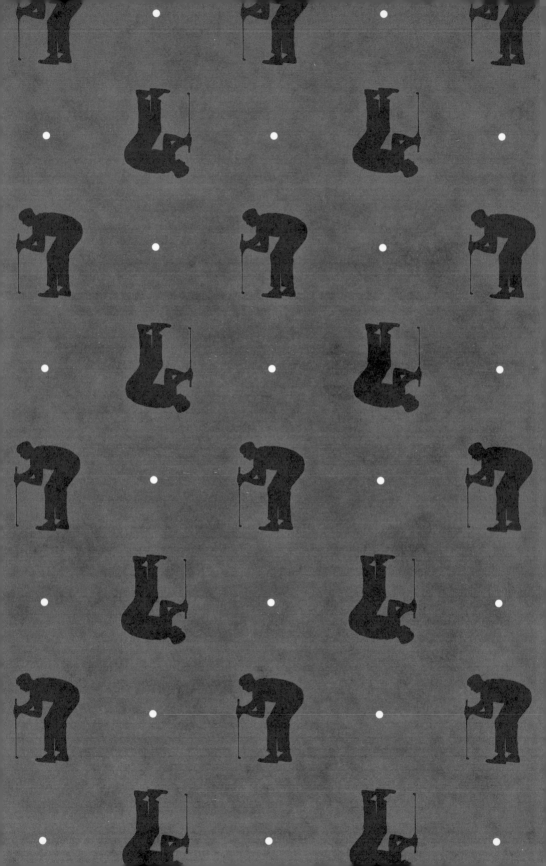